HOMICIDAL PSYCHO JUNGLE CAT

Other Books by Bill Watterson

Calvin and Hobbes
Something Under the Bed Is Drooling
Yukon Ho!
Weirdos from Another Planet
Revenge of the Baby-Sat
Scientific Progress Goes "Boink"
Attack of the Deranged Mutant Killer Monster Snow Goons
The Days Are Just *Packed*
The Calvin and Hobbes Tenth Anniversary Book
There's Treasure Everywhere
It's a Magical World

Treasury Collections

The Essential Calvin and Hobbes
The Lazy Sunday Book
The Authoritative Calvin and Hobbes
The Indispensable Calvin and Hobbes

HOMICIDAL PSYCHO JUNGLE CAT

A Calvin and Hobbes Collection by Bill Watterson

Andrews McMeel
Publishing®

a division of Andrews McMeel Universal

Calvin and Hobbes is distributed internationally by Universal Uclick.

Andrews McMeel Publishing
a division of Andrews McMeel Universal
1130 Walnut Street, Kansas City, Missouri 64106

www.andrewsmcmeel.com

ISBN: 978-0-8362-1769-8

Library of Congress Control Number: 94-71736

15 16 17 18 19 SDB 35 34 33 32 31

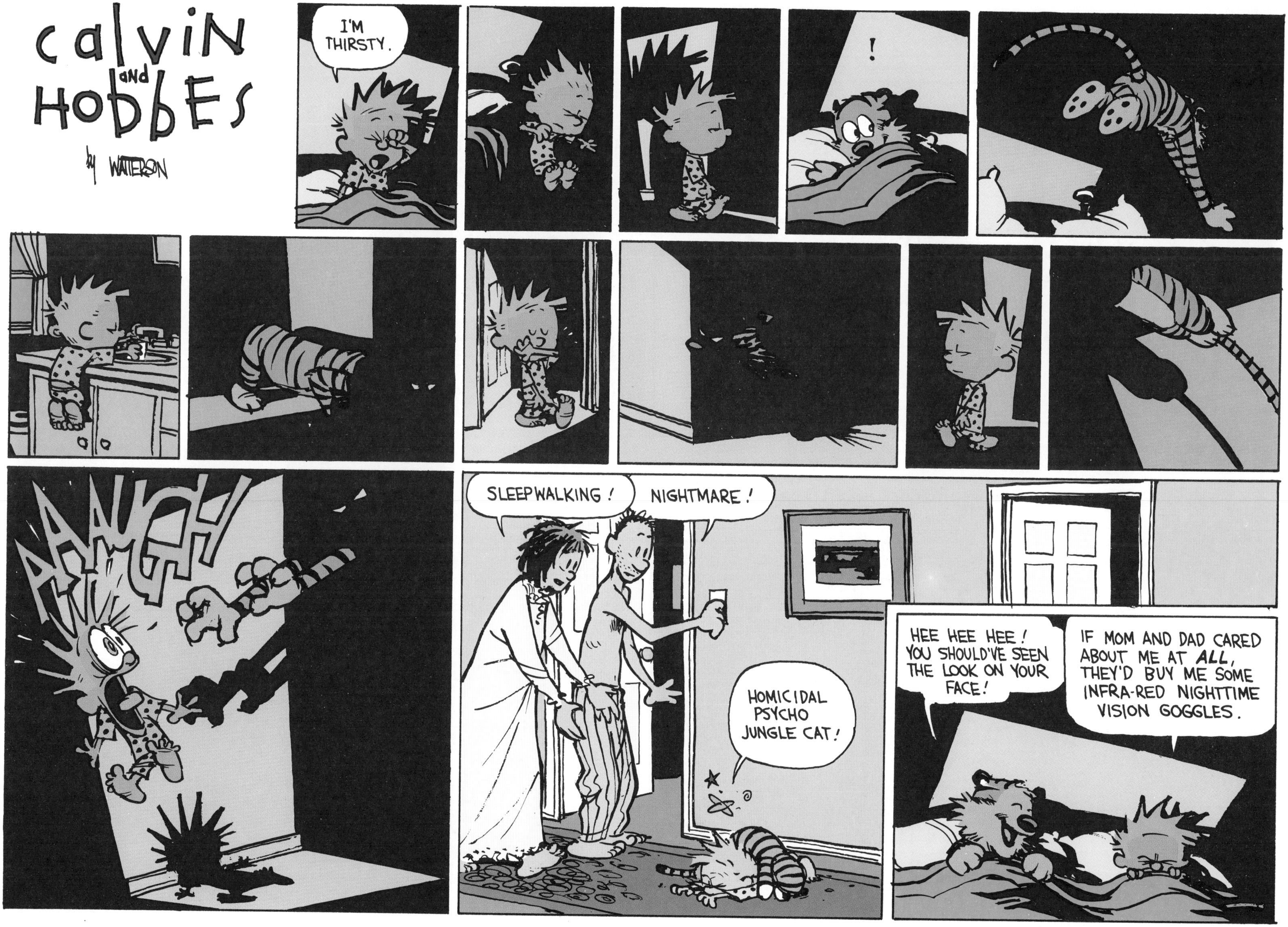
Calvin and Hobbes
by WATTERSON
I'M THIRSTY.
!
AAUGH!
SLEEPWALKING!
NIGHTMARE!
HOMICIDAL PSYCHO JUNGLE CAT!
HEE HEE HEE! YOU SHOULD'VE SEEN THE LOOK ON YOUR FACE!
IF MOM AND DAD CARED ABOUT ME AT ALL, THEY'D BUY ME SOME INFRA-RED NIGHTTIME VISION GOGGLES.

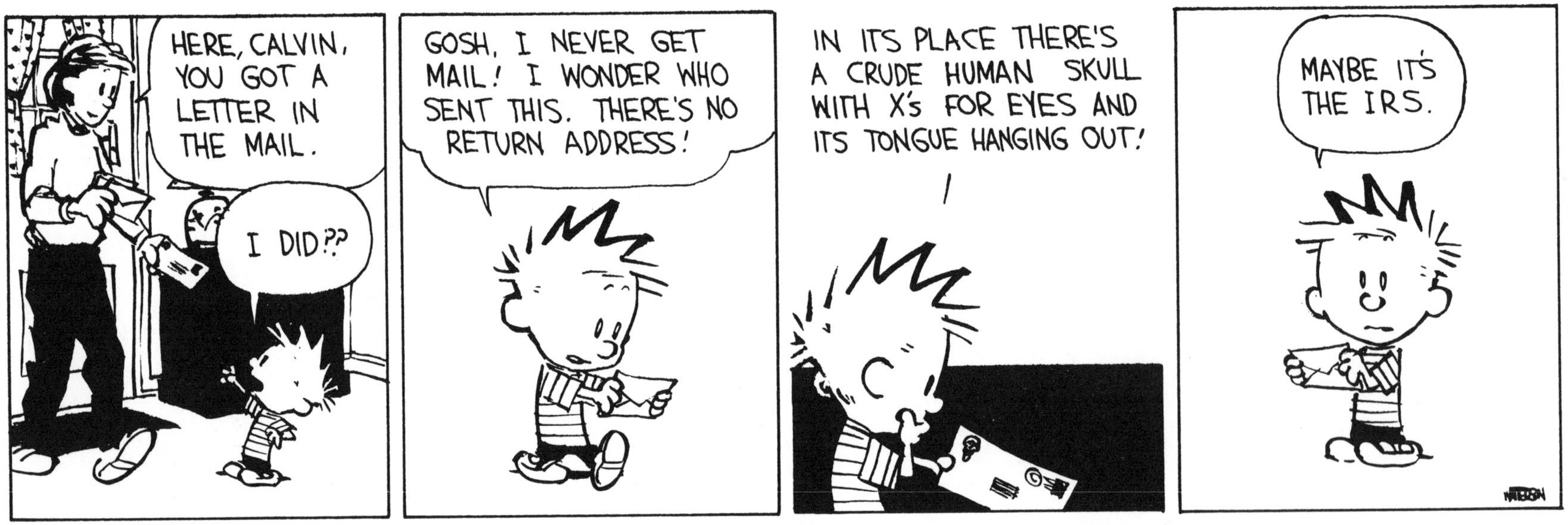
HERE, CALVIN, YOU GOT A LETTER IN THE MAIL.
I DID??
GOSH, I NEVER GET MAIL! I WONDER WHO SENT THIS. THERE'S NO RETURN ADDRESS!
IN ITS PLACE THERE'S A CRUDE HUMAN SKULL WITH X's FOR EYES AND ITS TONGUE HANGING OUT!
MAYBE IT'S THE IRS.

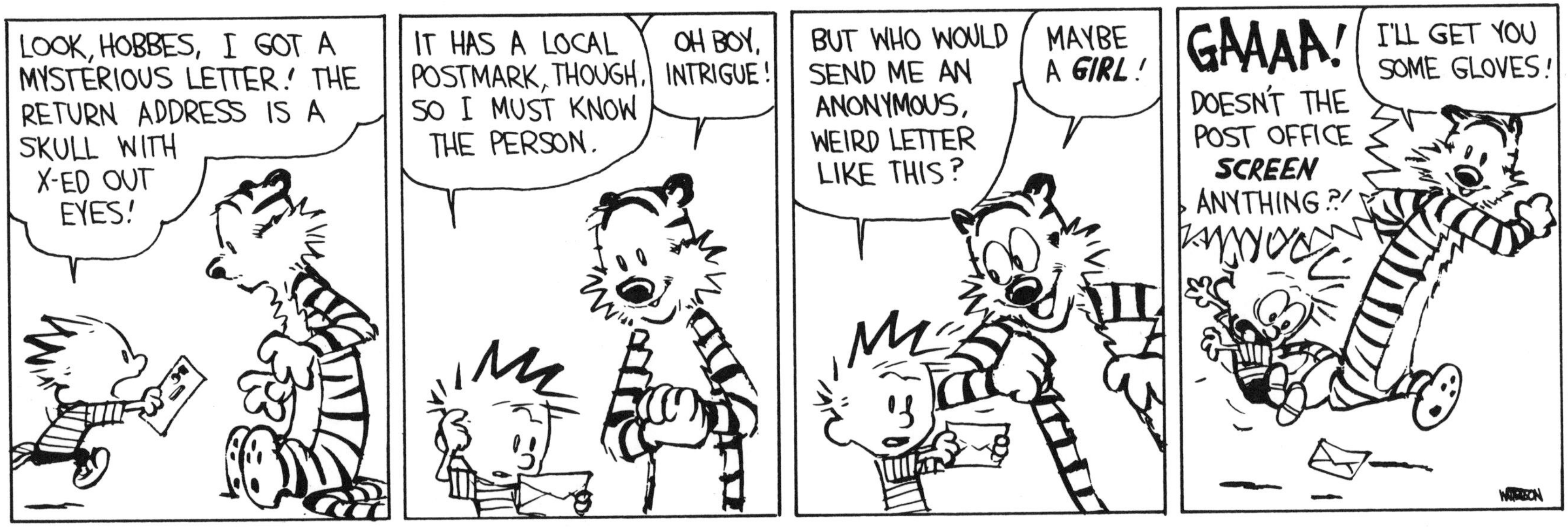
LOOK, HOBBES, I GOT A MYSTERIOUS LETTER! THE RETURN ADDRESS IS A SKULL WITH X-ED OUT EYES!
IT HAS A LOCAL POSTMARK, THOUGH, SO I MUST KNOW THE PERSON.
OH BOY, INTRIGUE!
BUT WHO WOULD SEND ME AN ANONYMOUS, WEIRD LETTER LIKE THIS?
MAYBE A **GIRL**!
GAAAA!
DOESN'T THE POST OFFICE **SCREEN** ANYTHING?!
I'LL GET YOU SOME GLOVES!

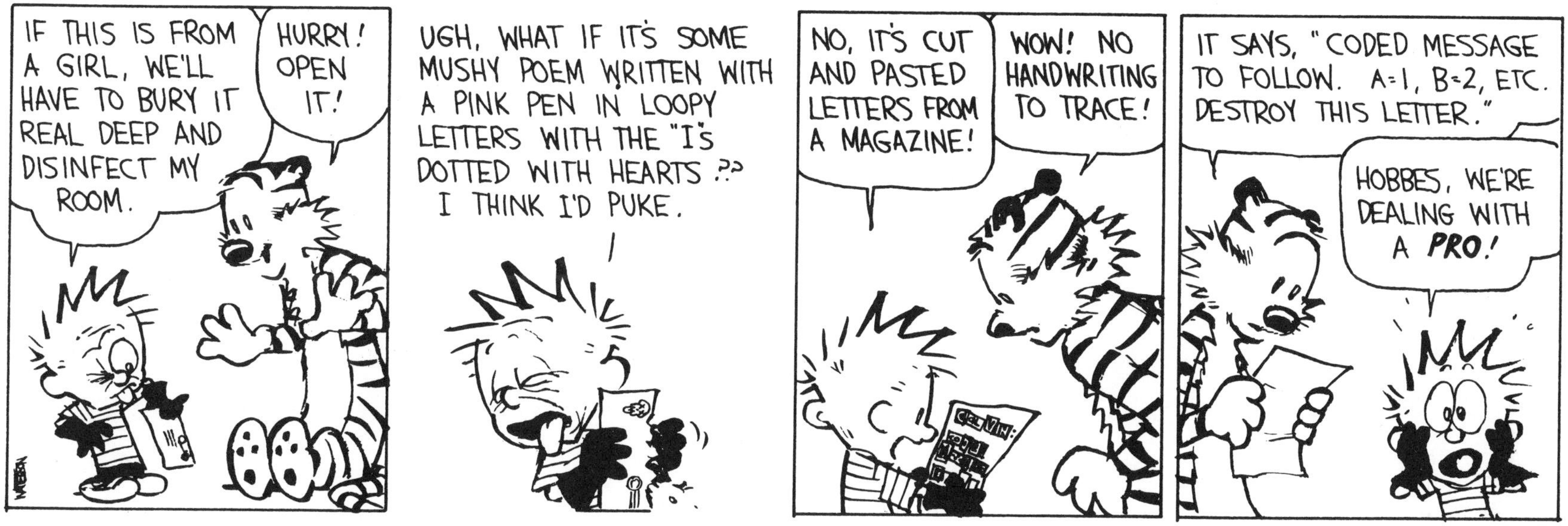
IF THIS IS FROM A GIRL, WE'LL HAVE TO BURY IT REAL DEEP AND DISINFECT MY ROOM.
HURRY! OPEN IT!
UGH, WHAT IF IT'S SOME MUSHY POEM WRITTEN WITH A PINK PEN IN LOOPY LETTERS WITH THE "I"S DOTTED WITH HEARTS ?? I THINK I'D PUKE.
NO, IT'S CUT AND PASTED LETTERS FROM A MAGAZINE!
WOW! NO HANDWRITING TO TRACE!
IT SAYS, "CODED MESSAGE TO FOLLOW. A=1, B=2, ETC. DESTROY THIS LETTER."
HOBBES, WE'RE DEALING WITH A PRO!

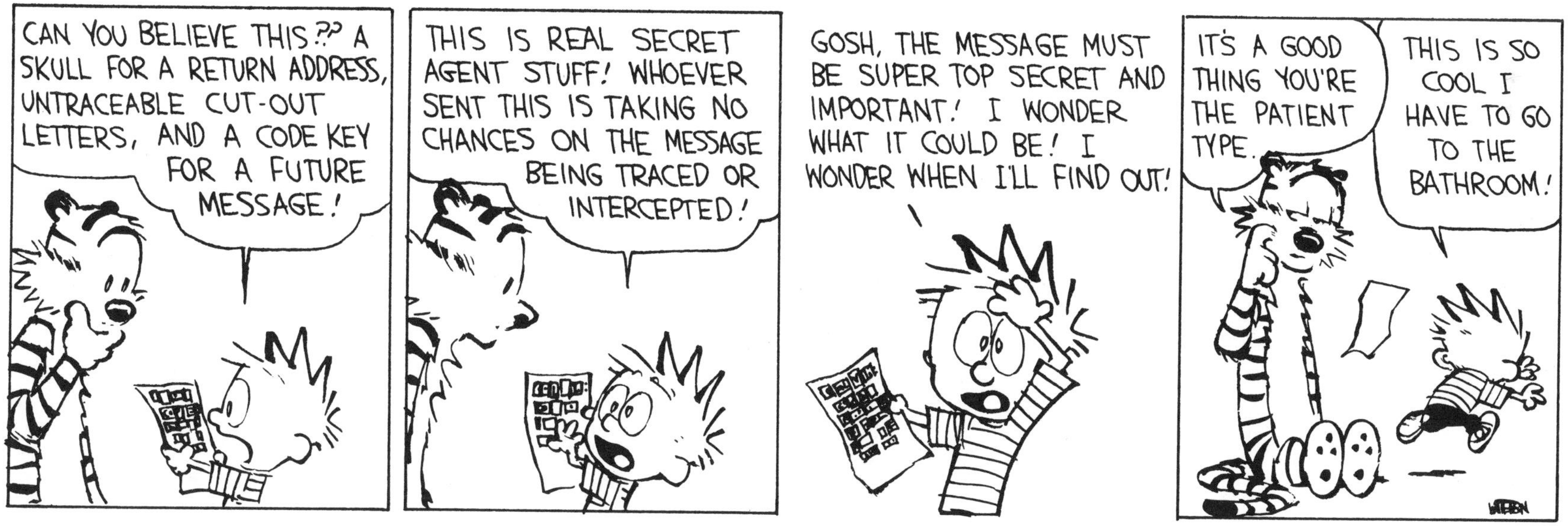
CAN YOU BELIEVE THIS?? A SKULL FOR A RETURN ADDRESS, UNTRACEABLE CUT-OUT LETTERS, AND A CODE KEY FOR A FUTURE MESSAGE!
THIS IS REAL SECRET AGENT STUFF! WHOEVER SENT THIS IS TAKING NO CHANCES ON THE MESSAGE BEING TRACED OR INTERCEPTED!
GOSH, THE MESSAGE MUST BE SUPER TOP SECRET AND IMPORTANT! I WONDER WHAT IT COULD BE! I WONDER WHEN I'LL FIND OUT!
IT'S A GOOD THING YOU'RE THE PATIENT TYPE.
THIS IS SO COOL I HAVE TO GO TO THE BATHROOM!

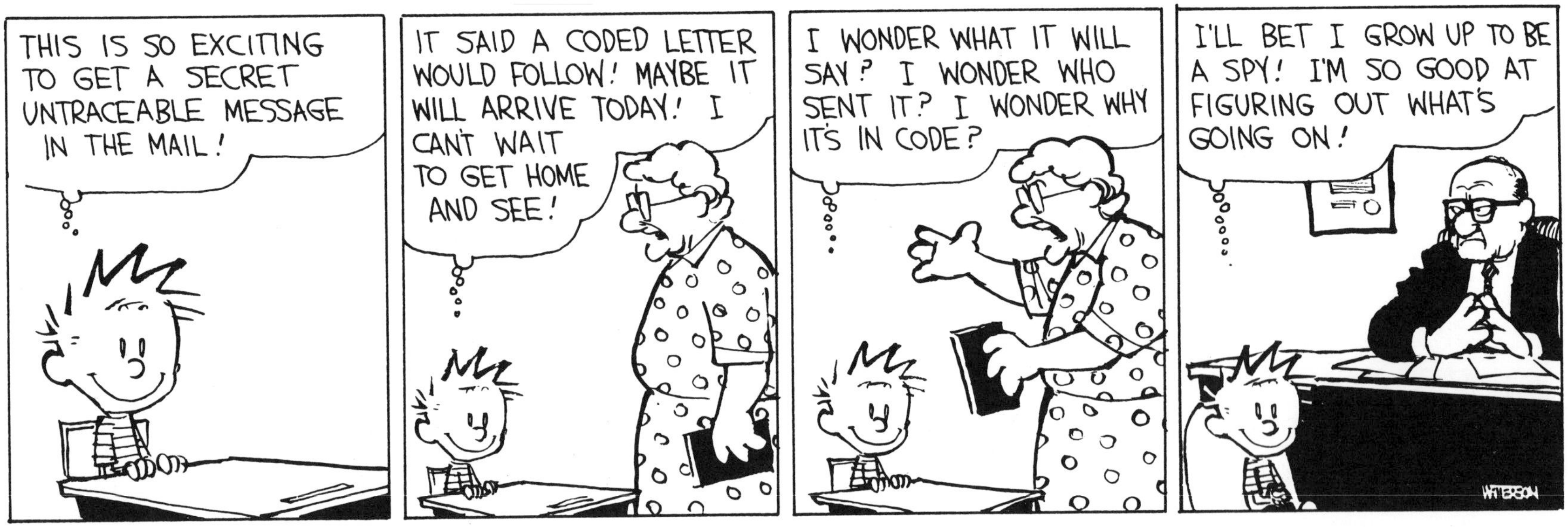
THIS IS SO EXCITING TO GET A SECRET UNTRACEABLE MESSAGE IN THE MAIL!
IT SAID A CODED LETTER WOULD FOLLOW! MAYBE IT WILL ARRIVE TODAY! I CAN'T WAIT TO GET HOME AND SEE!
I WONDER WHAT IT WILL SAY? I WONDER WHO SENT IT? I WONDER WHY IT'S IN CODE?
I'LL BET I GROW UP TO BE A SPY! I'M SO GOOD AT FIGURING OUT WHAT'S GOING ON!
WATTERSON

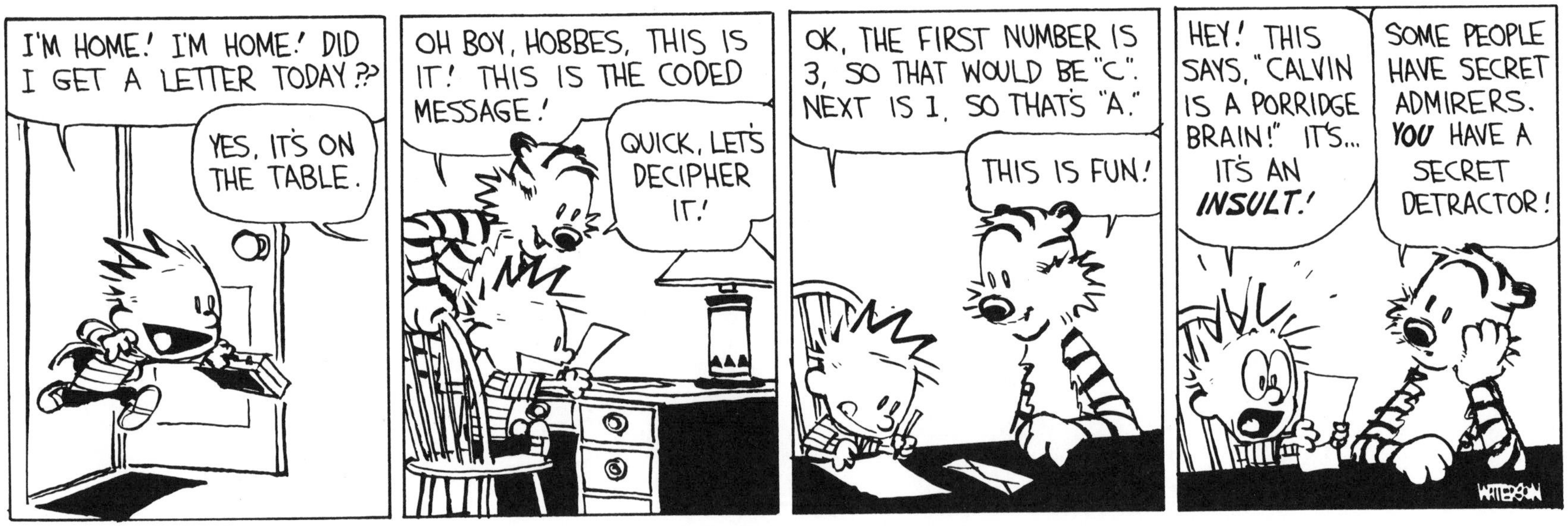
I'M HOME! I'M HOME! DID I GET A LETTER TODAY?!?
YES, IT'S ON THE TABLE.
OH BOY, HOBBES, THIS IS IT! THIS IS THE CODED MESSAGE!
QUICK, LET'S DECIPHER IT!
OK, THE FIRST NUMBER IS 3, SO THAT WOULD BE "C". NEXT IS 1, SO THAT'S "A."
THIS IS FUN!
HEY! THIS SAYS, "CALVIN IS A PORRIDGE BRAIN!" IT'S... IT'S AN INSULT!
SOME PEOPLE HAVE SECRET ADMIRERS. YOU HAVE A SECRET DETRACTOR!
WATTERSON

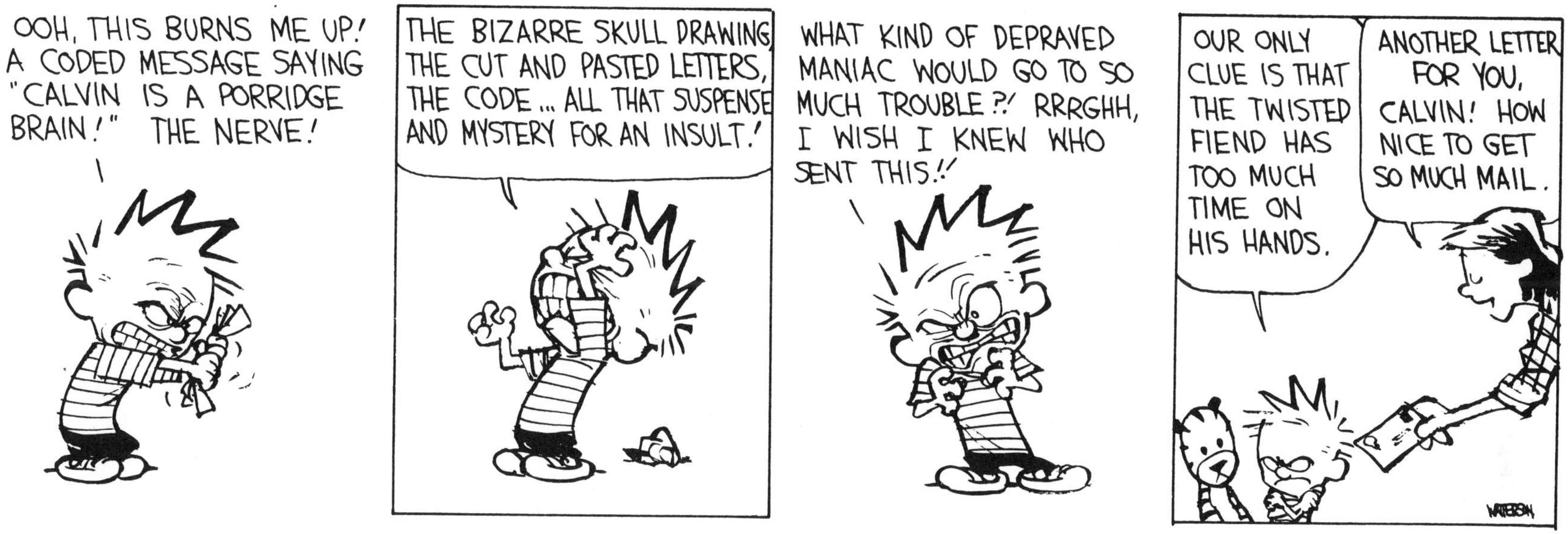

OOH, THIS BURNS ME UP! A CODED MESSAGE SAYING "CALVIN IS A PORRIDGE BRAIN!" THE NERVE!
THE BIZARRE SKULL DRAWING, THE CUT AND PASTED LETTERS, THE CODE... ALL THAT SUSPENSE AND MYSTERY FOR AN INSULT!
WHAT KIND OF DEPRAVED MANIAC WOULD GO TO SO MUCH TROUBLE?! RRRGHH, I WISH I KNEW WHO SENT THIS!!
OUR ONLY CLUE IS THAT THE TWISTED FIEND HAS TOO MUCH TIME ON HIS HANDS.
ANOTHER LETTER FOR YOU, CALVIN! HOW NICE TO GET SO MUCH MAIL.

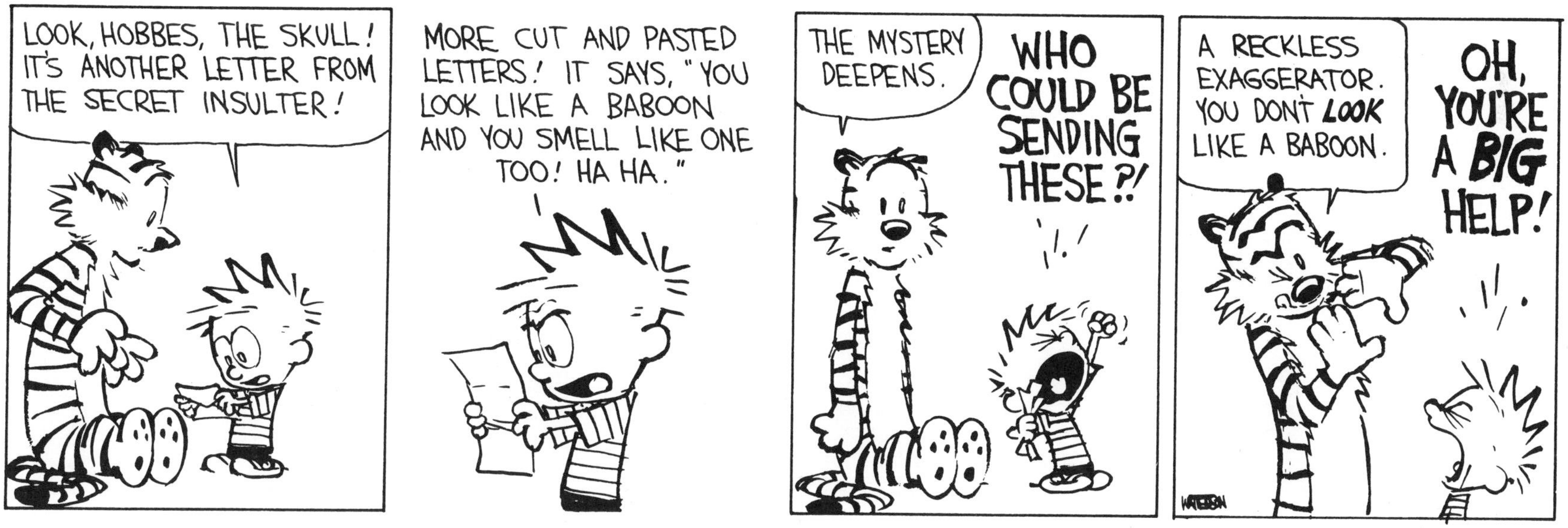

LOOK, HOBBES, THE SKULL! IT'S ANOTHER LETTER FROM THE SECRET INSULTER!
MORE CUT AND PASTED LETTERS! IT SAYS, "YOU LOOK LIKE A BABOON AND YOU SMELL LIKE ONE TOO! HA HA."
THE MYSTERY DEEPENS.
WHO COULD BE SENDING THESE?!
A RECKLESS EXAGGERATOR. YOU DON'T LOOK LIKE A BABOON.
OH, YOU'RE A BIG HELP!

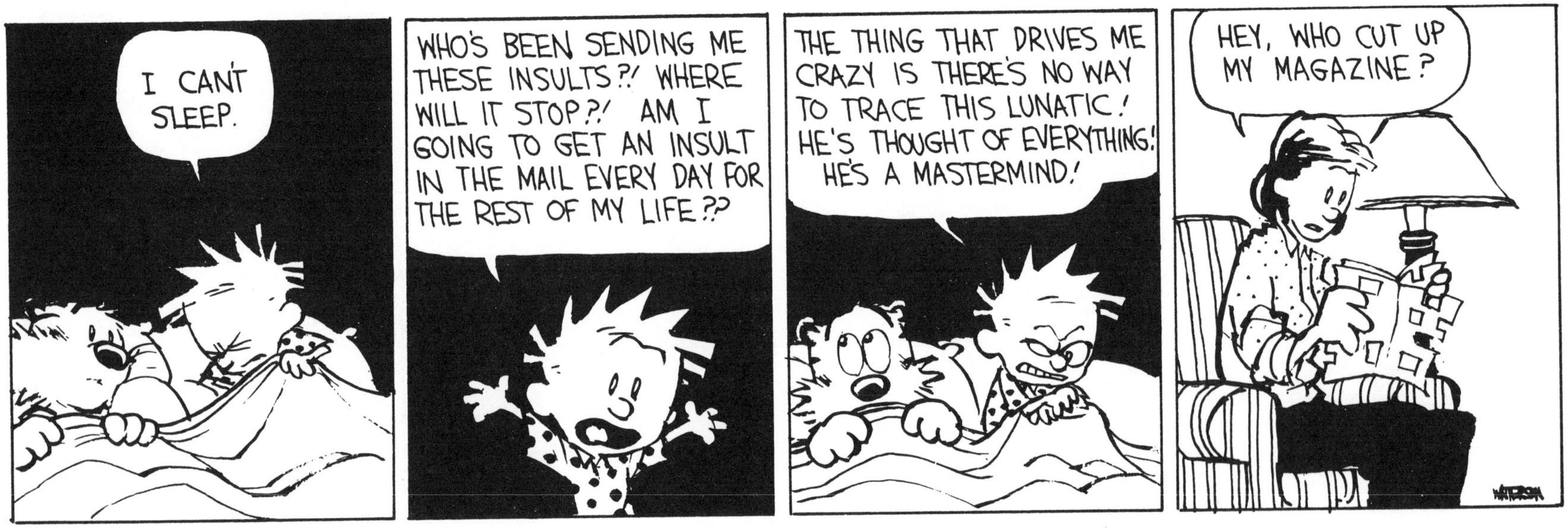
I CAN'T SLEEP.
WHO'S BEEN SENDING ME THESE INSULTS?! WHERE WILL IT STOP?! AM I GOING TO GET AN INSULT IN THE MAIL EVERY DAY FOR THE REST OF MY LIFE??
THE THING THAT DRIVES ME CRAZY IS THERE'S NO WAY TO TRACE THIS LUNATIC! HE'S THOUGHT OF EVERYTHING! HE'S A MASTERMIND!
HEY, WHO CUT UP MY MAGAZINE?

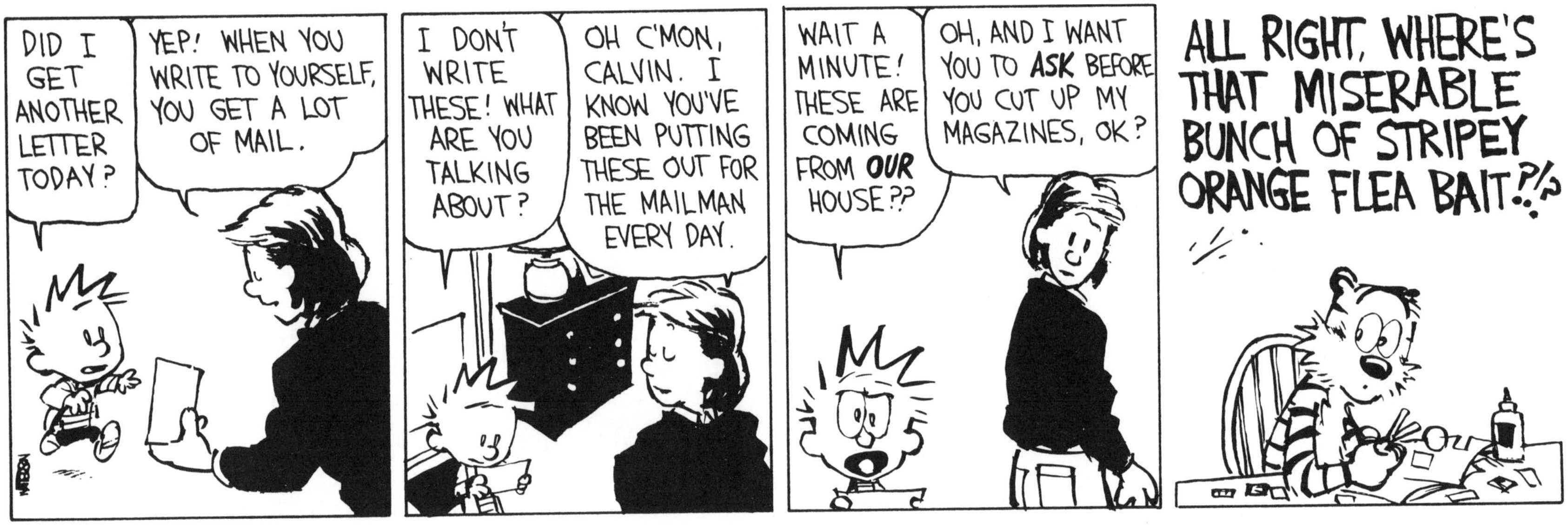
DID I GET ANOTHER LETTER TODAY?
YEP! WHEN YOU WRITE TO YOURSELF, YOU GET A LOT OF MAIL.
I DON'T WRITE THESE! WHAT ARE YOU TALKING ABOUT?
OH C'MON, CALVIN. I KNOW YOU'VE BEEN PUTTING THESE OUT FOR THE MAILMAN EVERY DAY.
WAIT A MINUTE! THESE ARE COMING FROM **OUR** HOUSE??
OH, AND I WANT YOU TO **ASK** BEFORE YOU CUT UP MY MAGAZINES, OK?
ALL RIGHT, WHERE'S THAT MISERABLE BUNCH OF STRIPEY ORANGE FLEA BAIT?!?

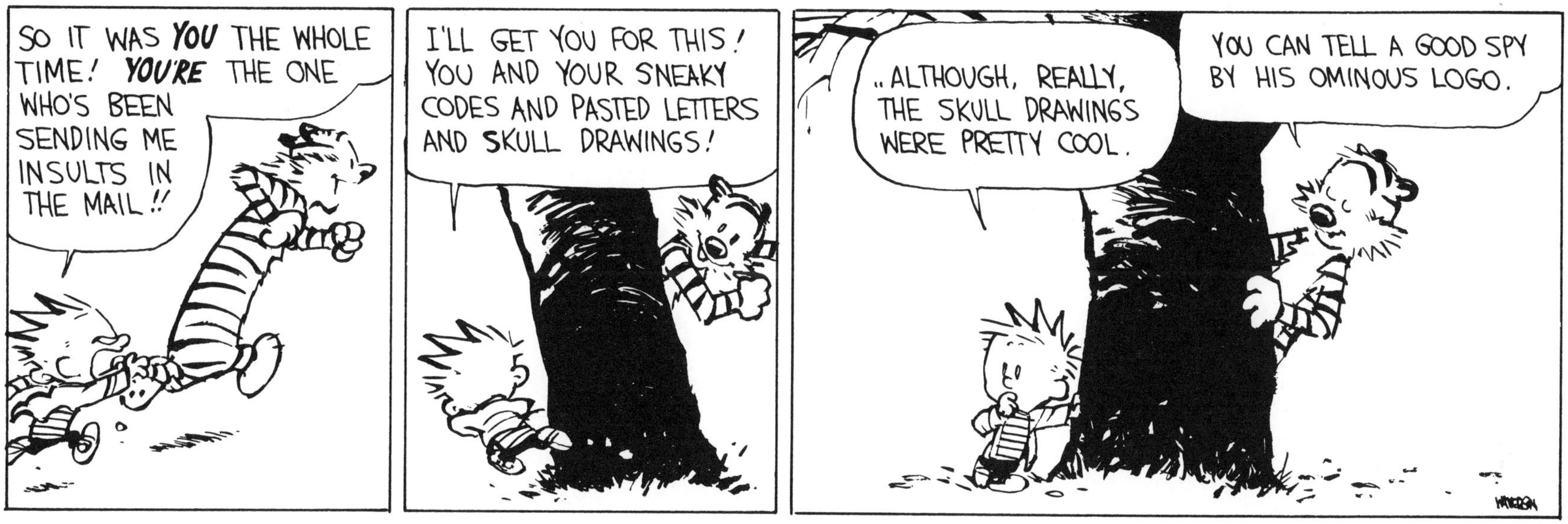
SO IT WAS YOU THE WHOLE TIME! YOU'RE THE ONE WHO'S BEEN SENDING ME INSULTS IN THE MAIL!!
I'LL GET YOU FOR THIS! YOU AND YOUR SNEAKY CODES AND PASTED LETTERS AND SKULL DRAWINGS!
..ALTHOUGH, REALLY, THE SKULL DRAWINGS WERE PRETTY COOL.
YOU CAN TELL A GOOD SPY BY HIS OMINOUS LOGO.

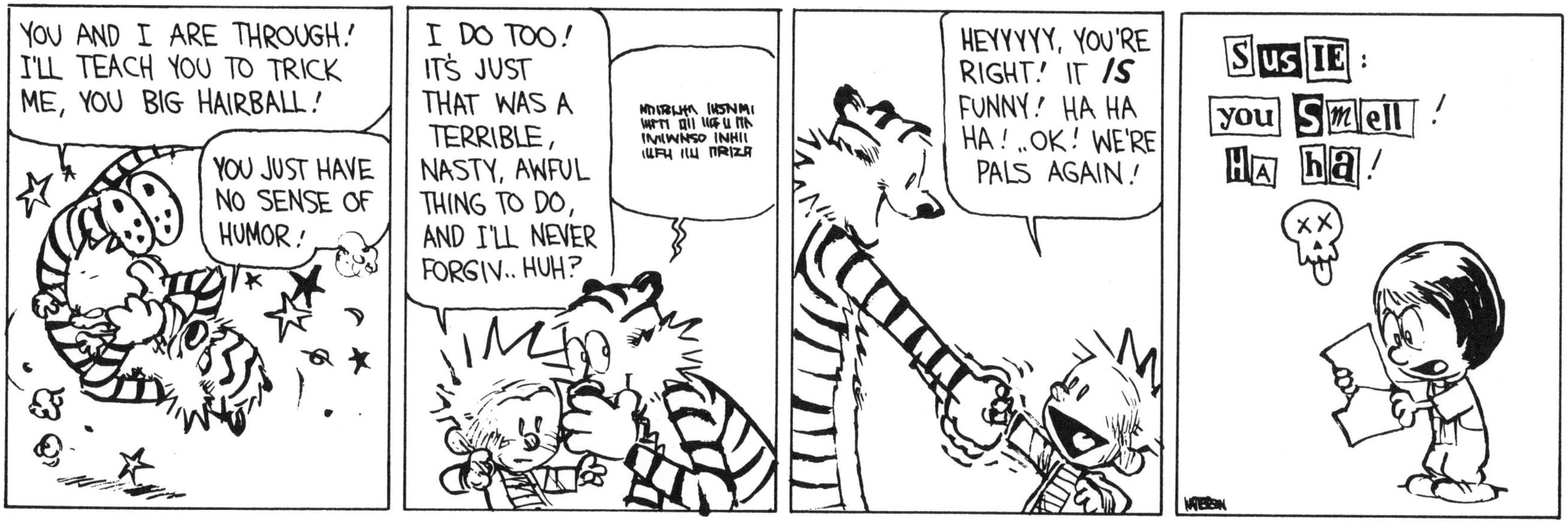
YOU AND I ARE THROUGH! I'LL TEACH YOU TO TRICK ME, YOU BIG HAIRBALL!
YOU JUST HAVE NO SENSE OF HUMOR!
I DO TOO! IT'S JUST THAT WAS A TERRIBLE, NASTY, AWFUL THING TO DO, AND I'LL NEVER FORGIV.. HUH?
HEYYYYY, YOU'RE RIGHT! IT IS FUNNY! HA HA HA! ..OK! WE'RE PALS AGAIN!
SUSIE:
you Smell!
HA ha!

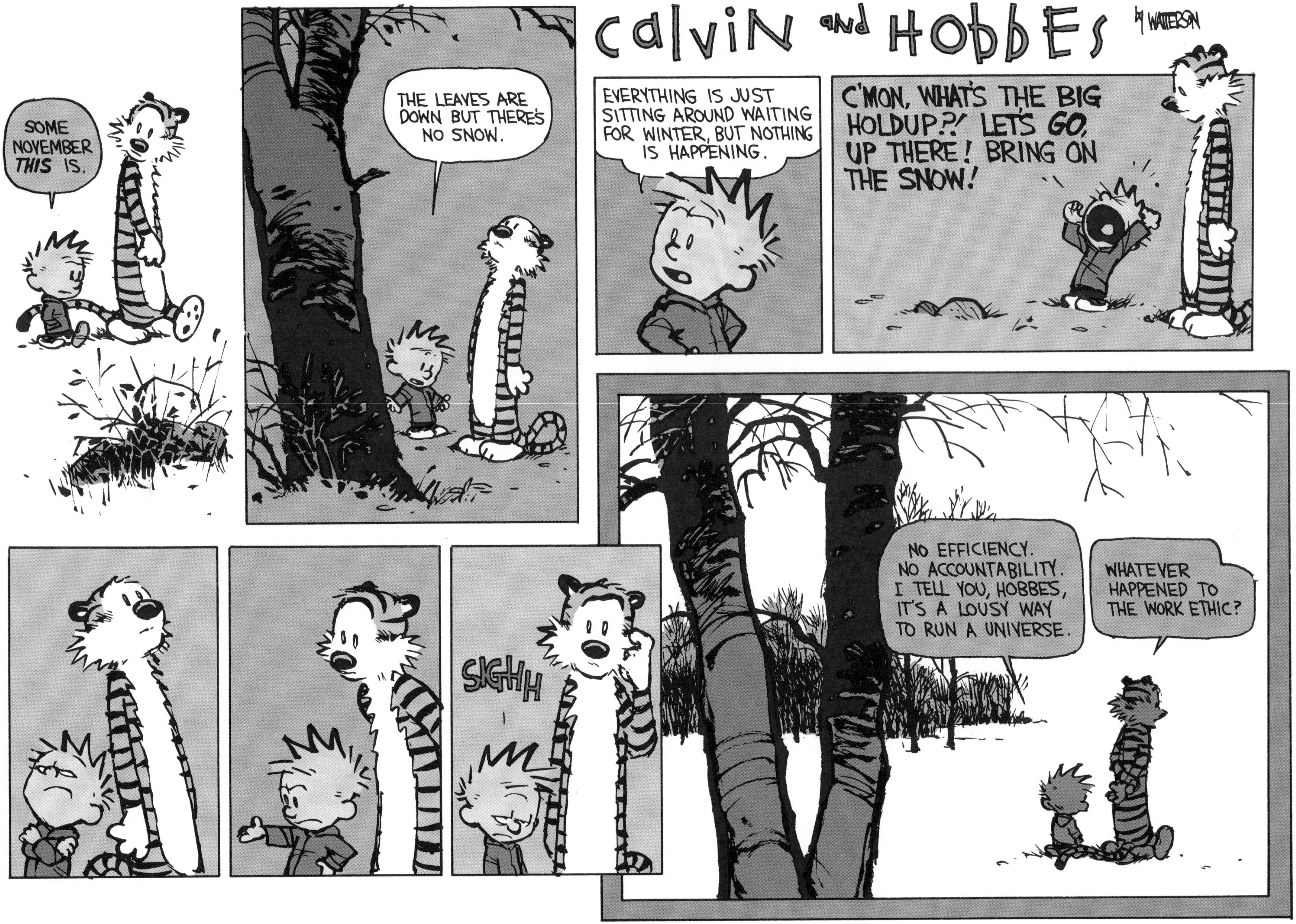
Calvin and HOBBES by WATTERSON
SOME NOVEMBER THIS IS.
THE LEAVES ARE DOWN BUT THERE'S NO SNOW.
EVERYTHING IS JUST SITTING AROUND WAITING FOR WINTER, BUT NOTHING IS HAPPENING.
C'MON, WHAT'S THE BIG HOLDUP?!' LET'S GO, UP THERE! BRING ON THE SNOW!
SIGHHH
NO EFFICIENCY. NO ACCOUNTABILITY. I TELL YOU, HOBBES, IT'S A LOUSY WAY TO RUN A UNIVERSE.
WHATEVER HAPPENED TO THE WORK ETHIC?

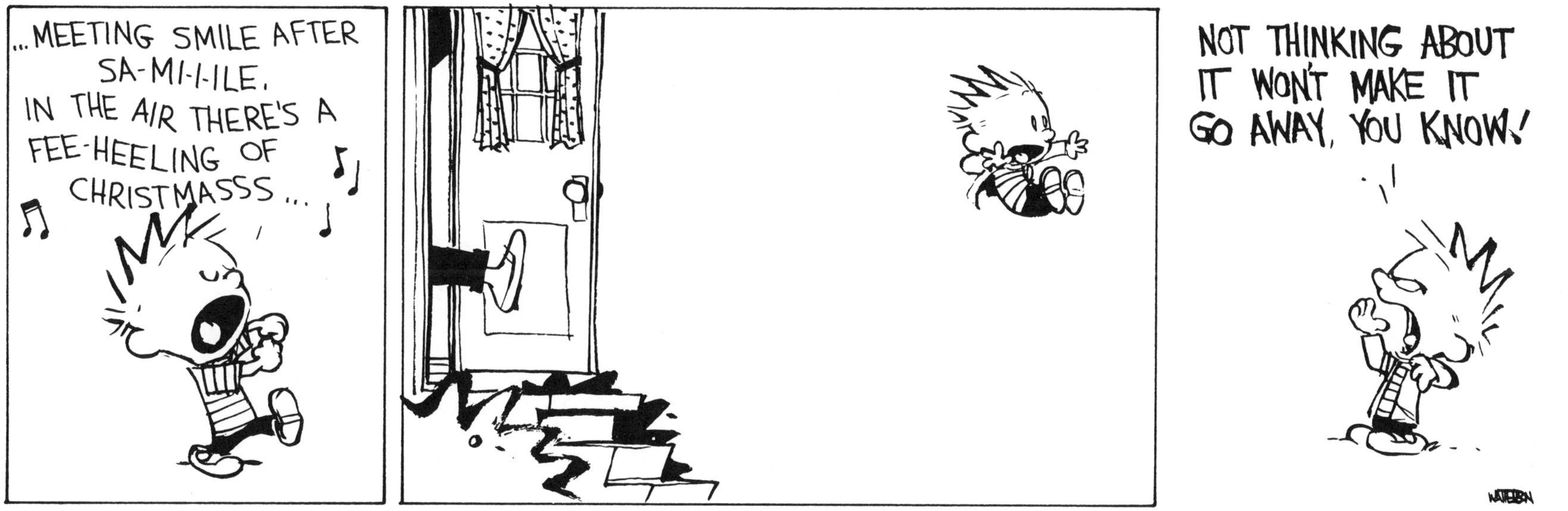
...MEETING SMILE AFTER SA-MI-I-ILE. IN THE AIR THERE'S A FEE-HEELING OF CHRISTMASSS ...
NOT THINKING ABOUT IT WON'T MAKE IT GO AWAY, YOU KNOW!
WATTERSON

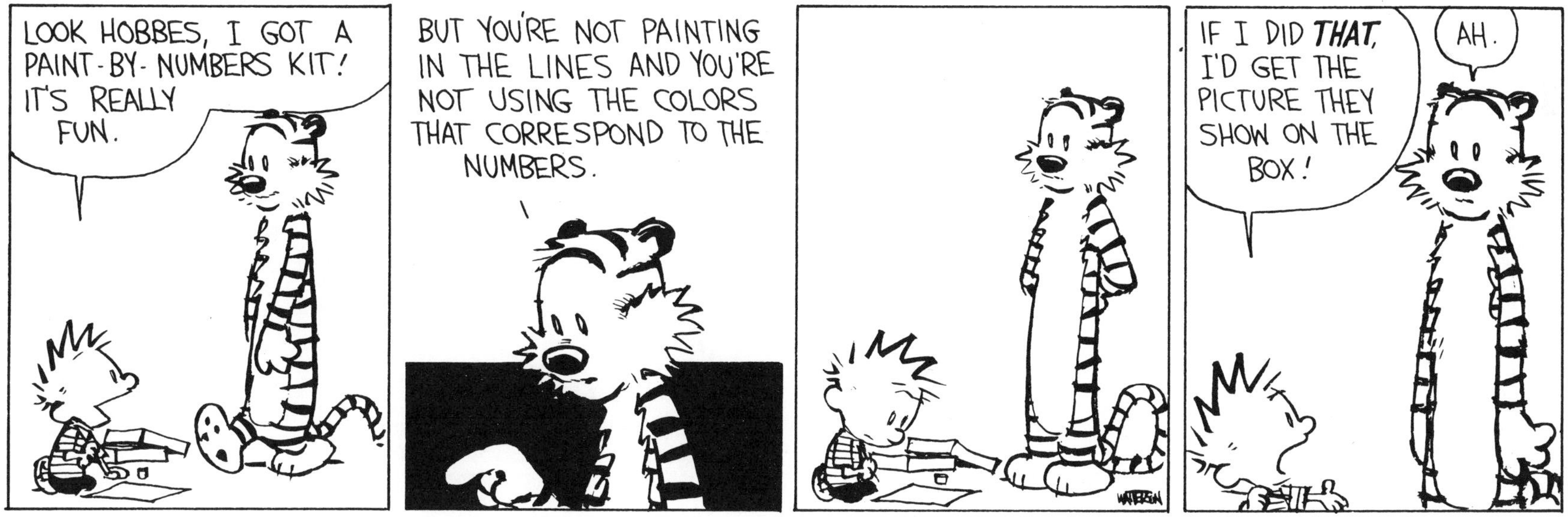
LOOK HOBBES, I GOT A PAINT-BY-NUMBERS KIT! IT'S REALLY FUN.
BUT YOU'RE NOT PAINTING IN THE LINES AND YOU'RE NOT USING THE COLORS THAT CORRESPOND TO THE NUMBERS.
WATTERSON
IF I DID **THAT**, I'D GET THE PICTURE THEY SHOW ON THE BOX!
AH.

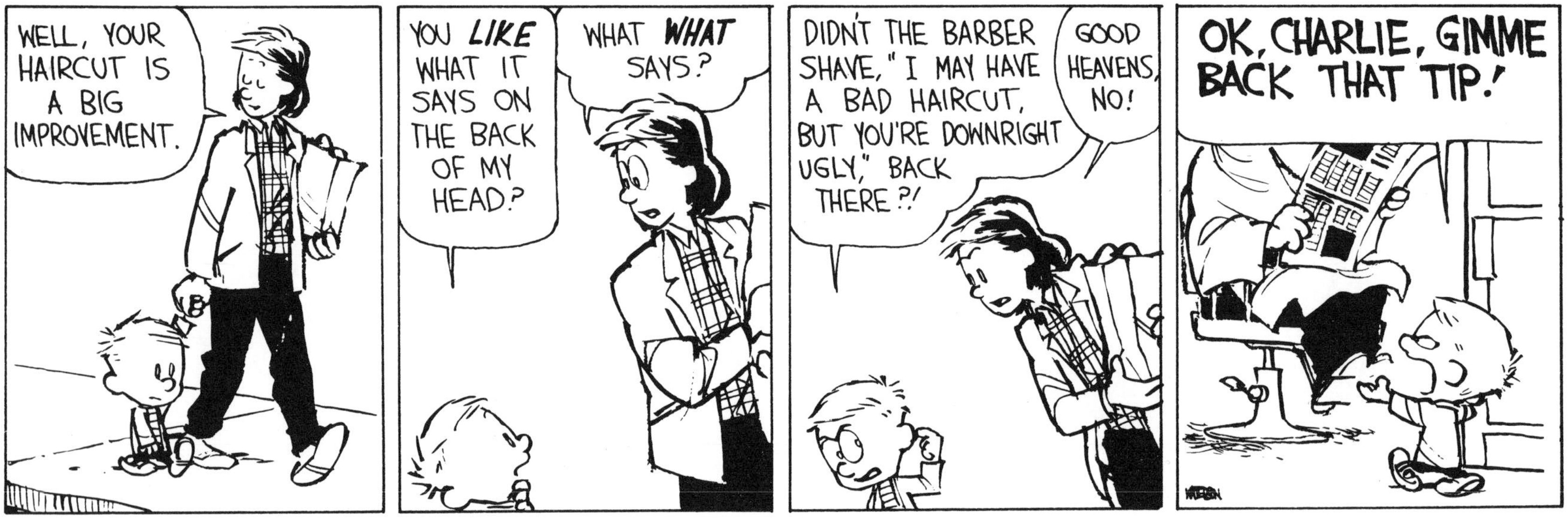
WELL, YOUR HAIRCUT IS A BIG IMPROVEMENT.
YOU **LIKE** WHAT IT SAYS ON THE BACK OF MY HEAD?
WHAT **WHAT** SAYS?
DIDN'T THE BARBER SHAVE, "I MAY HAVE A BAD HAIRCUT, BUT YOU'RE DOWNRIGHT UGLY," BACK THERE?!
GOOD HEAVENS, NO!
OK, CHARLIE, GIMME BACK THAT TIP!

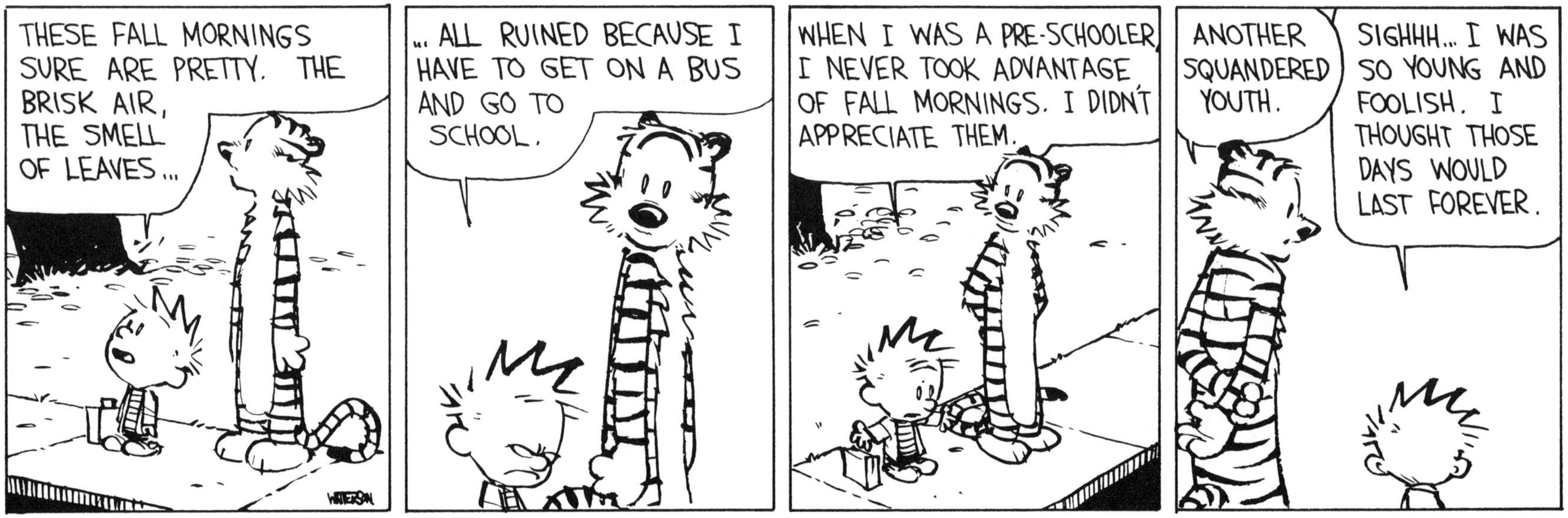
THESE FALL MORNINGS SURE ARE PRETTY. THE BRISK AIR, THE SMELL OF LEAVES...
...ALL RUINED BECAUSE I HAVE TO GET ON A BUS AND GO TO SCHOOL.
WHEN I WAS A PRE-SCHOOLER, I NEVER TOOK ADVANTAGE OF FALL MORNINGS. I DIDN'T APPRECIATE THEM.
ANOTHER SQUANDERED YOUTH.
SIGHHH... I WAS SO YOUNG AND FOOLISH. I THOUGHT THOSE DAYS WOULD LAST FOREVER.

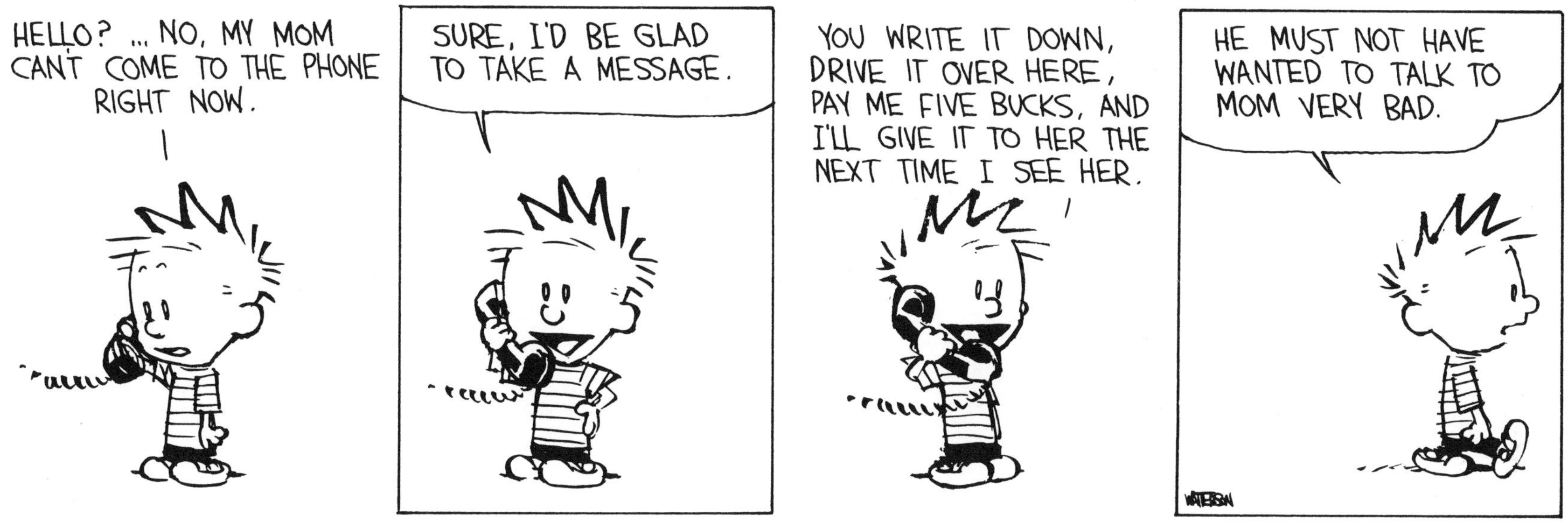
HELLO? ... NO, MY MOM CAN'T COME TO THE PHONE RIGHT NOW.
SURE, I'D BE GLAD TO TAKE A MESSAGE.
YOU WRITE IT DOWN, DRIVE IT OVER HERE, PAY ME FIVE BUCKS, AND I'LL GIVE IT TO HER THE NEXT TIME I SEE HER.
HE MUST NOT HAVE WANTED TO TALK TO MOM VERY BAD.
WATERSON

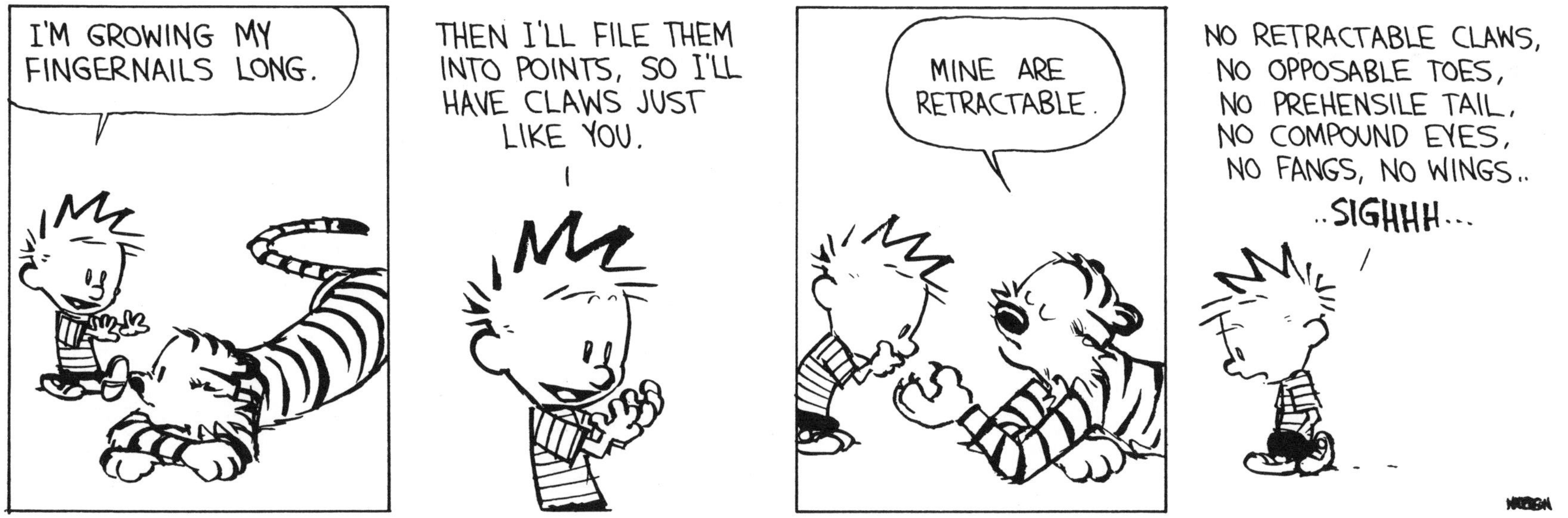
I'M GROWING MY FINGERNAILS LONG.
THEN I'LL FILE THEM INTO POINTS, SO I'LL HAVE CLAWS JUST LIKE YOU.
MINE ARE RETRACTABLE.
NO RETRACTABLE CLAWS, NO OPPOSABLE TOES, NO PREHENSILE TAIL, NO COMPOUND EYES, NO FANGS, NO WINGS..
..SIGHHH...
WATERSON

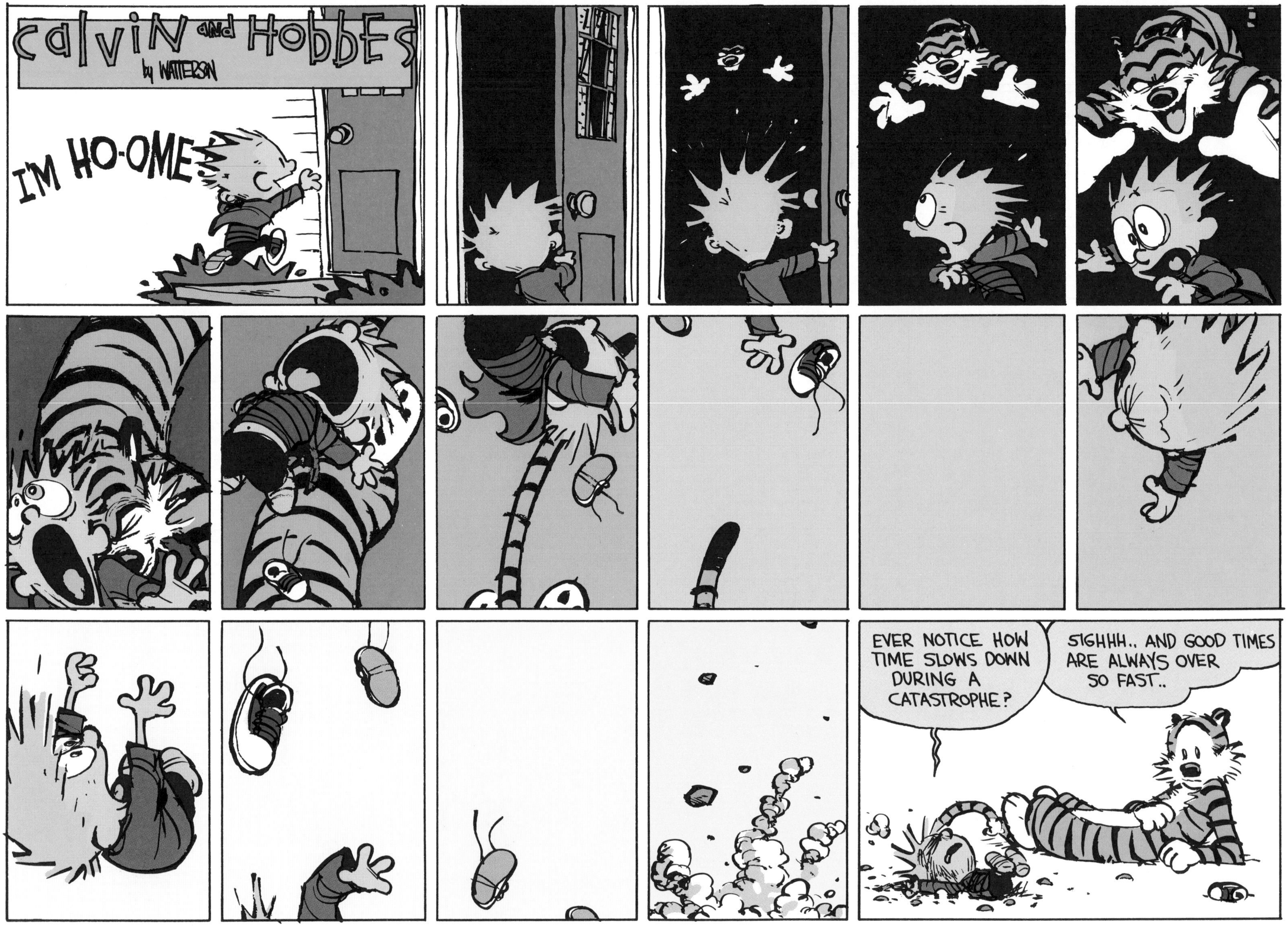
Calvin and Hobbes
by WATTERSON
I'M HO-OME!
EVER NOTICE HOW TIME SLOWS DOWN DURING A CATASTROPHE?
SIGHHH.. AND GOOD TIMES ARE ALWAYS OVER SO FAST..

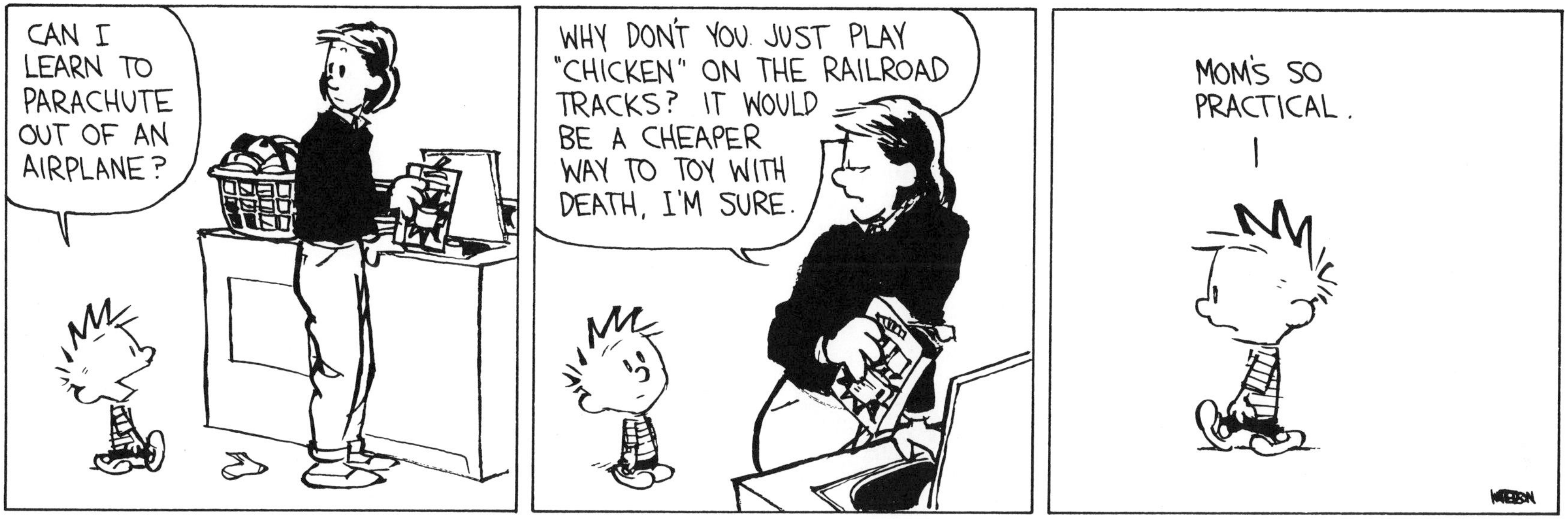
CAN I LEARN TO PARACHUTE OUT OF AN AIRPLANE?
WHY DON'T YOU JUST PLAY "CHICKEN" ON THE RAILROAD TRACKS? IT WOULD BE A CHEAPER WAY TO TOY WITH DEATH, I'M SURE.
MOM'S SO PRACTICAL.

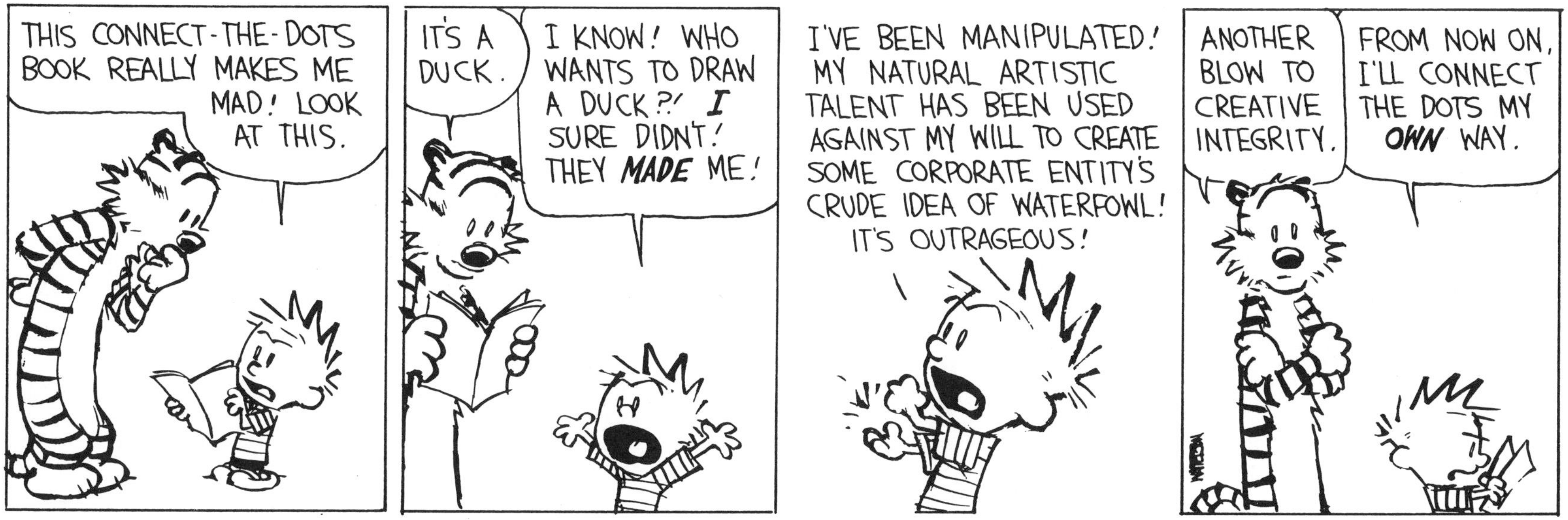
THIS CONNECT-THE-DOTS BOOK REALLY MAKES ME MAD! LOOK AT THIS.
IT'S A DUCK.
I KNOW! WHO WANTS TO DRAW A DUCK?! I SURE DIDN'T! THEY MADE ME!
I'VE BEEN MANIPULATED! MY NATURAL ARTISTIC TALENT HAS BEEN USED AGAINST MY WILL TO CREATE SOME CORPORATE ENTITY'S CRUDE IDEA OF WATERFOWL! IT'S OUTRAGEOUS!
ANOTHER BLOW TO CREATIVE INTEGRITY.
FROM NOW ON, I'LL CONNECT THE DOTS MY OWN WAY.

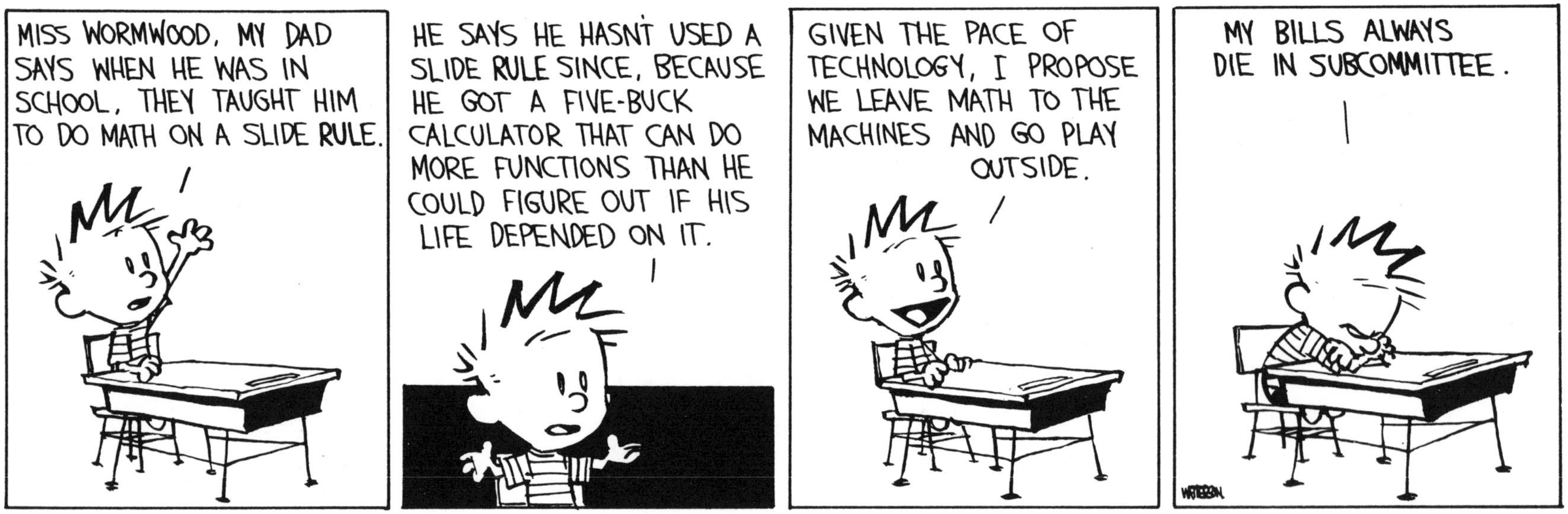
MISS WORMWOOD, MY DAD SAYS WHEN HE WAS IN SCHOOL, THEY TAUGHT HIM TO DO MATH ON A SLIDE RULE.
HE SAYS HE HASN'T USED A SLIDE RULE SINCE, BECAUSE HE GOT A FIVE-BUCK CALCULATOR THAT CAN DO MORE FUNCTIONS THAN HE COULD FIGURE OUT IF HIS LIFE DEPENDED ON IT.
GIVEN THE PACE OF TECHNOLOGY, I PROPOSE WE LEAVE MATH TO THE MACHINES AND GO PLAY OUTSIDE.
MY BILLS ALWAYS DIE IN SUBCOMMITTEE.
WATTERSON

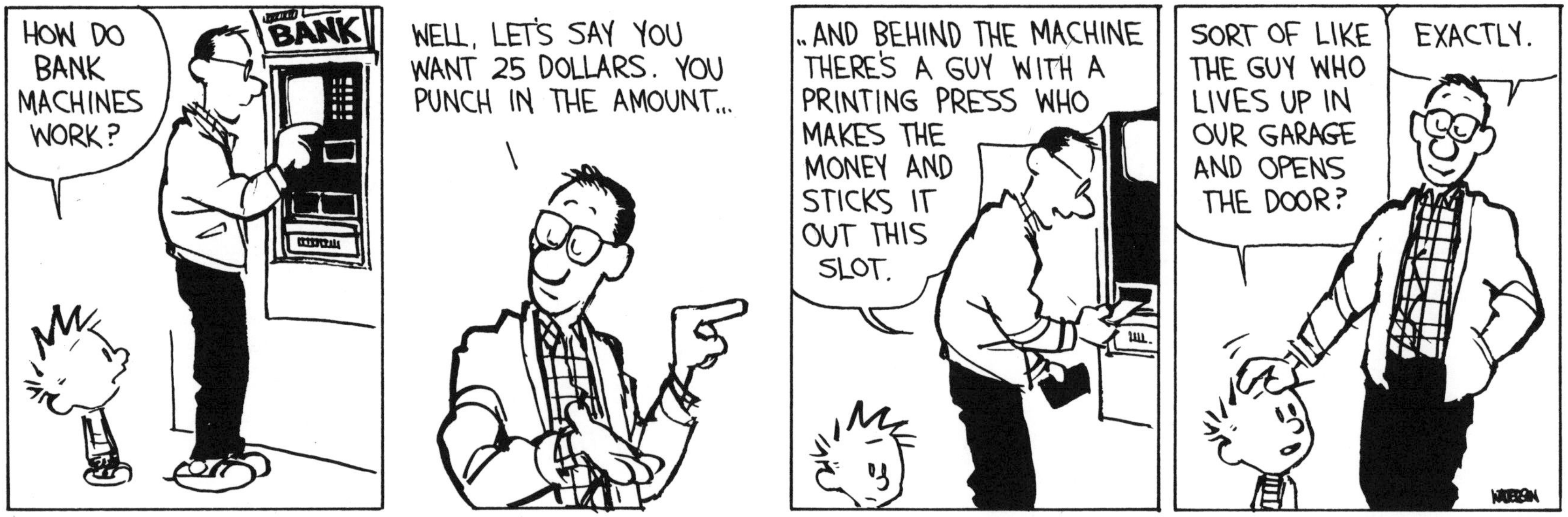
HOW DO BANK MACHINES WORK?
BANK
WELL, LET'S SAY YOU WANT 25 DOLLARS. YOU PUNCH IN THE AMOUNT...
..AND BEHIND THE MACHINE THERE'S A GUY WITH A PRINTING PRESS WHO MAKES THE MONEY AND STICKS IT OUT THIS SLOT.
SORT OF LIKE THE GUY WHO LIVES UP IN OUR GARAGE AND OPENS THE DOOR?
EXACTLY.
WATTERSON

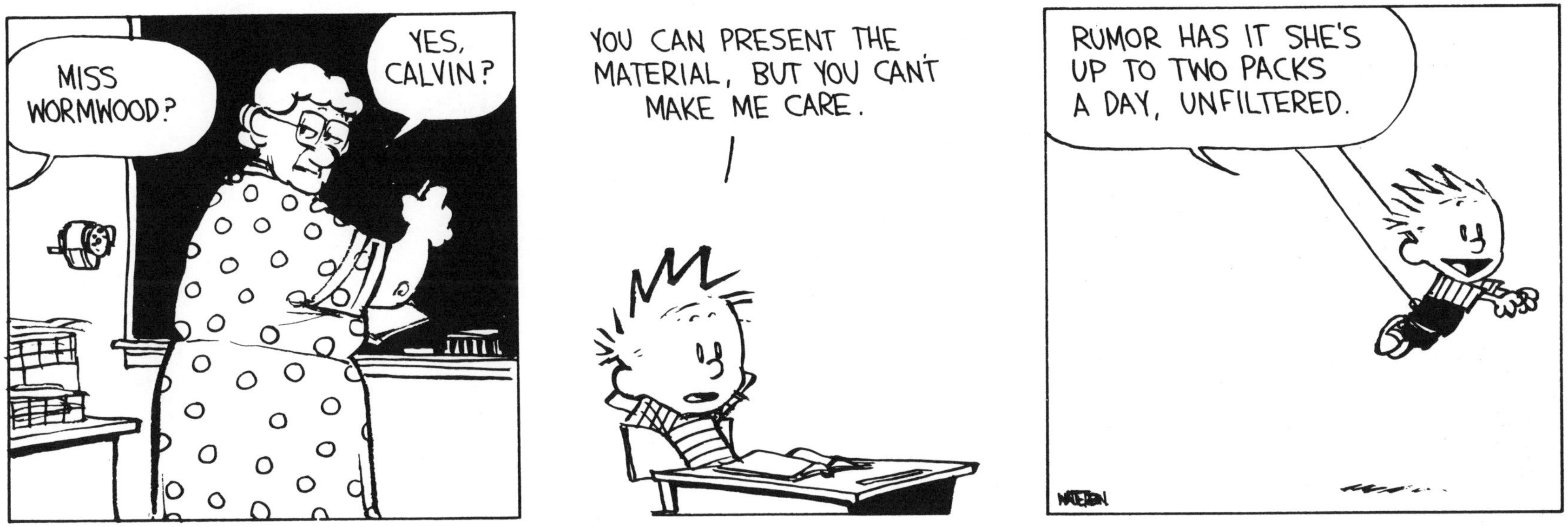
MISS WORMWOOD?
YES, CALVIN?
YOU CAN PRESENT THE MATERIAL, BUT YOU CAN'T MAKE ME CARE.
RUMOR HAS IT SHE'S UP TO TWO PACKS A DAY, UNFILTERED.

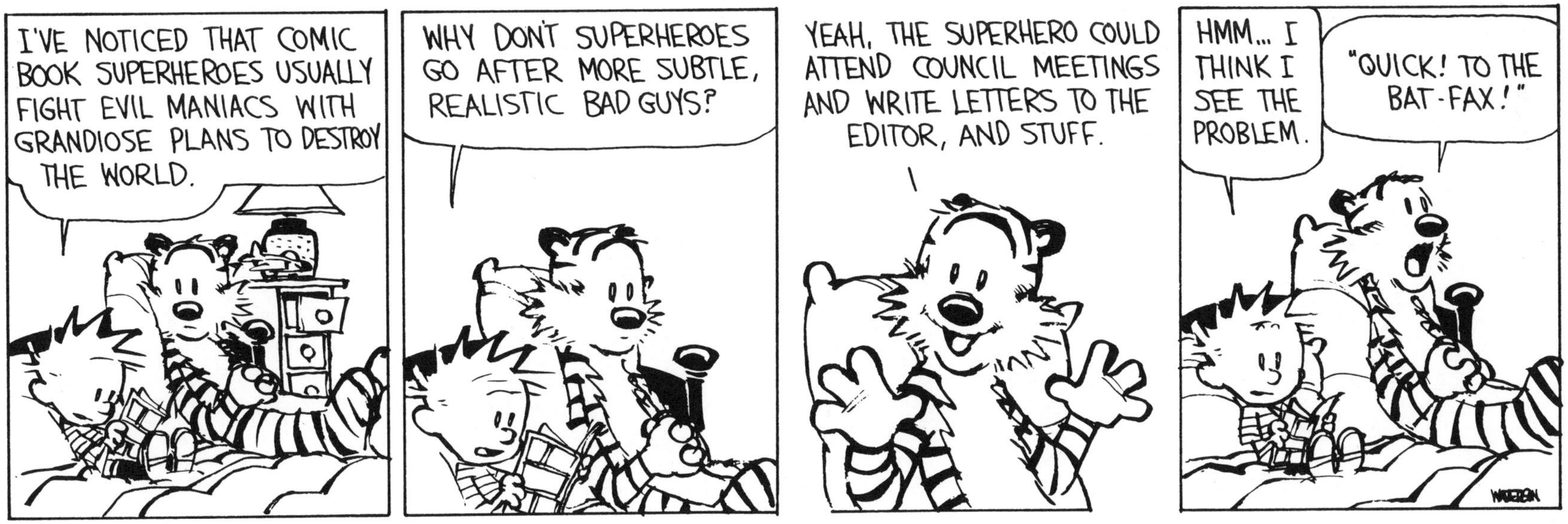
I'VE NOTICED THAT COMIC BOOK SUPERHEROES USUALLY FIGHT EVIL MANIACS WITH GRANDIOSE PLANS TO DESTROY THE WORLD.
WHY DON'T SUPERHEROES GO AFTER MORE SUBTLE, REALISTIC BAD GUYS?
YEAH, THE SUPERHERO COULD ATTEND COUNCIL MEETINGS AND WRITE LETTERS TO THE EDITOR, AND STUFF.
HMM... I THINK I SEE THE PROBLEM.
"QUICK! TO THE BAT-FAX!"

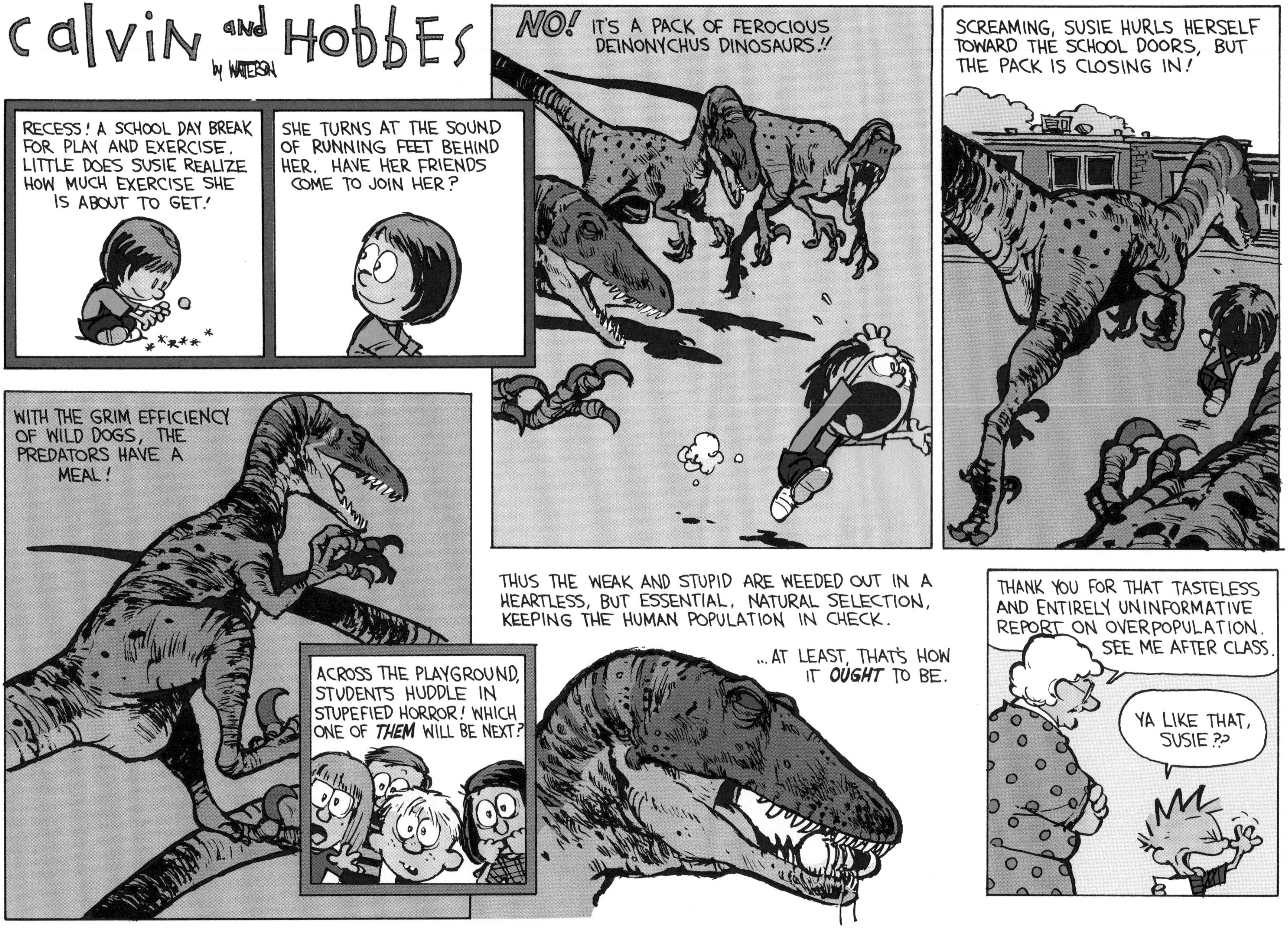

Calvin and Hobbes
by WATTERSON
RECESS! A SCHOOL DAY BREAK FOR PLAY AND EXERCISE. LITTLE DOES SUSIE REALIZE HOW MUCH EXERCISE SHE IS ABOUT TO GET!
SHE TURNS AT THE SOUND OF RUNNING FEET BEHIND HER. HAVE HER FRIENDS COME TO JOIN HER?
NO! IT'S A PACK OF FEROCIOUS DEINONYCHUS DINOSAURS!!
SCREAMING, SUSIE HURLS HERSELF TOWARD THE SCHOOL DOORS, BUT THE PACK IS CLOSING IN!
WITH THE GRIM EFFICIENCY OF WILD DOGS, THE PREDATORS HAVE A MEAL!
ACROSS THE PLAYGROUND, STUDENTS HUDDLE IN STUPEFIED HORROR! WHICH ONE OF THEM WILL BE NEXT?
THUS THE WEAK AND STUPID ARE WEEDED OUT IN A HEARTLESS, BUT ESSENTIAL, NATURAL SELECTION, KEEPING THE HUMAN POPULATION IN CHECK.
...AT LEAST, THAT'S HOW IT OUGHT TO BE.
THANK YOU FOR THAT TASTELESS AND ENTIRELY UNINFORMATIVE REPORT ON OVERPOPULATION. SEE ME AFTER CLASS.
YA LIKE THAT, SUSIE?

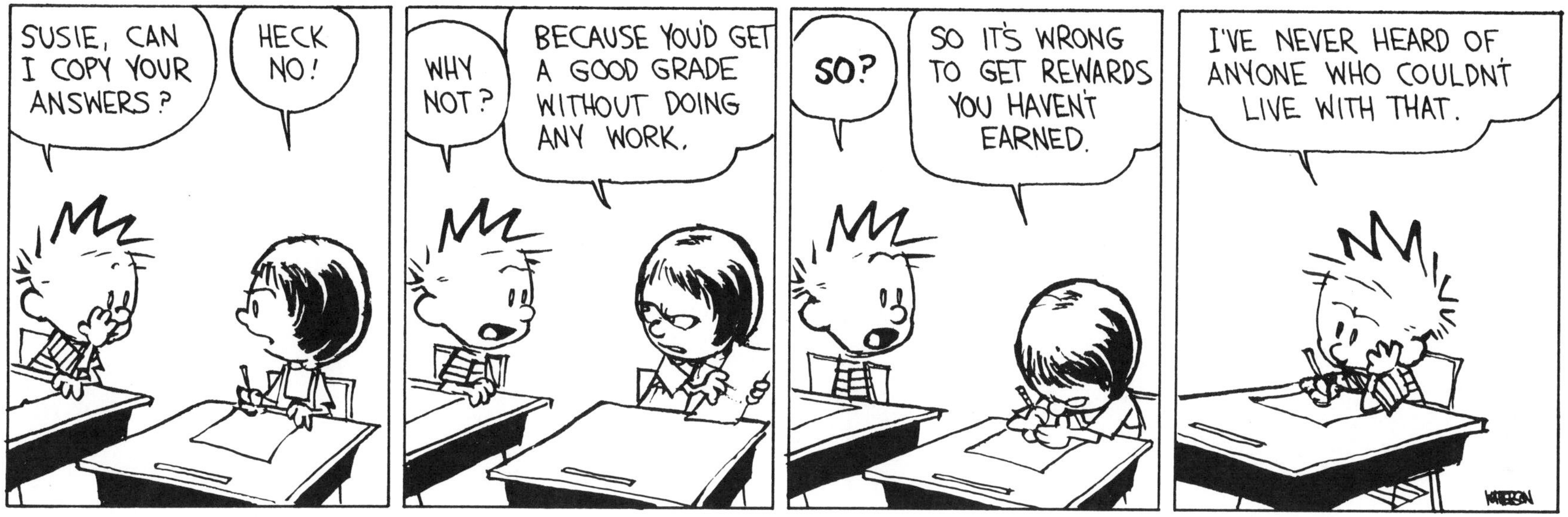
SUSIE, CAN I COPY YOUR ANSWERS?
HECK NO!
WHY NOT?
BECAUSE YOU'D GET A GOOD GRADE WITHOUT DOING ANY WORK.
SO?
SO IT'S WRONG TO GET REWARDS YOU HAVEN'T EARNED.
I'VE NEVER HEARD OF ANYONE WHO COULDN'T LIVE WITH THAT.

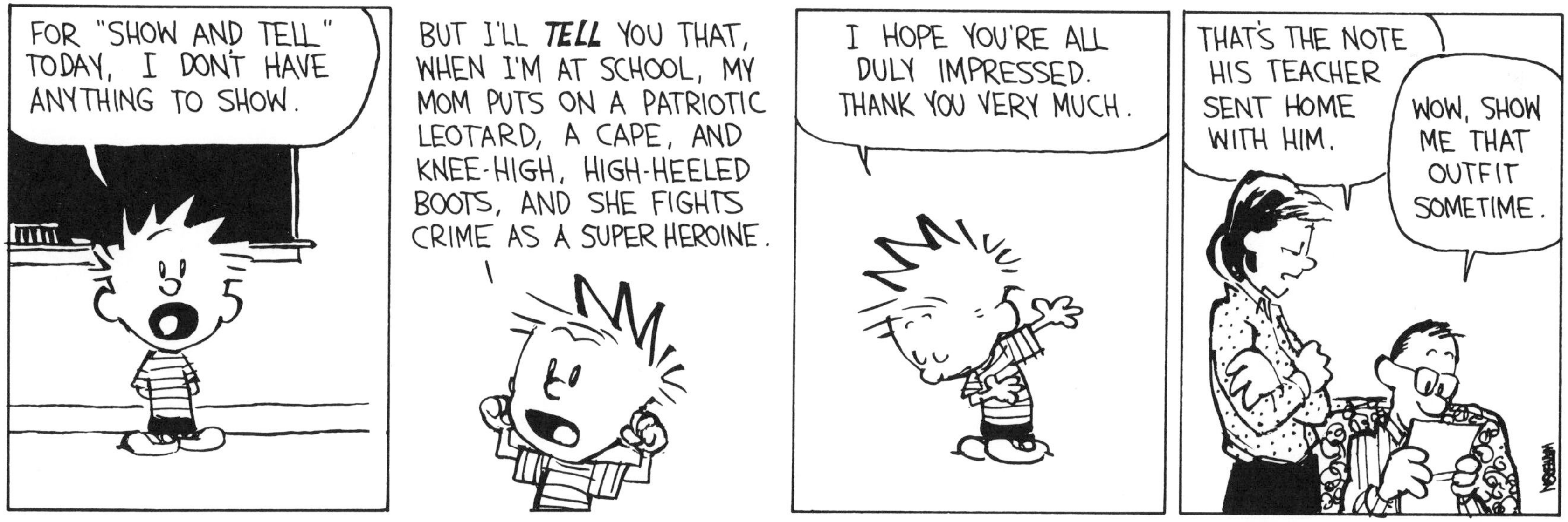
FOR "SHOW AND TELL" TODAY, I DON'T HAVE ANYTHING TO SHOW.
BUT I'LL TELL YOU THAT, WHEN I'M AT SCHOOL, MY MOM PUTS ON A PATRIOTIC LEOTARD, A CAPE, AND KNEE-HIGH, HIGH-HEELED BOOTS, AND SHE FIGHTS CRIME AS A SUPER HEROINE.
I HOPE YOU'RE ALL DULY IMPRESSED. THANK YOU VERY MUCH.
THAT'S THE NOTE HIS TEACHER SENT HOME WITH HIM.
WOW, SHOW ME THAT OUTFIT SOMETIME.

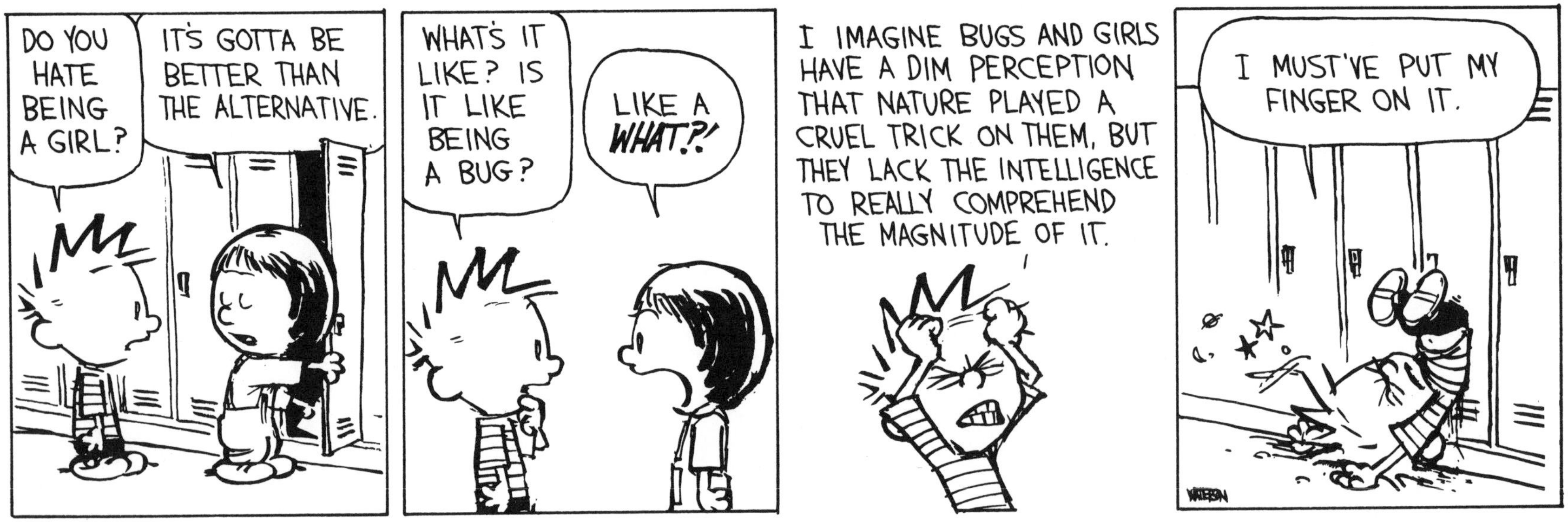
DO YOU HATE BEING A GIRL?
IT'S GOTTA BE BETTER THAN THE ALTERNATIVE.
WHAT'S IT LIKE? IS IT LIKE BEING A BUG?
LIKE A *WHAT?!*
I IMAGINE BUGS AND GIRLS HAVE A DIM PERCEPTION THAT NATURE PLAYED A CRUEL TRICK ON THEM, BUT THEY LACK THE INTELLIGENCE TO REALLY COMPREHEND THE MAGNITUDE OF IT.
I MUST'VE PUT MY FINGER ON IT.

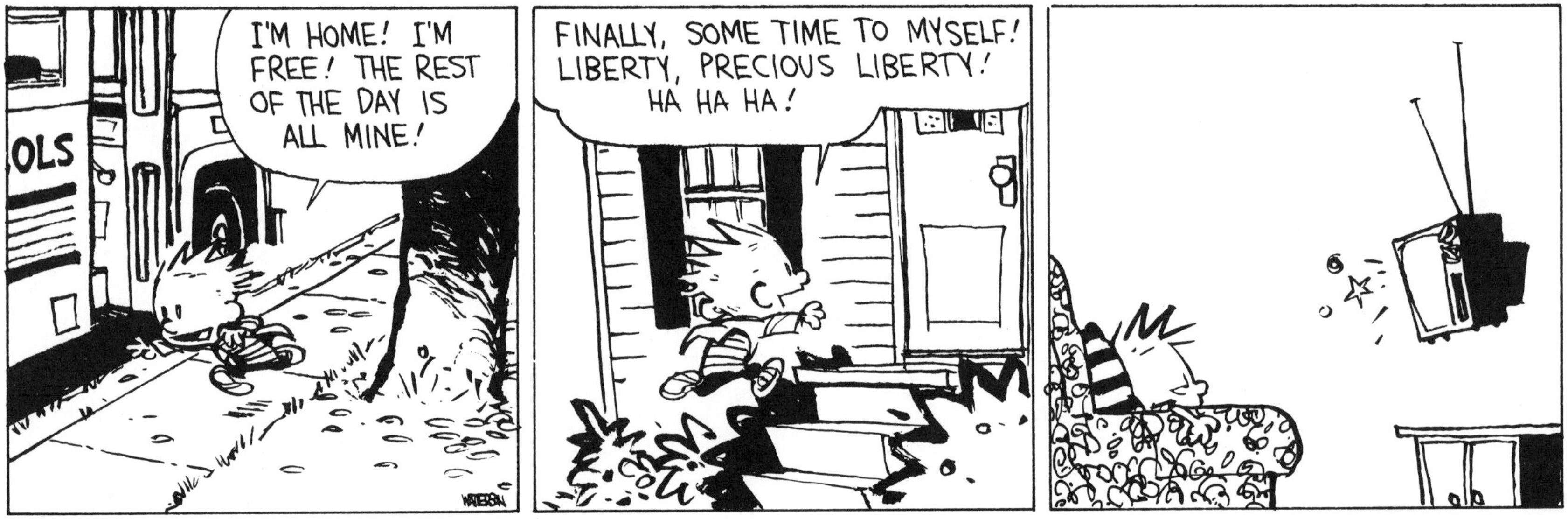
OLS
I'M HOME! I'M FREE! THE REST OF THE DAY IS ALL MINE!
FINALLY, SOME TIME TO MYSELF! LIBERTY, PRECIOUS LIBERTY! HA HA HA!

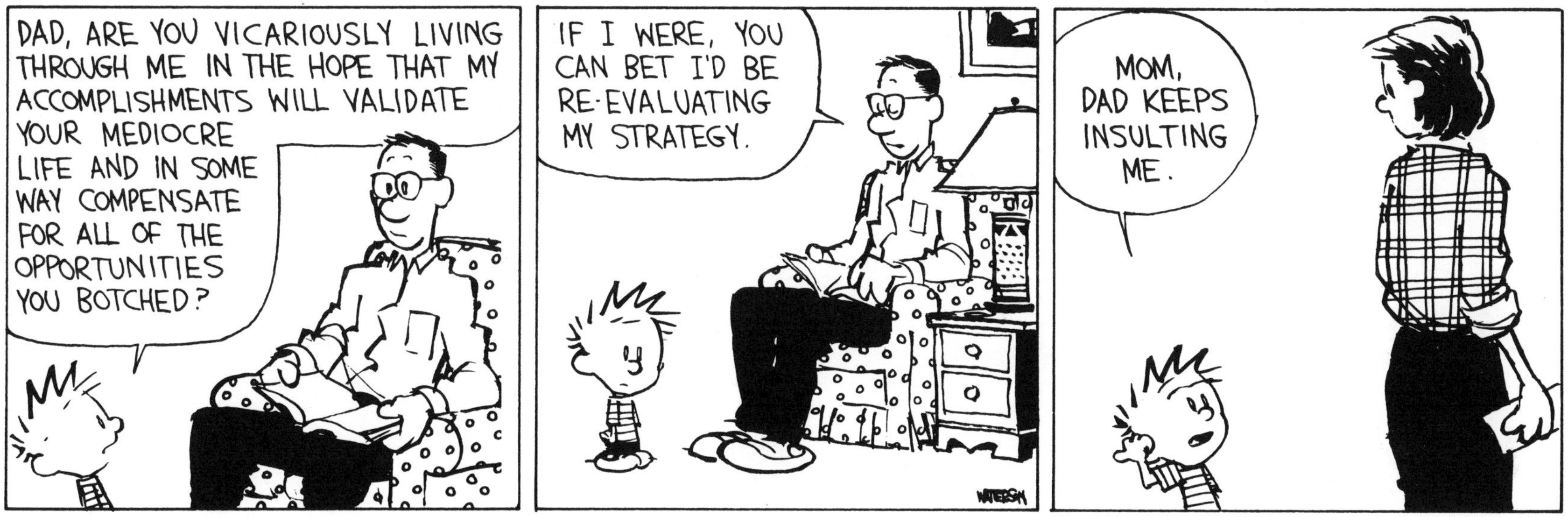
DAD, ARE YOU VICARIOUSLY LIVING THROUGH ME IN THE HOPE THAT MY ACCOMPLISHMENTS WILL VALIDATE YOUR MEDIOCRE LIFE AND IN SOME WAY COMPENSATE FOR ALL OF THE OPPORTUNITIES YOU BOTCHED?
IF I WERE, YOU CAN BET I'D BE RE-EVALUATING MY STRATEGY.
MOM, DAD KEEPS INSULTING ME.

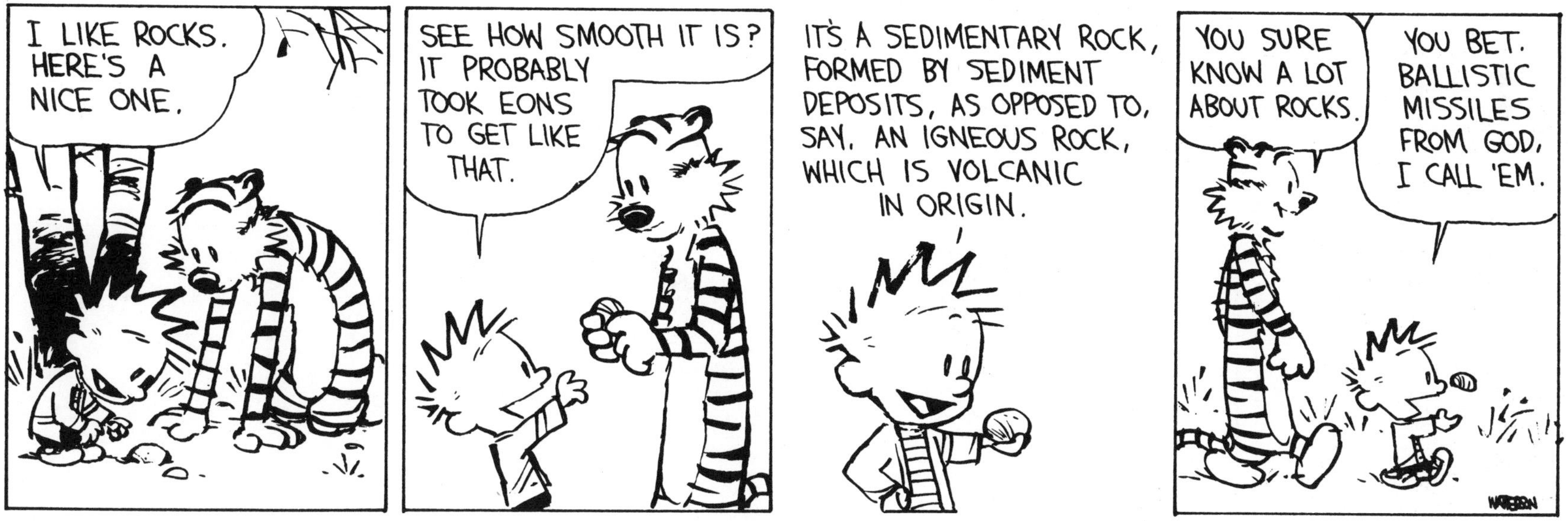
I LIKE ROCKS. HERE'S A NICE ONE.
SEE HOW SMOOTH IT IS? IT PROBABLY TOOK EONS TO GET LIKE THAT.
IT'S A SEDIMENTARY ROCK, FORMED BY SEDIMENT DEPOSITS, AS OPPOSED TO, SAY, AN IGNEOUS ROCK, WHICH IS VOLCANIC IN ORIGIN.
YOU SURE KNOW A LOT ABOUT ROCKS.
YOU BET. BALLISTIC MISSILES FROM GOD, I CALL 'EM.

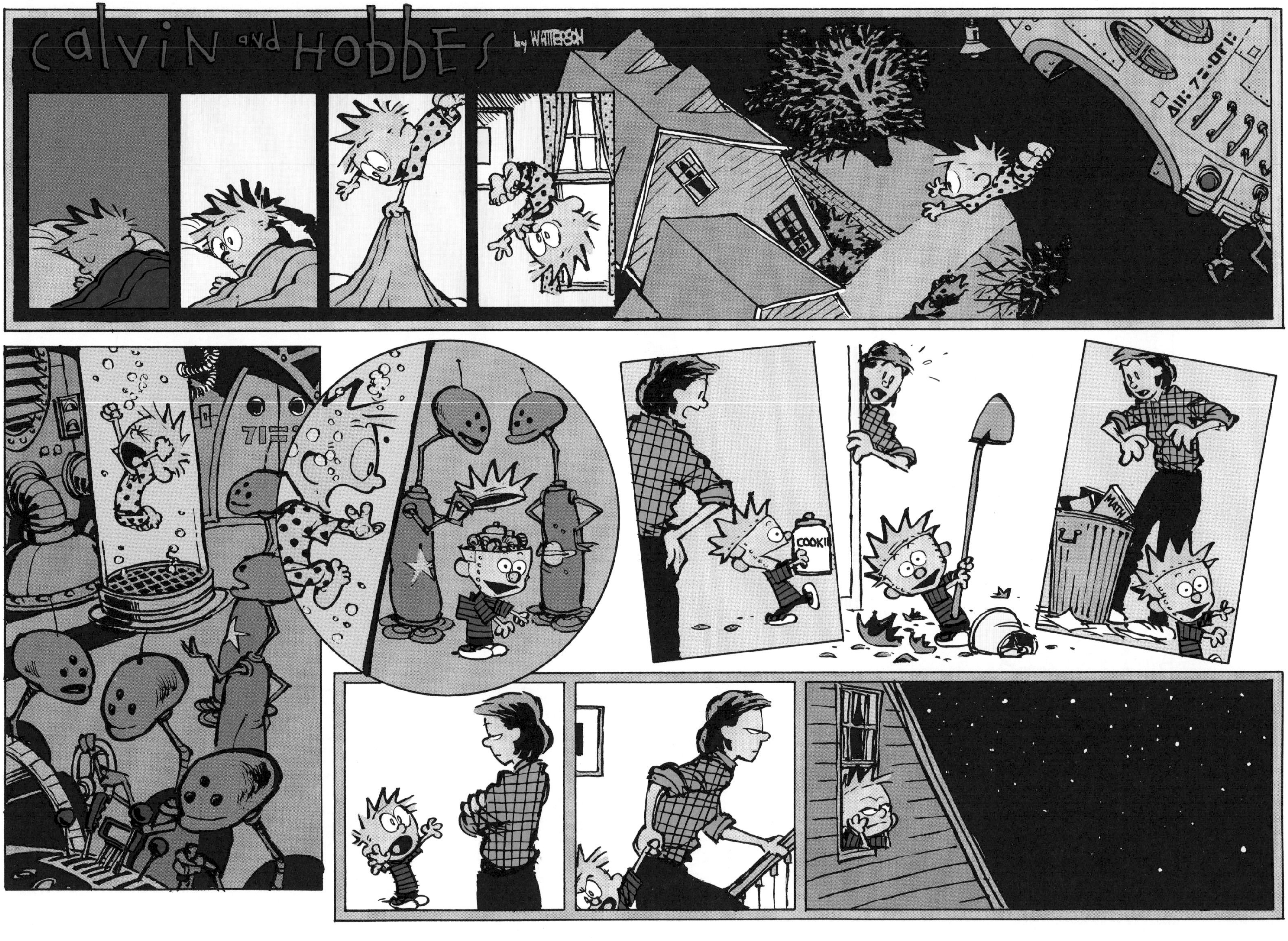
Calvin and HOBBES
by WATTERSON
COOKI
MATH

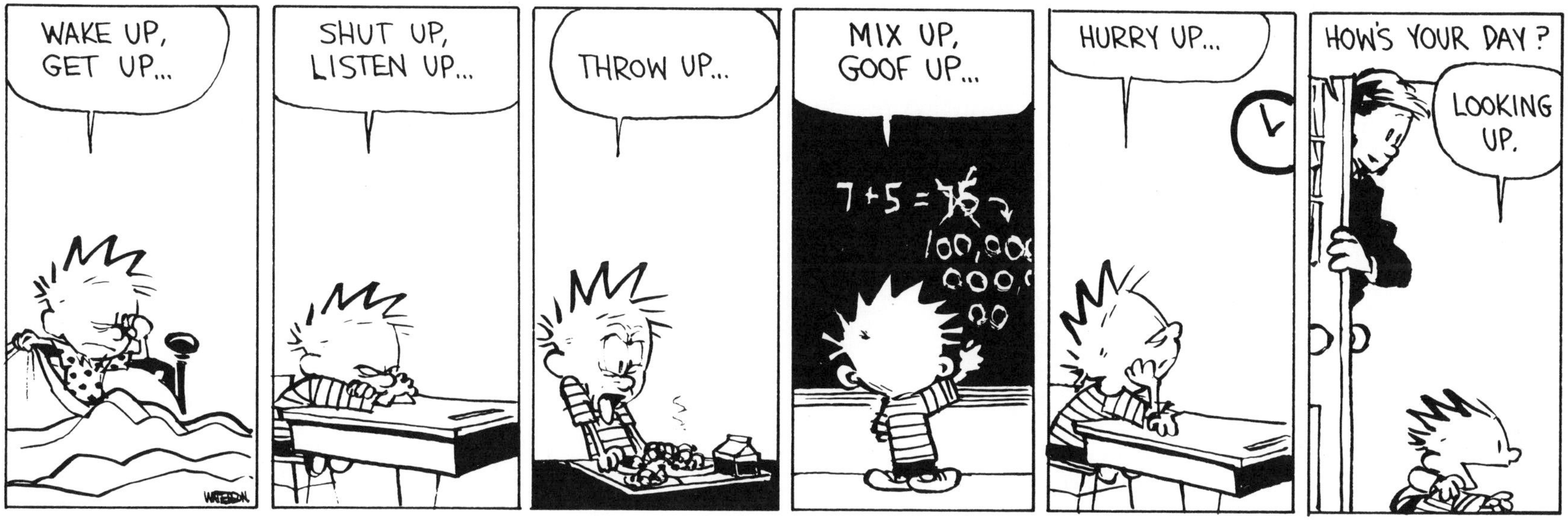
WAKE UP, GET UP...
SHUT UP, LISTEN UP...
THROW UP...
MIX UP, GOOF UP...
7+5=
HURRY UP...
HOW'S YOUR DAY?
LOOKING UP.

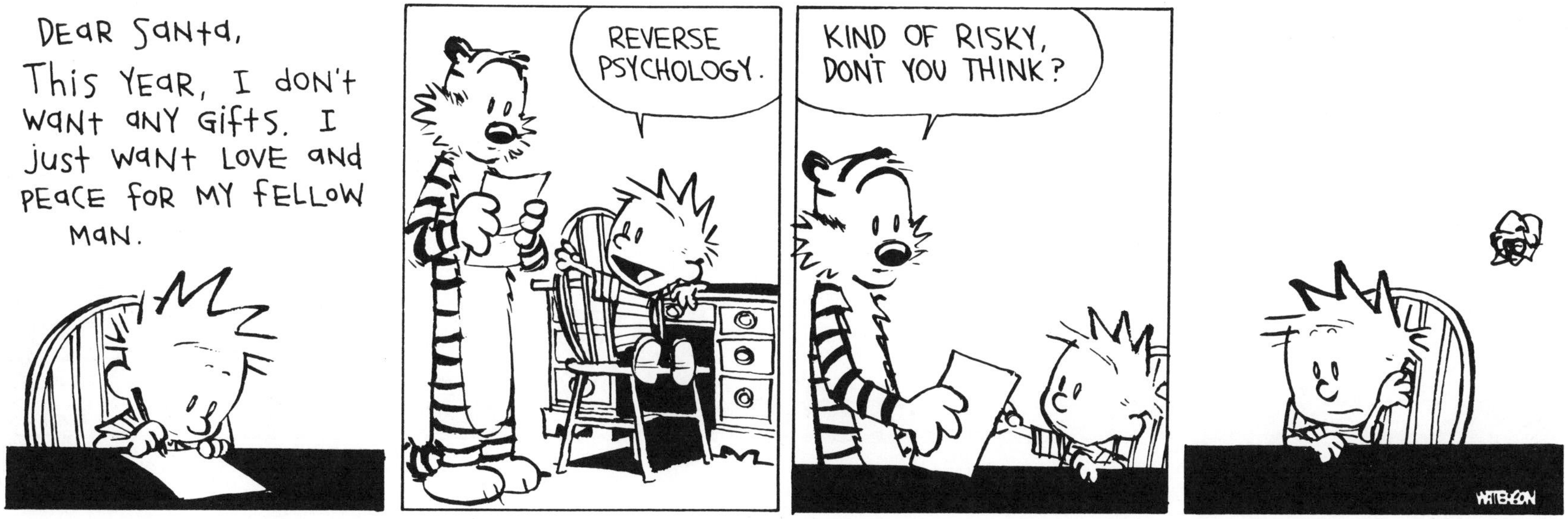
Dear Santa,
This Year, I don't want any Gifts. I just want Love and Peace for my fellow man.
REVERSE PSYCHOLOGY.
KIND OF RISKY, DON'T YOU THINK?

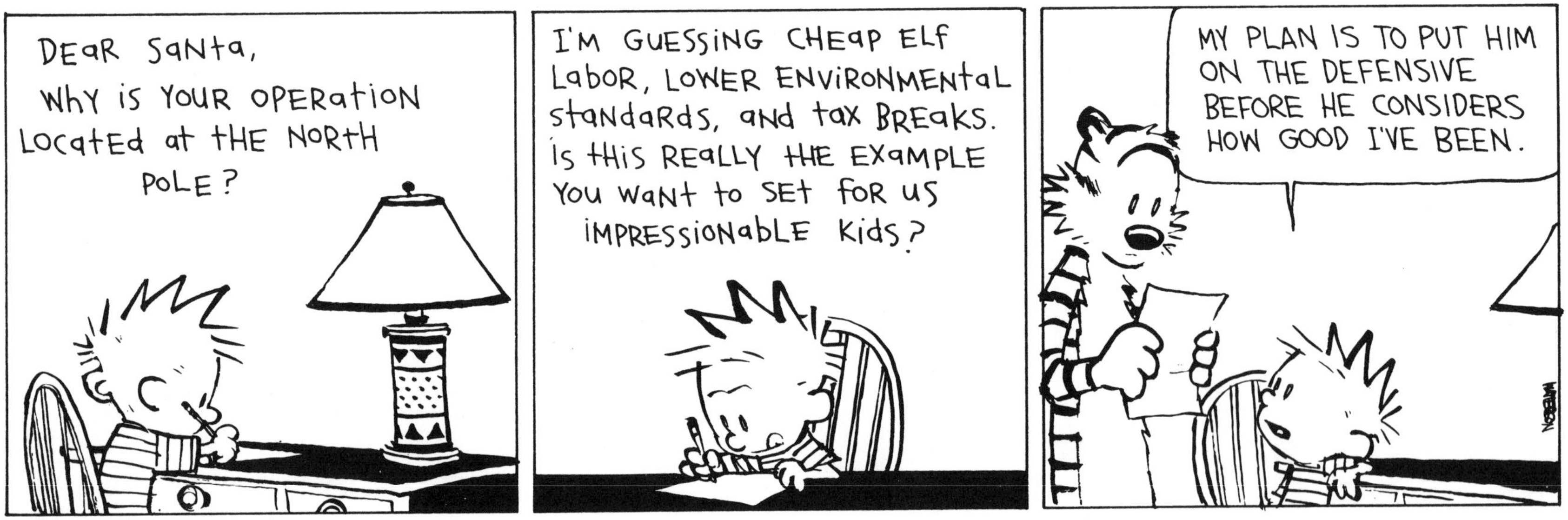
DEAR SANTA,
WHY IS YOUR OPERATION LOCATED AT THE NORTH POLE?
I'M GUESSING CHEAP ELF LABOR, LOWER ENVIRONMENTAL STANDARDS, AND TAX BREAKS. IS THIS REALLY THE EXAMPLE YOU WANT TO SET FOR US IMPRESSIONABLE KIDS?
MY PLAN IS TO PUT HIM ON THE DEFENSIVE BEFORE HE CONSIDERS HOW GOOD I'VE BEEN.

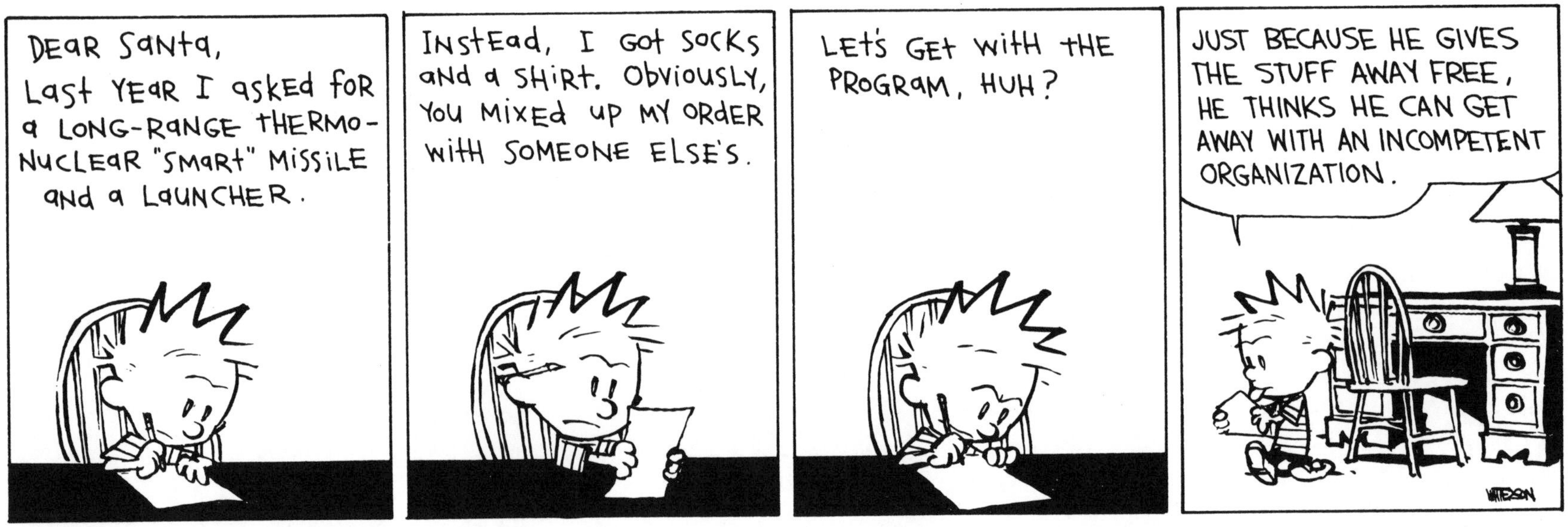
DEAR SANTA,
LAST YEAR I ASKED FOR A LONG-RANGE THERMO-NUCLEAR "SMART" MISSILE AND A LAUNCHER.
INSTEAD, I GOT SOCKS AND A SHIRT. OBVIOUSLY, YOU MIXED UP MY ORDER WITH SOMEONE ELSE'S.
LET'S GET WITH THE PROGRAM, HUH?
JUST BECAUSE HE GIVES THE STUFF AWAY FREE, HE THINKS HE CAN GET AWAY WITH AN INCOMPETENT ORGANIZATION.
WATTERSON

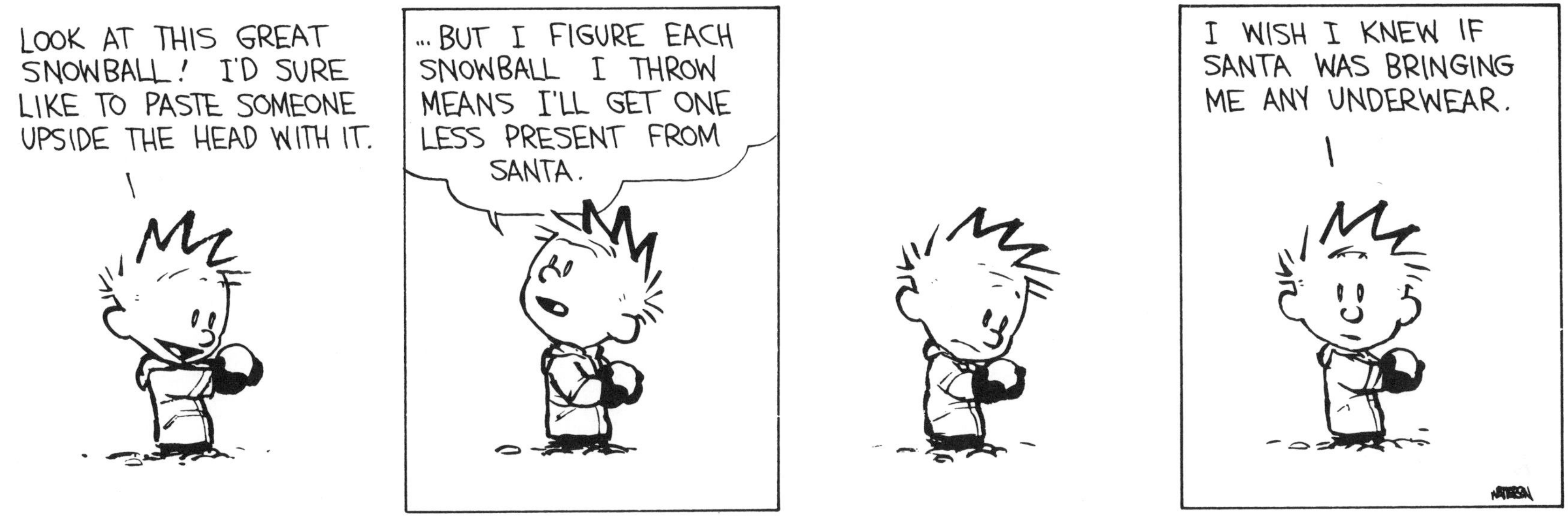
LOOK AT THIS GREAT SNOWBALL! I'D SURE LIKE TO PASTE SOMEONE UPSIDE THE HEAD WITH IT.
...BUT I FIGURE EACH SNOWBALL I THROW MEANS I'LL GET ONE LESS PRESENT FROM SANTA.
I WISH I KNEW IF SANTA WAS BRINGING ME ANY UNDERWEAR.

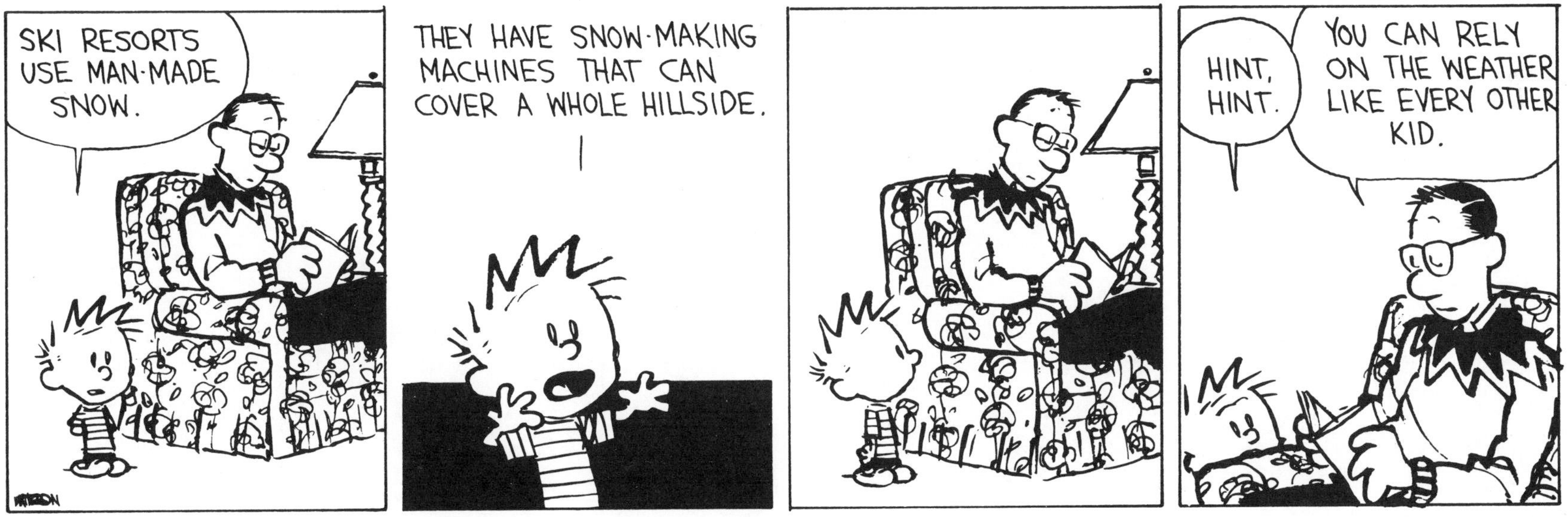
SKI RESORTS USE MAN-MADE SNOW.
THEY HAVE SNOW-MAKING MACHINES THAT CAN COVER A WHOLE HILLSIDE.
HINT, HINT.
YOU CAN RELY ON THE WEATHER LIKE EVERY OTHER KID.

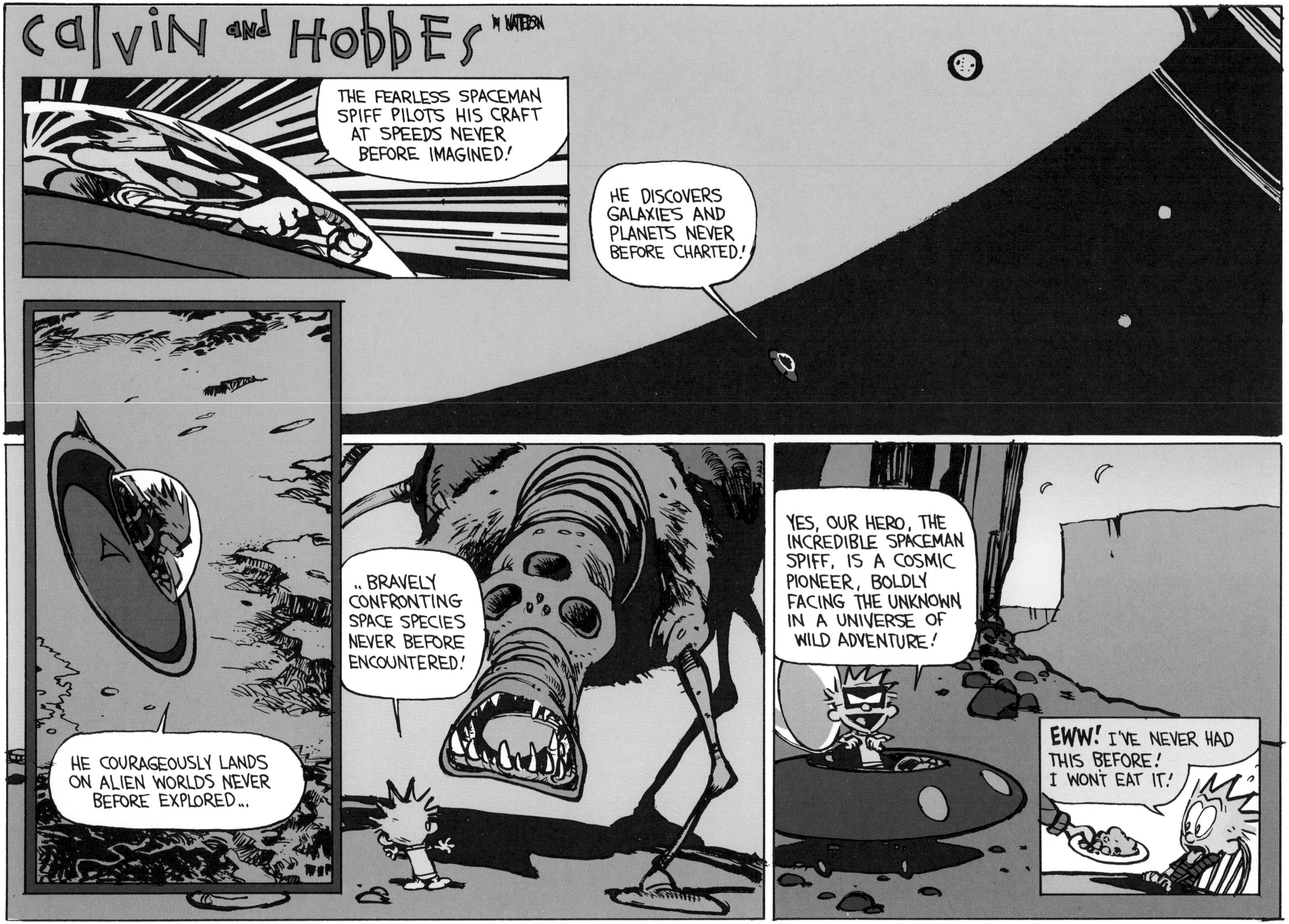
Calvin and Hobbes
by WATTERSON
THE FEARLESS SPACEMAN SPIFF PILOTS HIS CRAFT AT SPEEDS NEVER BEFORE IMAGINED!
HE DISCOVERS GALAXIES AND PLANETS NEVER BEFORE CHARTED!
HE COURAGEOUSLY LANDS ON ALIEN WORLDS NEVER BEFORE EXPLORED...
..BRAVELY CONFRONTING SPACE SPECIES NEVER BEFORE ENCOUNTERED!
YES, OUR HERO, THE INCREDIBLE SPACEMAN SPIFF, IS A COSMIC PIONEER, BOLDLY FACING THE UNKNOWN IN A UNIVERSE OF WILD ADVENTURE!
EWW! I'VE NEVER HAD THIS BEFORE! I WON'T EAT IT!

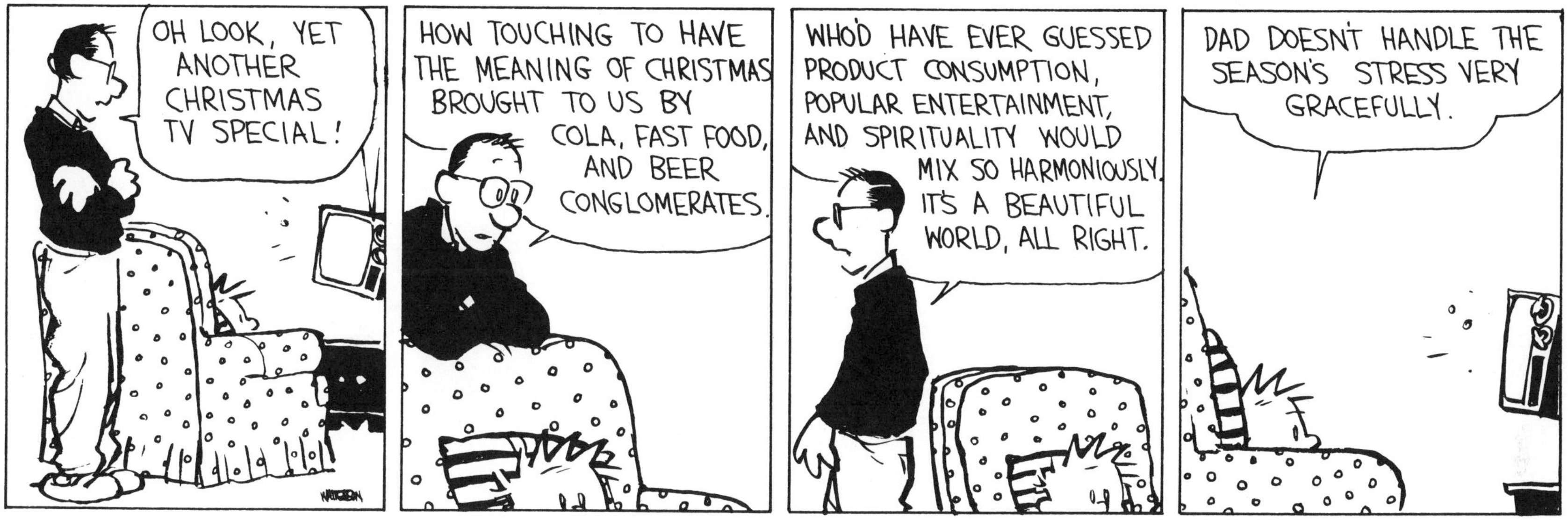
OH LOOK, YET ANOTHER CHRISTMAS TV SPECIAL!
HOW TOUCHING TO HAVE THE MEANING OF CHRISTMAS BROUGHT TO US BY COLA, FAST FOOD, AND BEER CONGLOMERATES.
WHO'D HAVE EVER GUESSED PRODUCT CONSUMPTION, POPULAR ENTERTAINMENT, AND SPIRITUALITY WOULD MIX SO HARMONIOUSLY. IT'S A BEAUTIFUL WORLD, ALL RIGHT.
DAD DOESN'T HANDLE THE SEASON'S STRESS VERY GRACEFULLY.

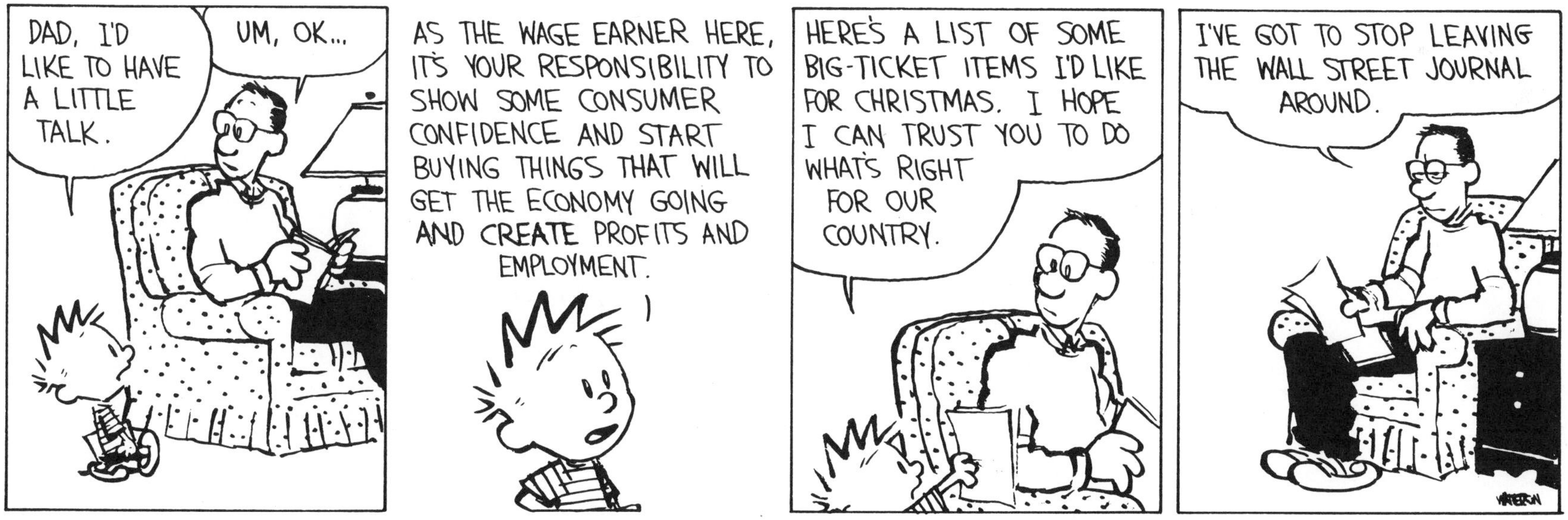
DAD, I'D LIKE TO HAVE A LITTLE TALK.
UM, OK...
AS THE WAGE EARNER HERE, IT'S YOUR RESPONSIBILITY TO SHOW SOME CONSUMER CONFIDENCE AND START BUYING THINGS THAT WILL GET THE ECONOMY GOING AND CREATE PROFITS AND EMPLOYMENT.
HERE'S A LIST OF SOME BIG-TICKET ITEMS I'D LIKE FOR CHRISTMAS. I HOPE I CAN TRUST YOU TO DO WHAT'S RIGHT FOR OUR COUNTRY.
I'VE GOT TO STOP LEAVING THE WALL STREET JOURNAL AROUND.

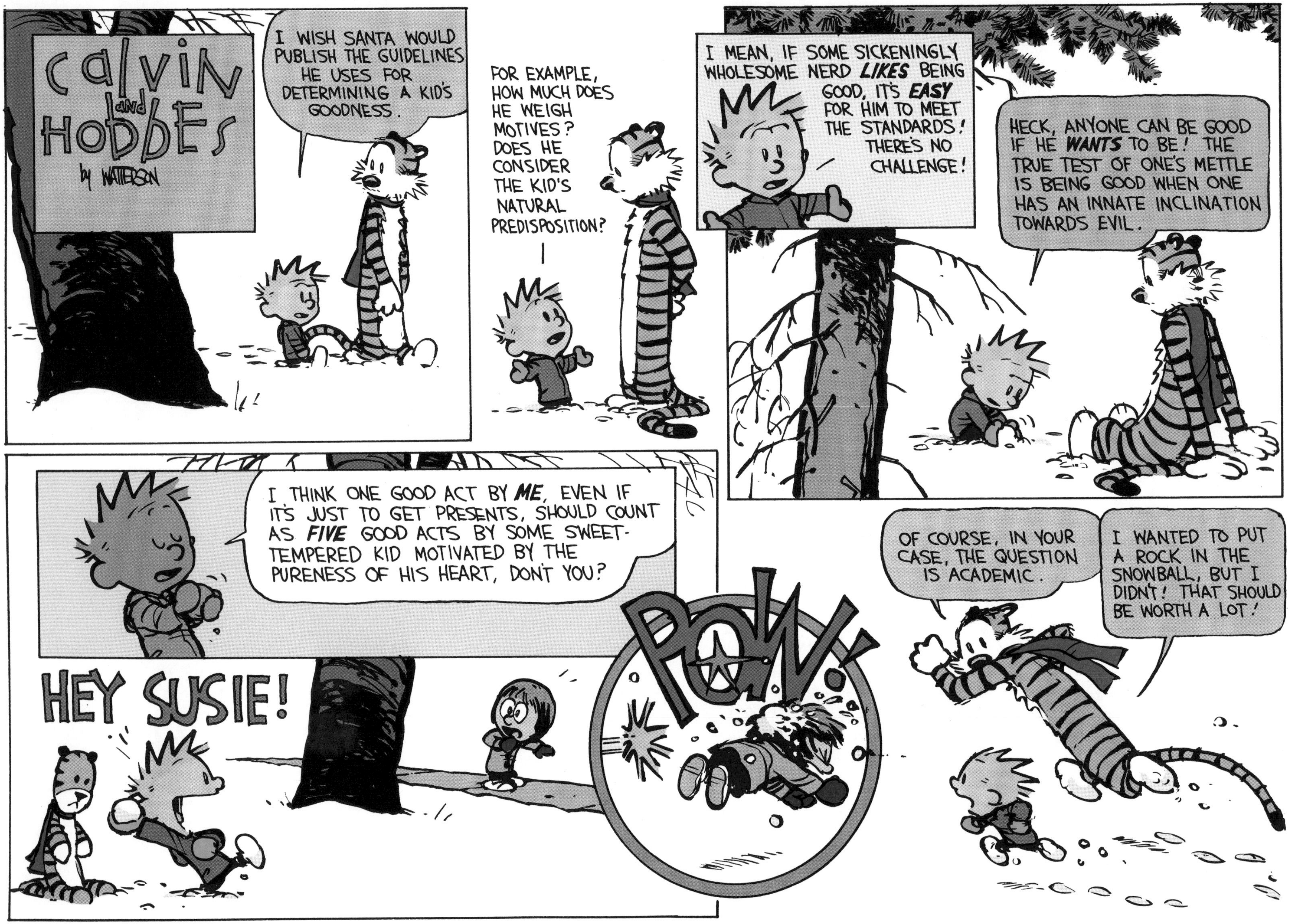
Calvin and Hobbes
by WATTERSON
I WISH SANTA WOULD PUBLISH THE GUIDELINES HE USES FOR DETERMINING A KID'S GOODNESS.
FOR EXAMPLE, HOW MUCH DOES HE WEIGH MOTIVES? DOES HE CONSIDER THE KID'S NATURAL PREDISPOSITION?
I MEAN, IF SOME SICKENINGLY WHOLESOME NERD LIKES BEING GOOD, IT'S EASY FOR HIM TO MEET THE STANDARDS! THERE'S NO CHALLENGE!
HECK, ANYONE CAN BE GOOD IF HE WANTS TO BE! THE TRUE TEST OF ONE'S METTLE IS BEING GOOD WHEN ONE HAS AN INNATE INCLINATION TOWARDS EVIL.
I THINK ONE GOOD ACT BY ME, EVEN IF IT'S JUST TO GET PRESENTS, SHOULD COUNT AS FIVE GOOD ACTS BY SOME SWEET-TEMPERED KID MOTIVATED BY THE PURENESS OF HIS HEART, DON'T YOU?
HEY SUSIE!
POW!
OF COURSE, IN YOUR CASE, THE QUESTION IS ACADEMIC.
I WANTED TO PUT A ROCK IN THE SNOWBALL, BUT I DIDN'T! THAT SHOULD BE WORTH A LOT!

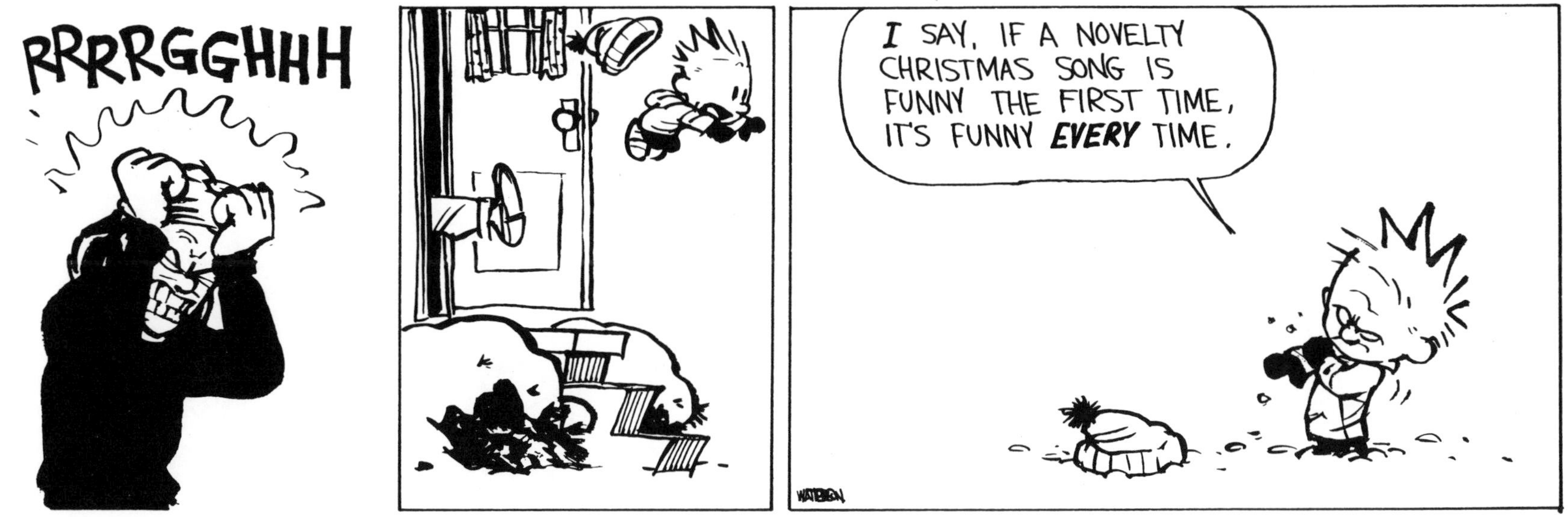
RRRRGGHHH
I SAY, IF A NOVELTY CHRISTMAS SONG IS FUNNY THE FIRST TIME, IT'S FUNNY **EVERY** TIME.

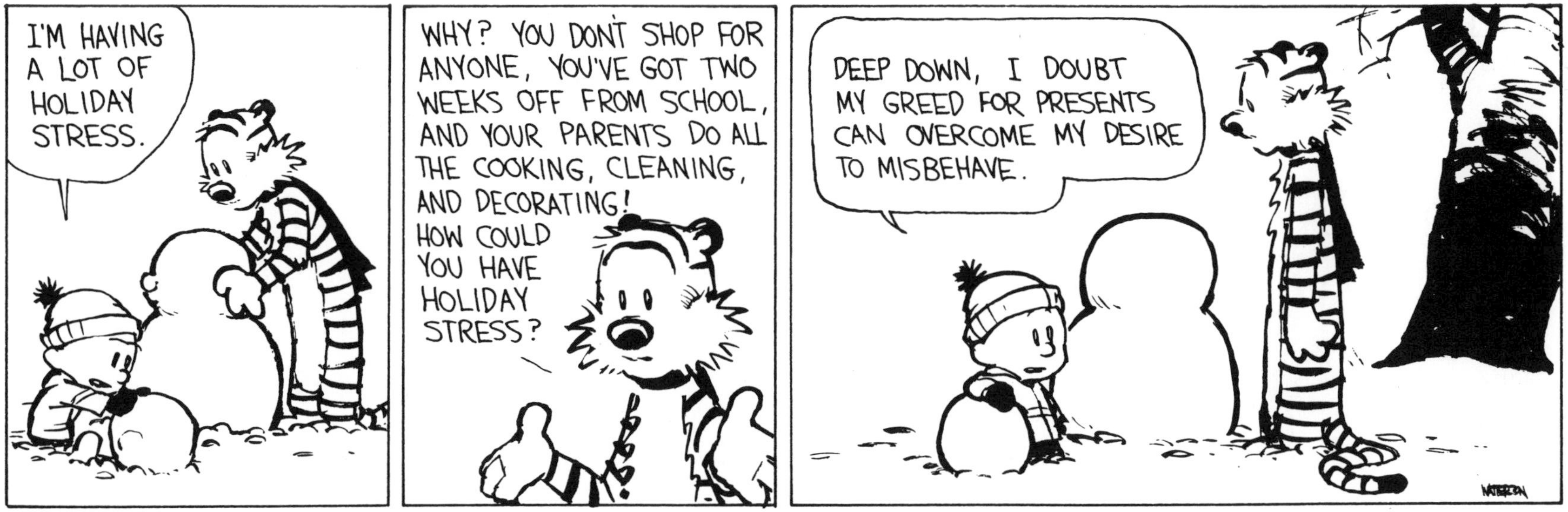
I'M HAVING A LOT OF HOLIDAY STRESS.
WHY? YOU DON'T SHOP FOR ANYONE, YOU'VE GOT TWO WEEKS OFF FROM SCHOOL, AND YOUR PARENTS DO ALL THE COOKING, CLEANING, AND DECORATING! HOW COULD YOU HAVE HOLIDAY STRESS?
DEEP DOWN, I DOUBT MY GREED FOR PRESENTS CAN OVERCOME MY DESIRE TO MISBEHAVE.

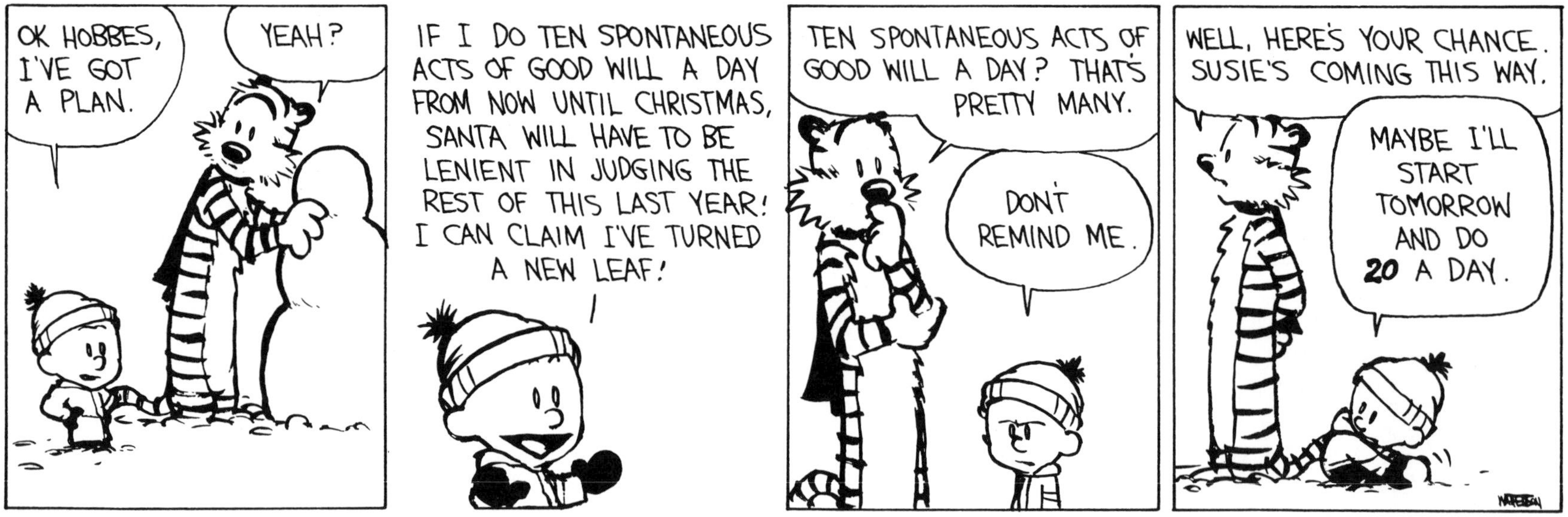
OK HOBBES, I'VE GOT A PLAN.
YEAH?
IF I DO TEN SPONTANEOUS ACTS OF GOOD WILL A DAY FROM NOW UNTIL CHRISTMAS, SANTA WILL HAVE TO BE LENIENT IN JUDGING THE REST OF THIS LAST YEAR! I CAN CLAIM I'VE TURNED A NEW LEAF!
TEN SPONTANEOUS ACTS OF GOOD WILL A DAY? THAT'S PRETTY MANY.
DON'T REMIND ME.
WELL, HERE'S YOUR CHANCE. SUSIE'S COMING THIS WAY.
MAYBE I'LL START TOMORROW AND DO **20** A DAY.

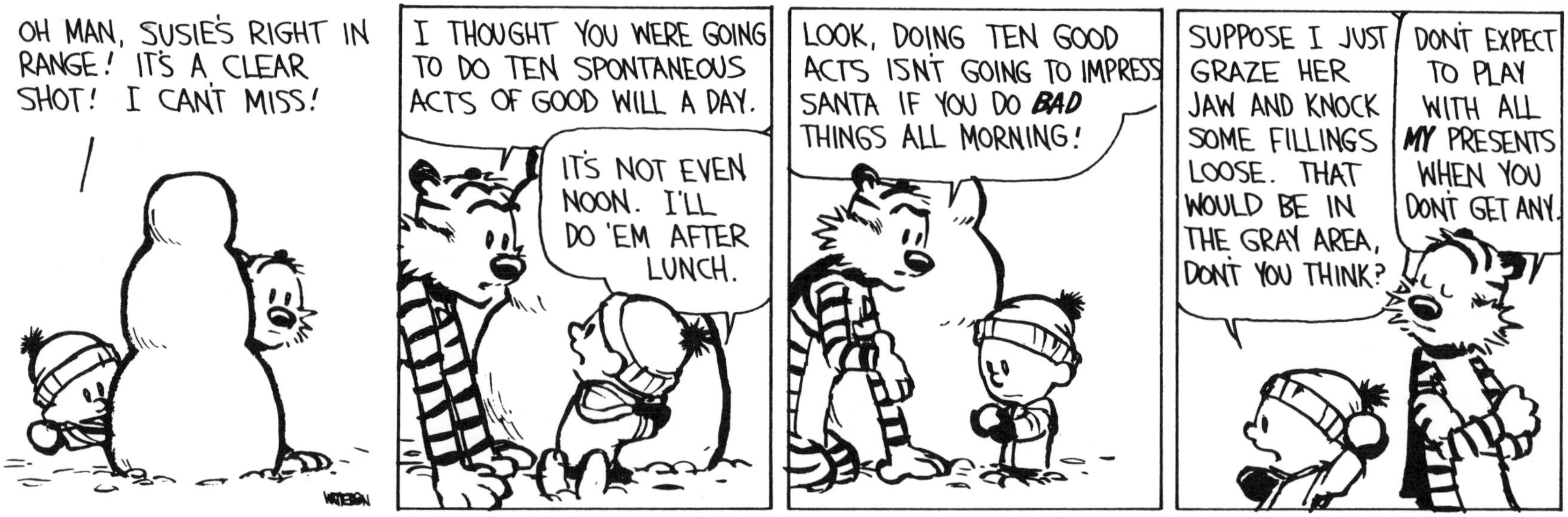
OH MAN, SUSIE'S RIGHT IN RANGE! IT'S A CLEAR SHOT! I CAN'T MISS!
I THOUGHT YOU WERE GOING TO DO TEN SPONTANEOUS ACTS OF GOOD WILL A DAY.
IT'S NOT EVEN NOON. I'LL DO 'EM AFTER LUNCH.
LOOK, DOING TEN GOOD ACTS ISN'T GOING TO IMPRESS SANTA IF YOU DO **BAD** THINGS ALL MORNING!
SUPPOSE I JUST GRAZE HER JAW AND KNOCK SOME FILLINGS LOOSE. THAT WOULD BE IN THE GRAY AREA, DON'T YOU THINK?
DON'T EXPECT TO PLAY WITH ALL **MY** PRESENTS WHEN YOU DON'T GET ANY.

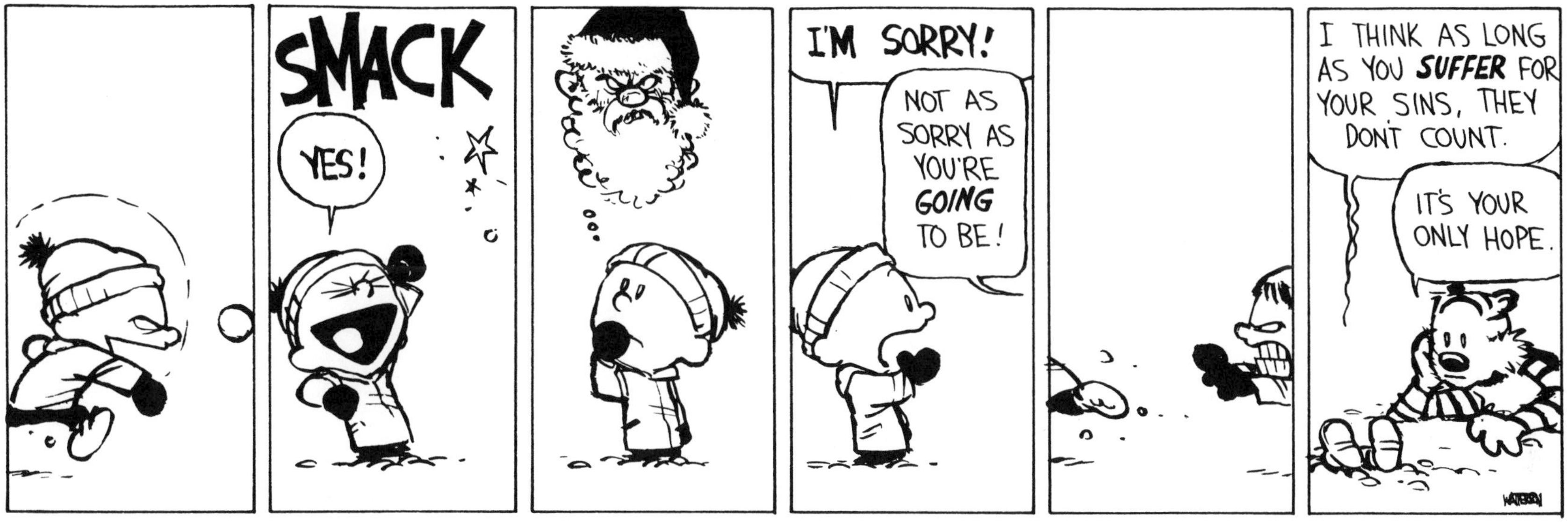
SMACK
YES!
I'M SORRY!
NOT AS SORRY AS YOU'RE **GOING** TO BE!
I THINK AS LONG AS YOU **SUFFER** FOR YOUR SINS, THEY DON'T COUNT.
IT'S YOUR ONLY HOPE.

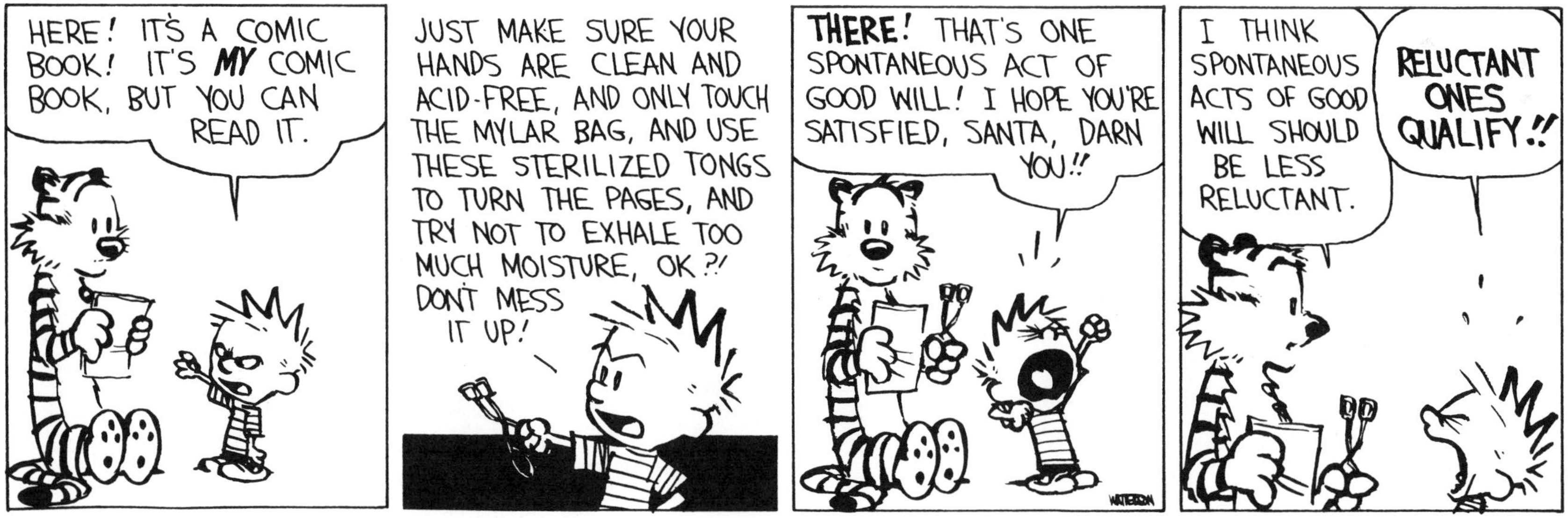
HERE! IT'S A COMIC BOOK! IT'S **MY** COMIC BOOK, BUT YOU CAN READ IT.
JUST MAKE SURE YOUR HANDS ARE CLEAN AND ACID-FREE, AND ONLY TOUCH THE MYLAR BAG, AND USE THESE STERILIZED TONGS TO TURN THE PAGES, AND TRY NOT TO EXHALE TOO MUCH MOISTURE, OK?! DON'T MESS IT UP!
THERE! THAT'S ONE SPONTANEOUS ACT OF GOOD WILL! I HOPE YOU'RE SATISFIED, SANTA, DARN YOU!!
I THINK SPONTANEOUS ACTS OF GOOD WILL SHOULD BE LESS RELUCTANT.
RELUCTANT ONES QUALIFY!!

34

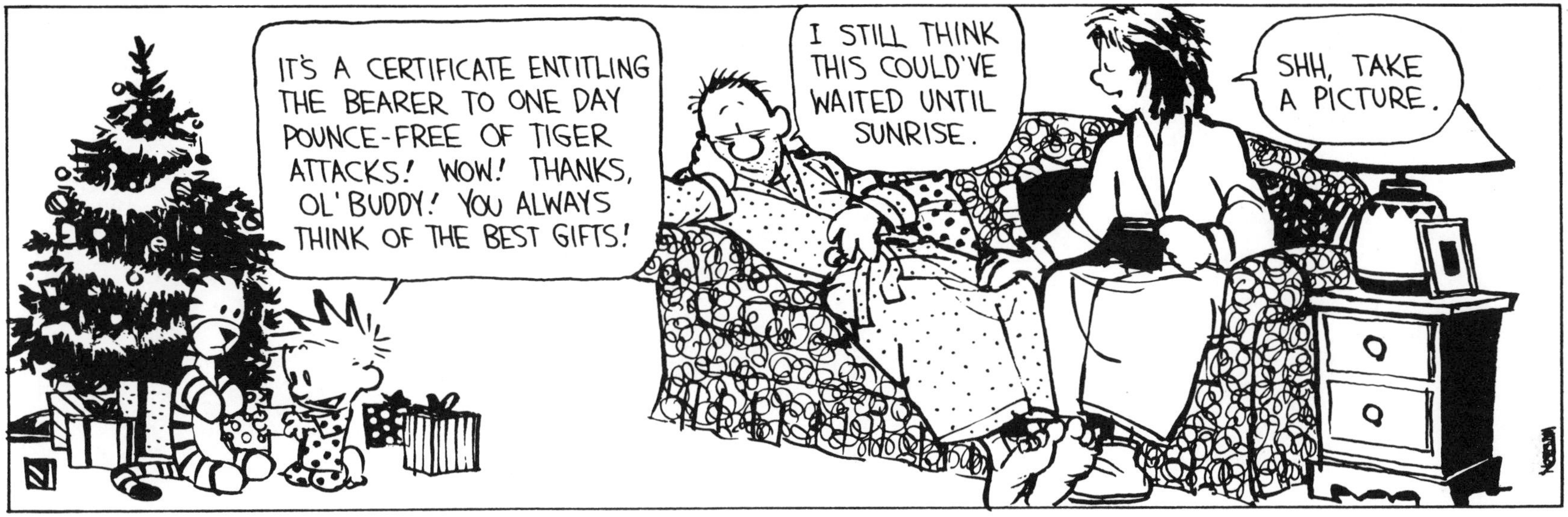
IT'S A CERTIFICATE ENTITLING THE BEARER TO ONE DAY POUNCE-FREE OF TIGER ATTACKS! WOW! THANKS, OL' BUDDY! YOU ALWAYS THINK OF THE BEST GIFTS!
I STILL THINK THIS COULD'VE WAITED UNTIL SUNRISE.
SHH, TAKE A PICTURE.

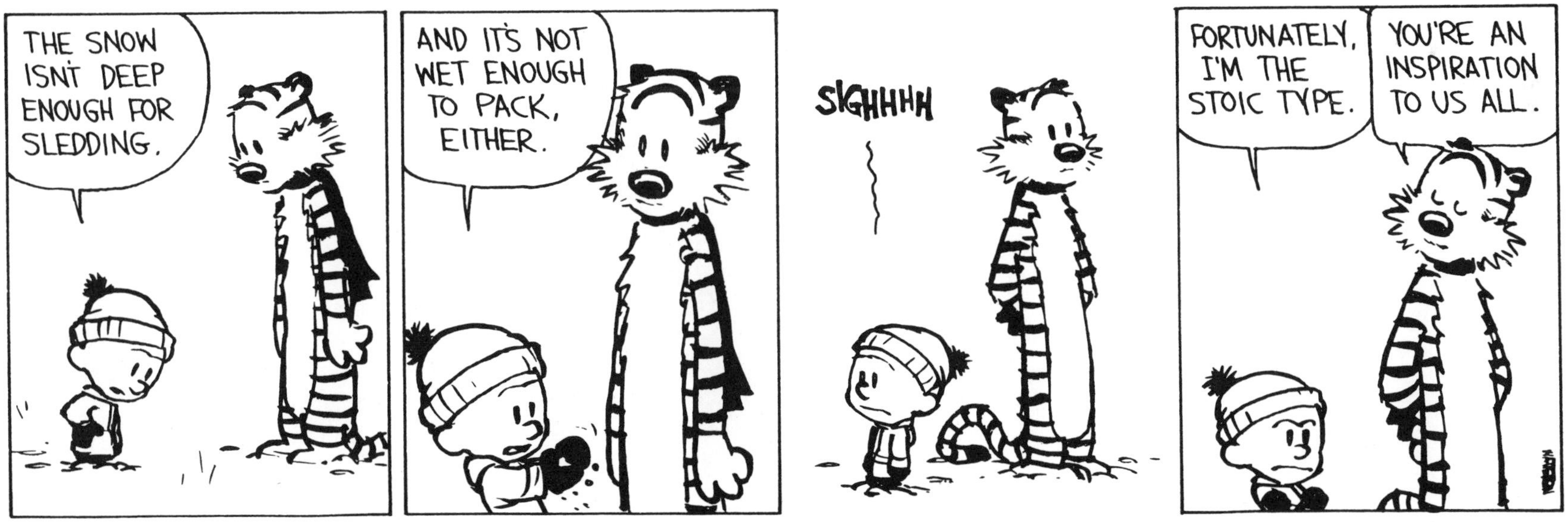
THE SNOW ISN'T DEEP ENOUGH FOR SLEDDING.
AND IT'S NOT WET ENOUGH TO PACK, EITHER.
SIGHHHH
FORTUNATELY, I'M THE STOIC TYPE.
YOU'RE AN INSPIRATION TO US ALL.

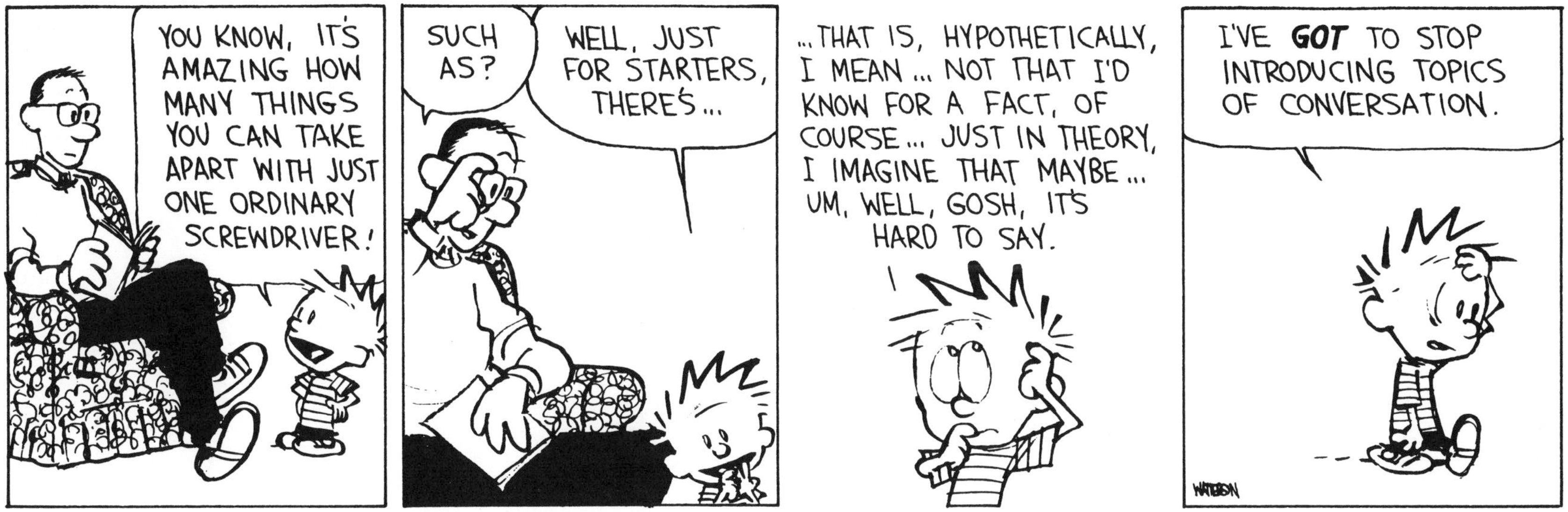
YOU KNOW, IT'S AMAZING HOW MANY THINGS YOU CAN TAKE APART WITH JUST ONE ORDINARY SCREWDRIVER!
SUCH AS?
WELL, JUST FOR STARTERS, THERE'S...
...THAT IS, HYPOTHETICALLY, I MEAN... NOT THAT I'D KNOW FOR A FACT, OF COURSE... JUST IN THEORY, I IMAGINE THAT MAYBE... UM, WELL, GOSH, IT'S HARD TO SAY.
I'VE **GOT** TO STOP INTRODUCING TOPICS OF CONVERSATION.
WATSON

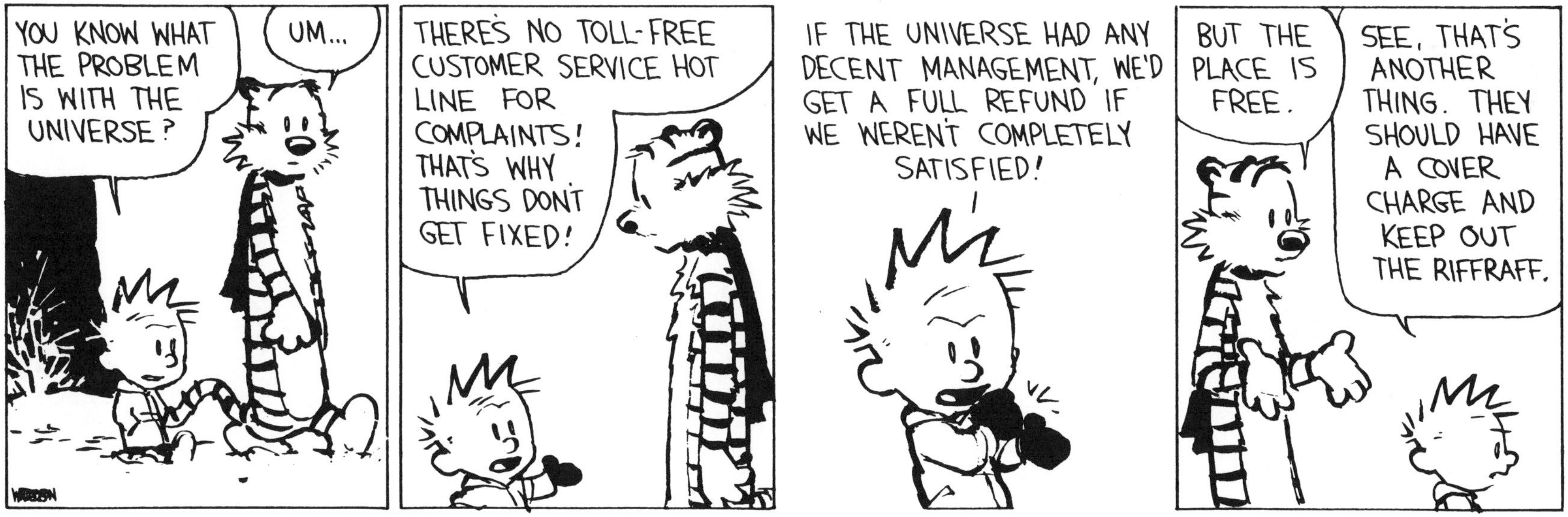
YOU KNOW WHAT THE PROBLEM IS WITH THE UNIVERSE?
UM...
WATSON
THERE'S NO TOLL-FREE CUSTOMER SERVICE HOT LINE FOR COMPLAINTS! THAT'S WHY THINGS DON'T GET FIXED!
IF THE UNIVERSE HAD ANY DECENT MANAGEMENT, WE'D GET A FULL REFUND IF WE WEREN'T COMPLETELY SATISFIED!
BUT THE PLACE IS FREE.
SEE, THAT'S ANOTHER THING. THEY SHOULD HAVE A COVER CHARGE AND KEEP OUT THE RIFFRAFF.

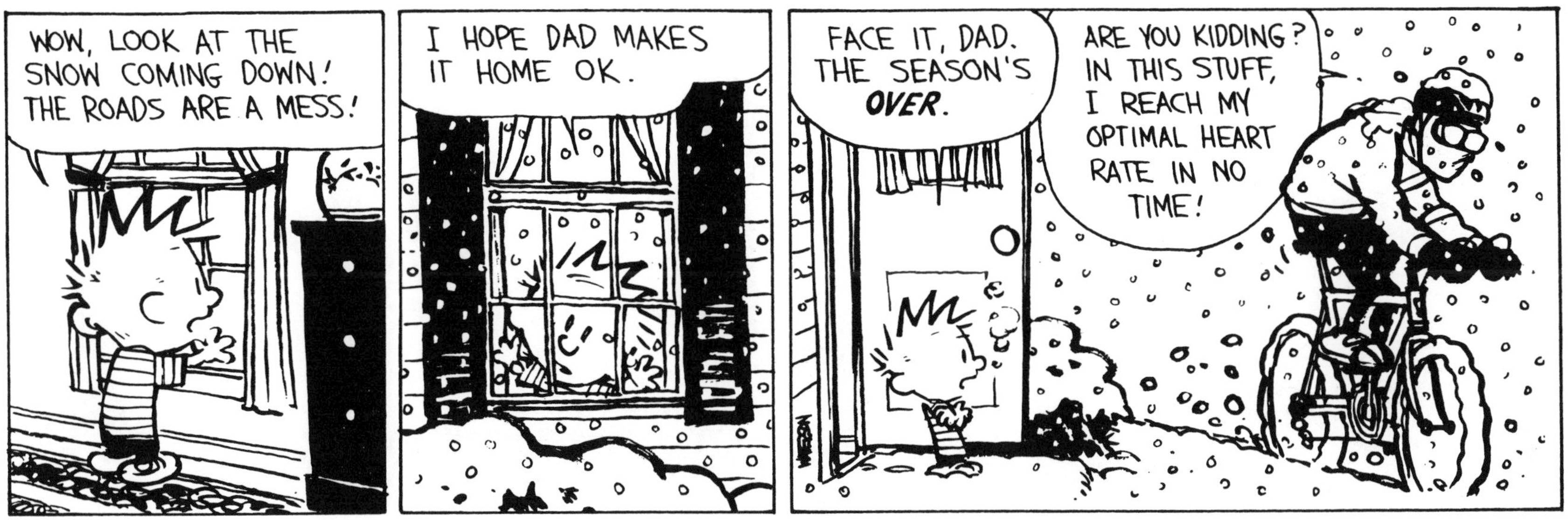
WOW, LOOK AT THE SNOW COMING DOWN! THE ROADS ARE A MESS!
I HOPE DAD MAKES IT HOME OK.
FACE IT, DAD. THE SEASON'S **OVER**.
ARE YOU KIDDING? IN THIS STUFF, I REACH MY OPTIMAL HEART RATE IN NO TIME!

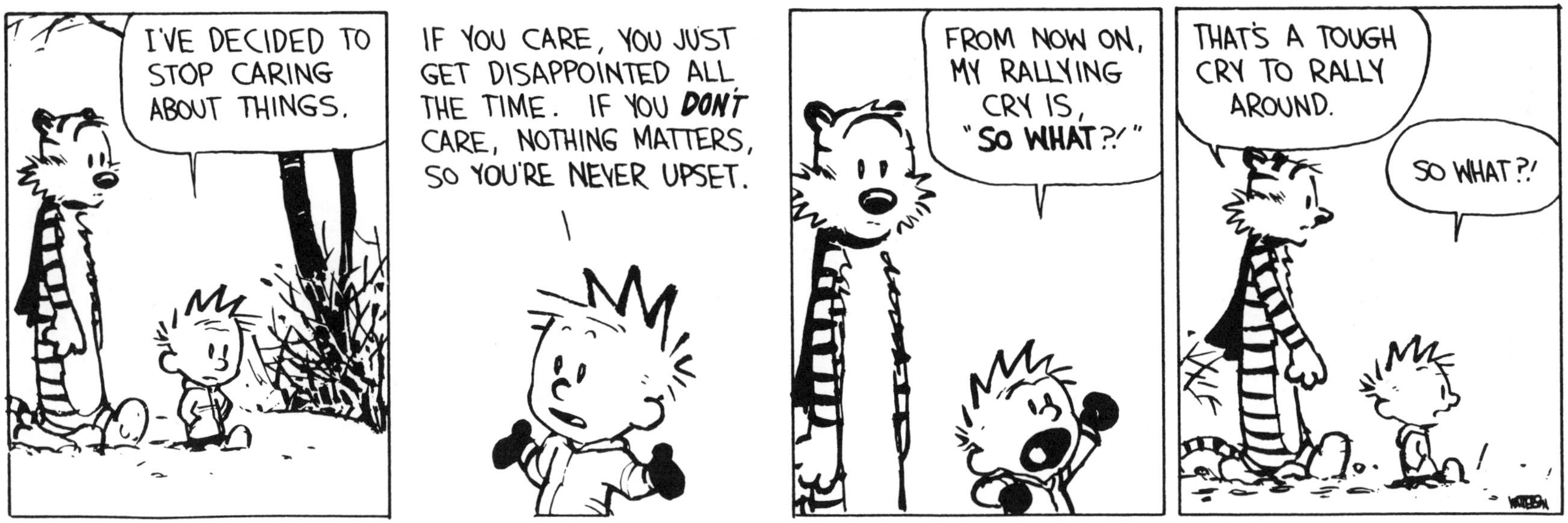
I'VE DECIDED TO STOP CARING ABOUT THINGS.
IF YOU CARE, YOU JUST GET DISAPPOINTED ALL THE TIME. IF YOU **DON'T** CARE, NOTHING MATTERS, SO YOU'RE NEVER UPSET.
FROM NOW ON, MY RALLYING CRY IS, "**SO WHAT**?!"
THAT'S A TOUGH CRY TO RALLY AROUND.
SO WHAT?!

40

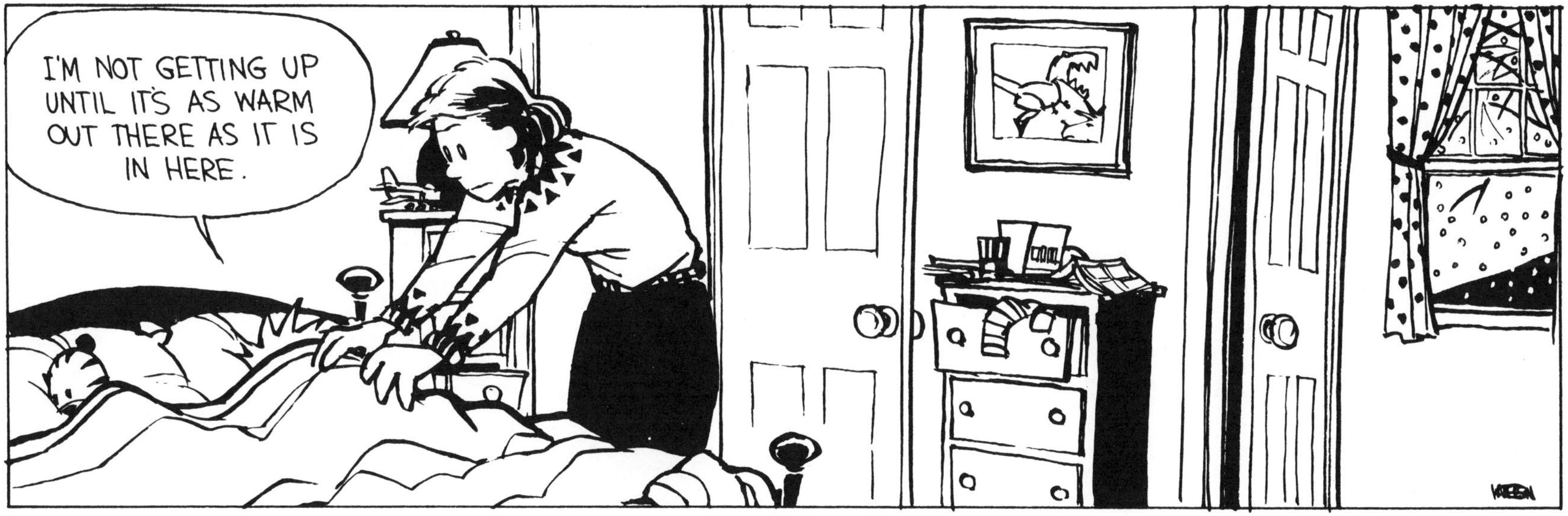
I'M NOT GETTING UP UNTIL IT'S AS WARM OUT THERE AS IT IS IN HERE.

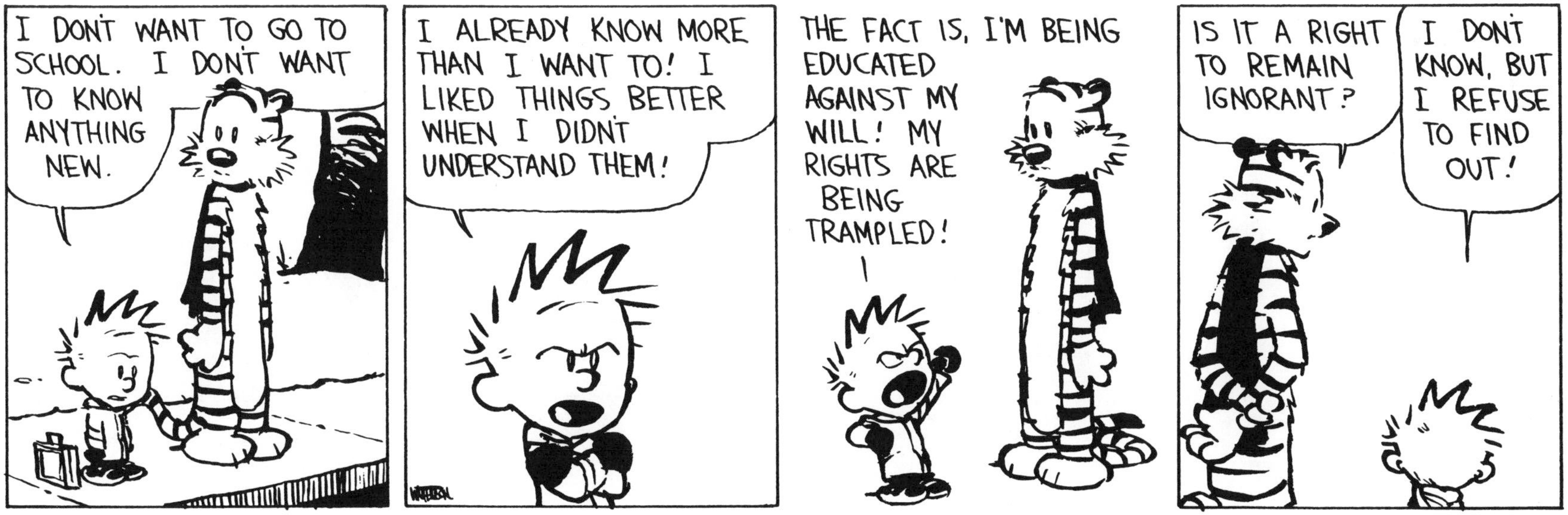
I DON'T WANT TO GO TO SCHOOL. I DON'T WANT TO KNOW ANYTHING NEW.
I ALREADY KNOW MORE THAN I WANT TO! I LIKED THINGS BETTER WHEN I DIDN'T UNDERSTAND THEM!
THE FACT IS, I'M BEING EDUCATED AGAINST MY WILL! MY RIGHTS ARE BEING TRAMPLED!
IS IT A RIGHT TO REMAIN IGNORANT?
I DON'T KNOW, BUT I REFUSE TO FIND OUT!

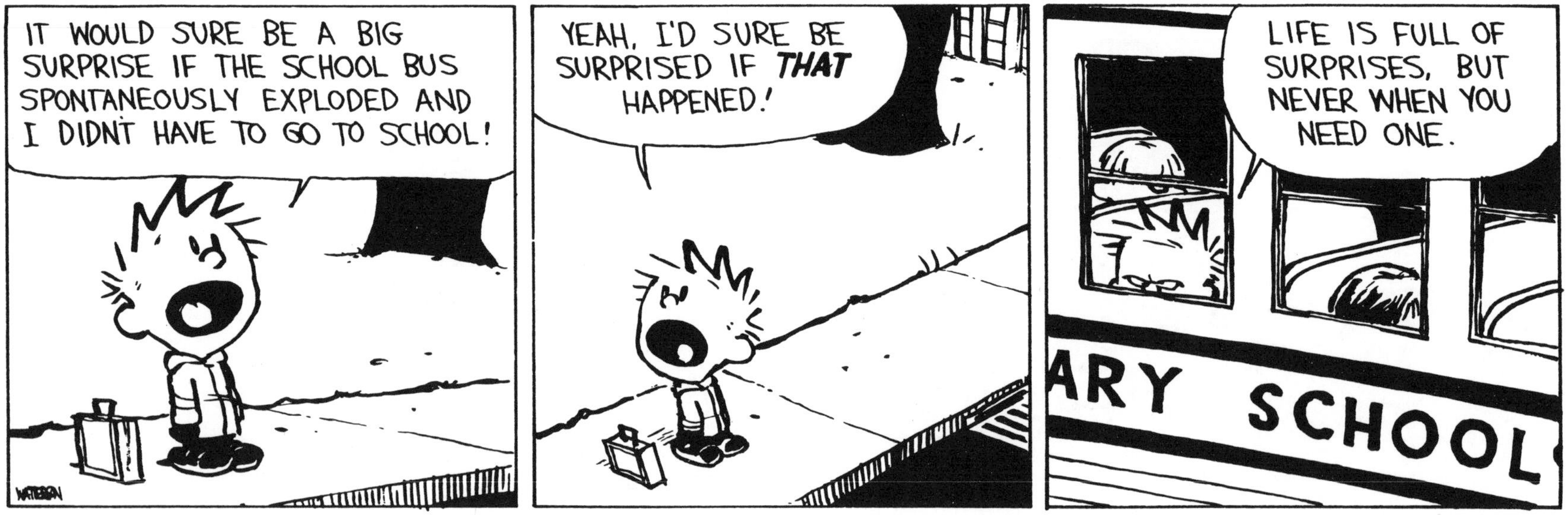
IT WOULD SURE BE A BIG SURPRISE IF THE SCHOOL BUS SPONTANEOUSLY EXPLODED AND I DIDN'T HAVE TO GO TO SCHOOL!
YEAH, I'D SURE BE SURPRISED IF THAT HAPPENED!
LIFE IS FULL OF SURPRISES, BUT NEVER WHEN YOU NEED ONE.
ARY SCHOOL

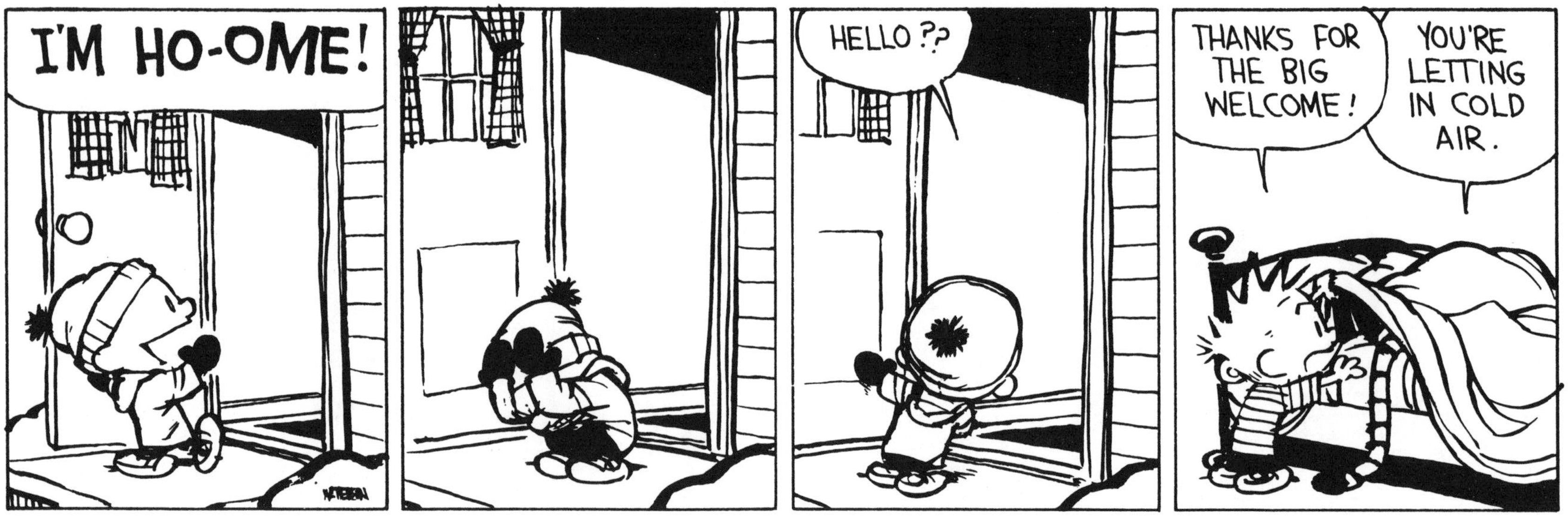
I'M HO-OME!
HELLO ??
THANKS FOR THE BIG WELCOME!
YOU'RE LETTING IN COLD AIR.

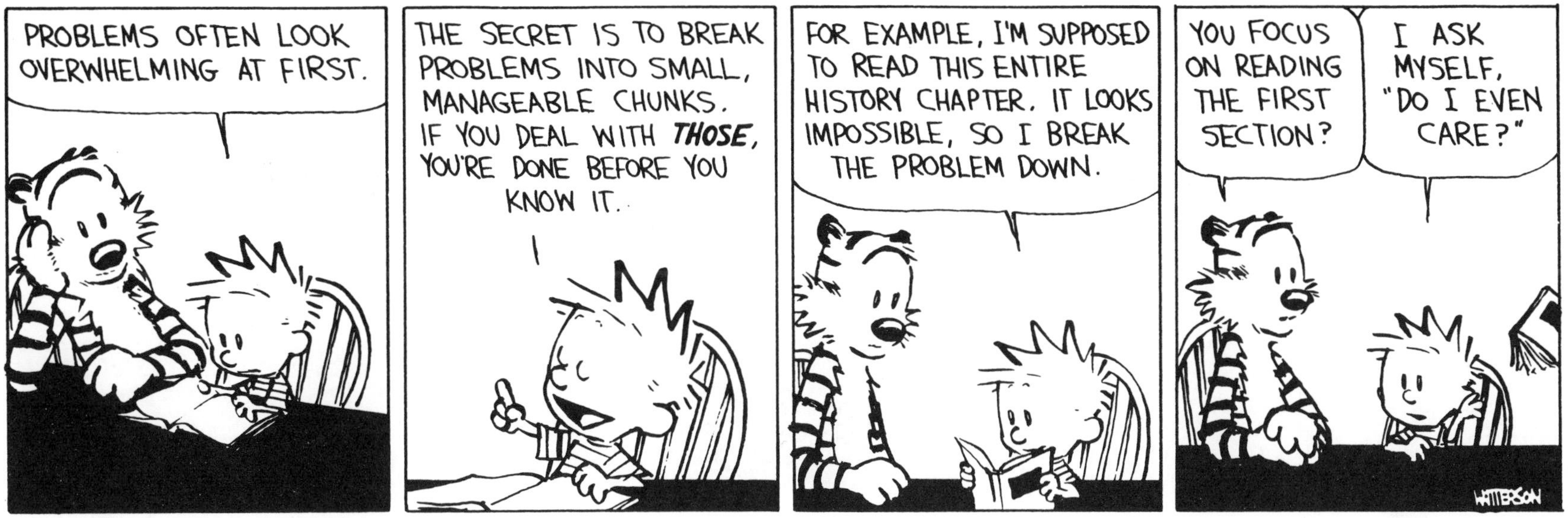
PROBLEMS OFTEN LOOK OVERWHELMING AT FIRST.
THE SECRET IS TO BREAK PROBLEMS INTO SMALL, MANAGEABLE CHUNKS. IF YOU DEAL WITH **THOSE**, YOU'RE DONE BEFORE YOU KNOW IT.
FOR EXAMPLE, I'M SUPPOSED TO READ THIS ENTIRE HISTORY CHAPTER. IT LOOKS IMPOSSIBLE, SO I BREAK THE PROBLEM DOWN.
YOU FOCUS ON READING THE FIRST SECTION?
I ASK MYSELF, "DO I EVEN CARE?"

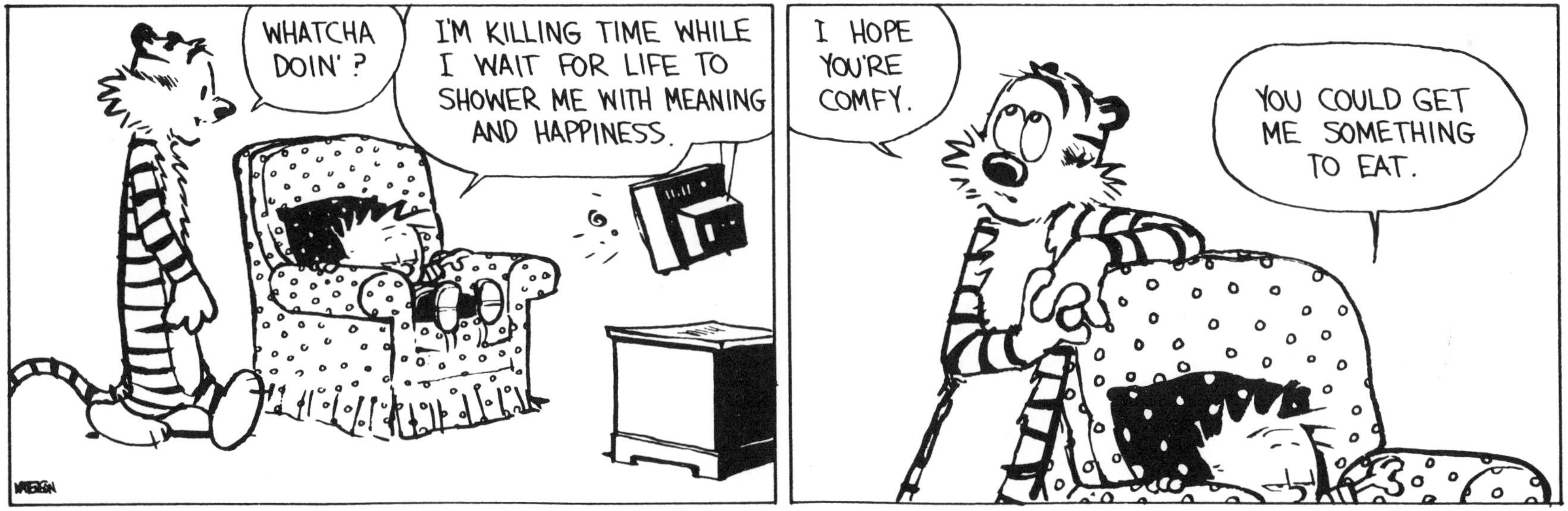
WHATCHA DOIN'?
I'M KILLING TIME WHILE I WAIT FOR LIFE TO SHOWER ME WITH MEANING AND HAPPINESS.
I HOPE YOU'RE COMFY.
YOU COULD GET ME SOMETHING TO EAT.

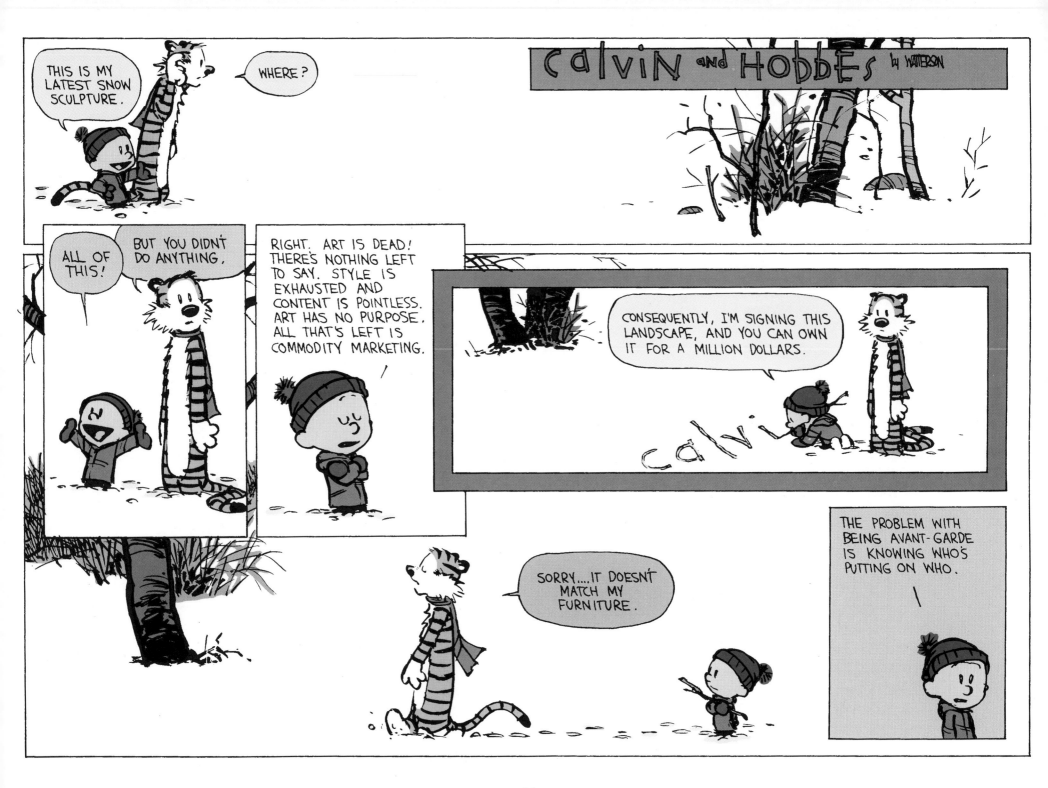

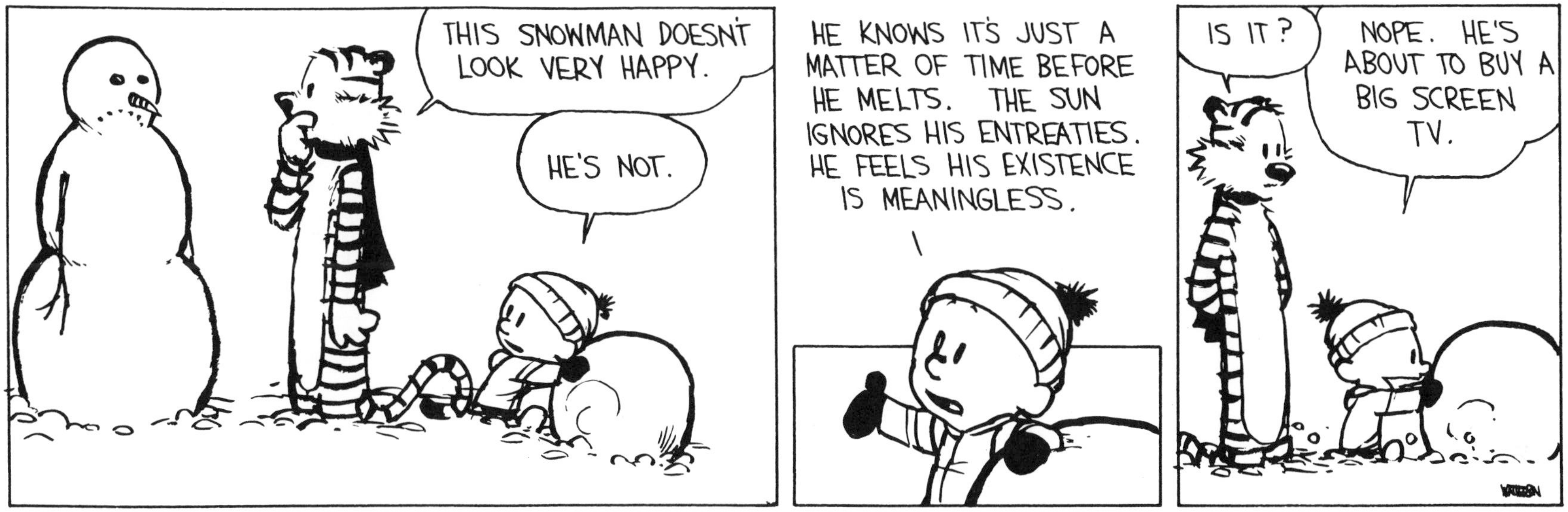
THIS SNOWMAN DOESN'T LOOK VERY HAPPY.
HE'S NOT.
HE KNOWS IT'S JUST A MATTER OF TIME BEFORE HE MELTS. THE SUN IGNORES HIS ENTREATIES. HE FEELS HIS EXISTENCE IS MEANINGLESS.
IS IT?
NOPE. HE'S ABOUT TO BUY A BIG SCREEN TV.

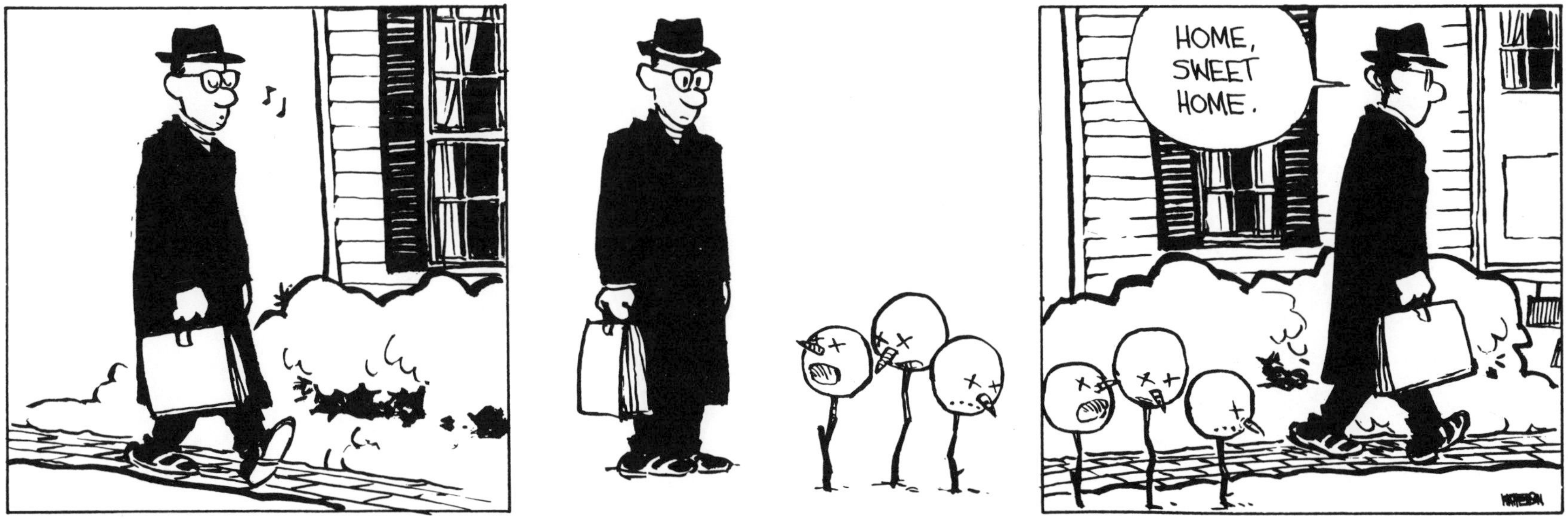
HOME, SWEET HOME.

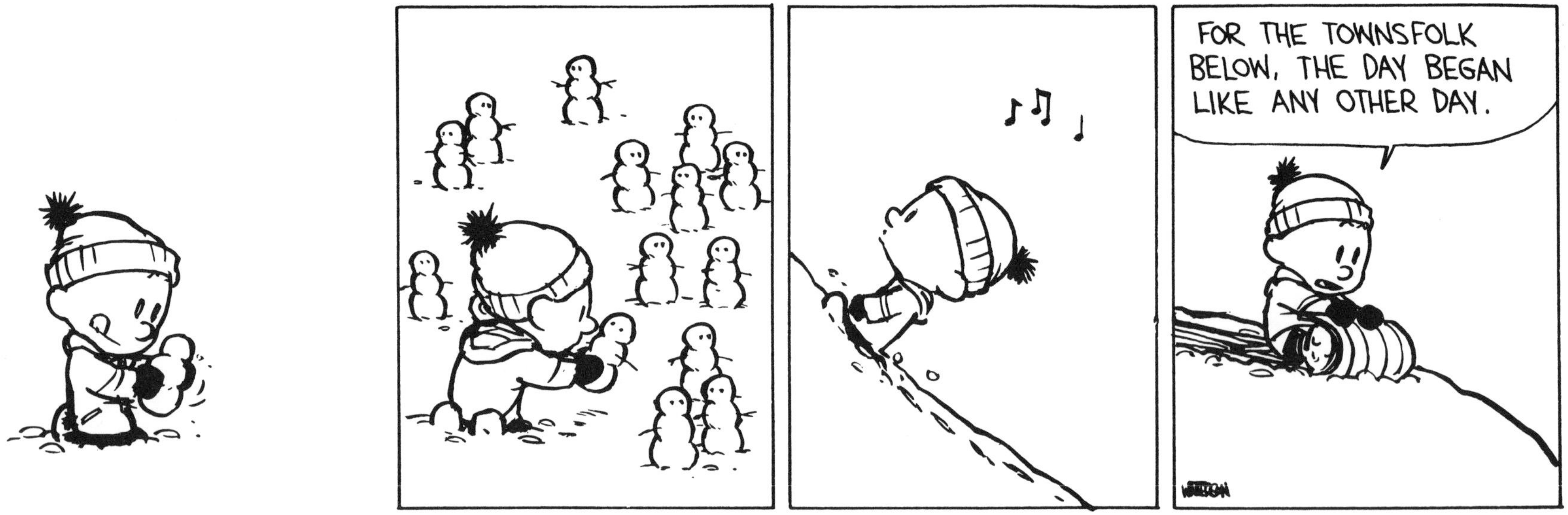
FOR THE TOWNSFOLK BELOW, THE DAY BEGAN LIKE ANY OTHER DAY.

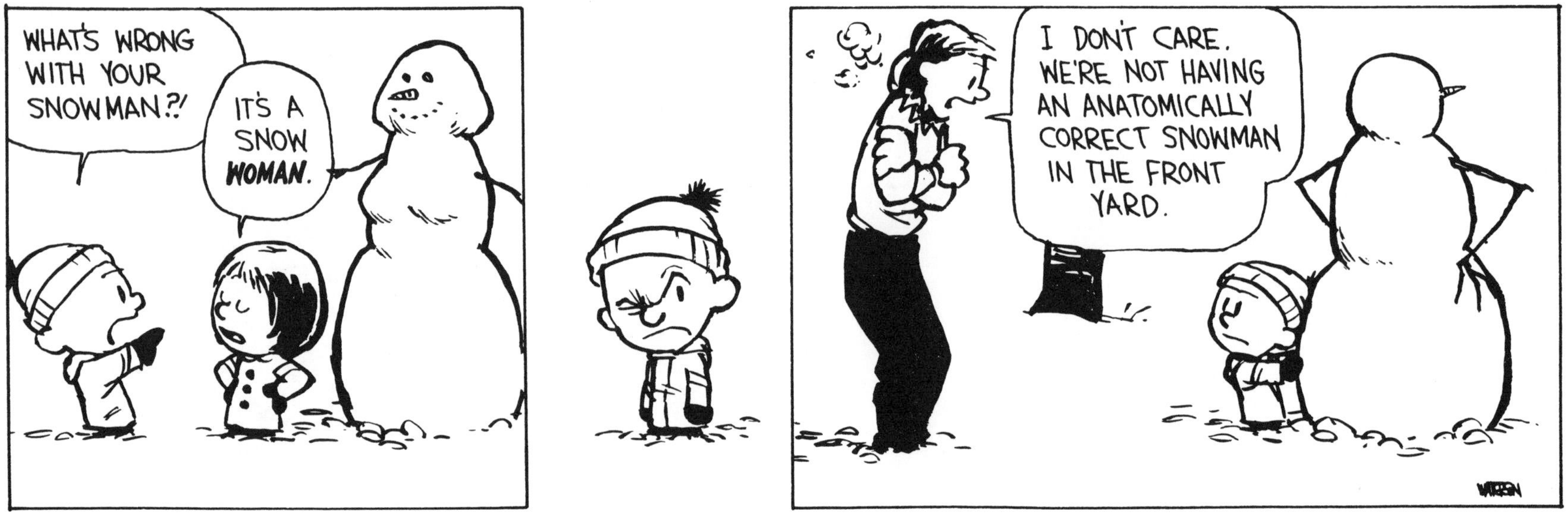
WHAT'S WRONG WITH YOUR SNOWMAN?!
IT'S A SNOW **WOMAN**.
I DON'T CARE. WE'RE NOT HAVING AN ANATOMICALLY CORRECT SNOWMAN IN THE FRONT YARD.

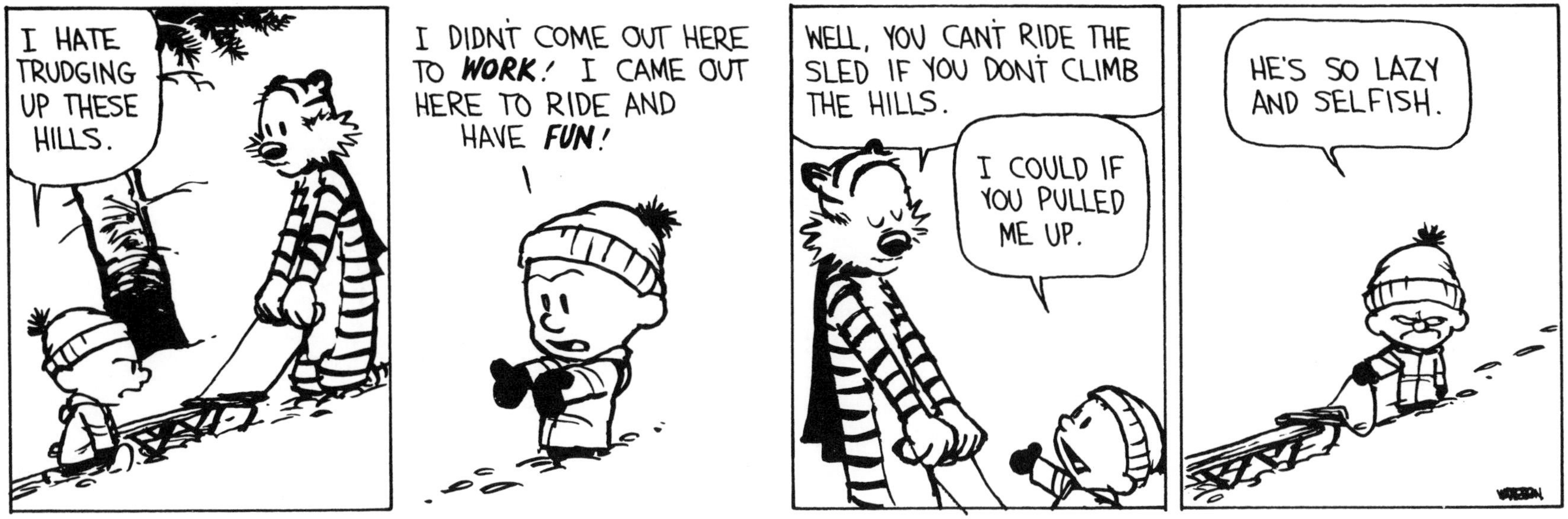
I HATE TRUDGING UP THESE HILLS.
I DIDN'T COME OUT HERE TO ***WORK***! I CAME OUT HERE TO RIDE AND HAVE ***FUN***!
WELL, YOU CAN'T RIDE THE SLED IF YOU DON'T CLIMB THE HILLS.
I COULD IF YOU PULLED ME UP.
HE'S SO LAZY AND SELFISH.

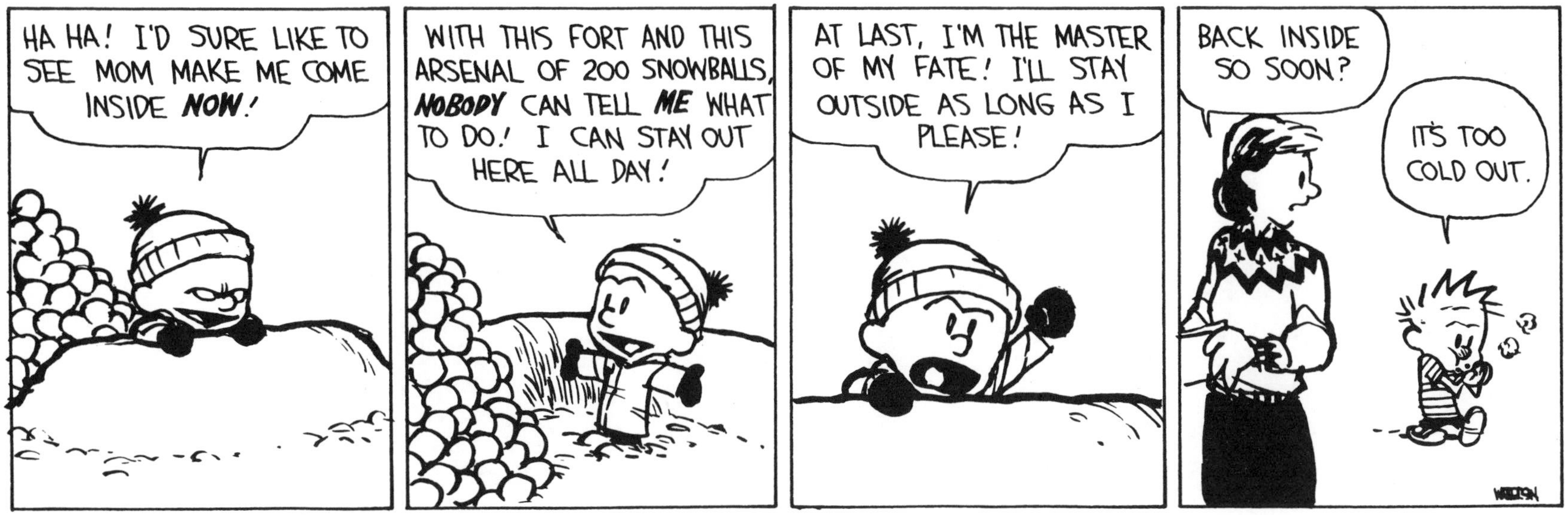
HA HA! I'D SURE LIKE TO SEE MOM MAKE ME COME INSIDE ***NOW***!
WITH THIS FORT AND THIS ARSENAL OF 200 SNOWBALLS, ***NOBODY*** CAN TELL ***ME*** WHAT TO DO! I CAN STAY OUT HERE ALL DAY!
AT LAST, I'M THE MASTER OF MY FATE! I'LL STAY OUTSIDE AS LONG AS I PLEASE!
BACK INSIDE SO SOON?
IT'S TOO COLD OUT.

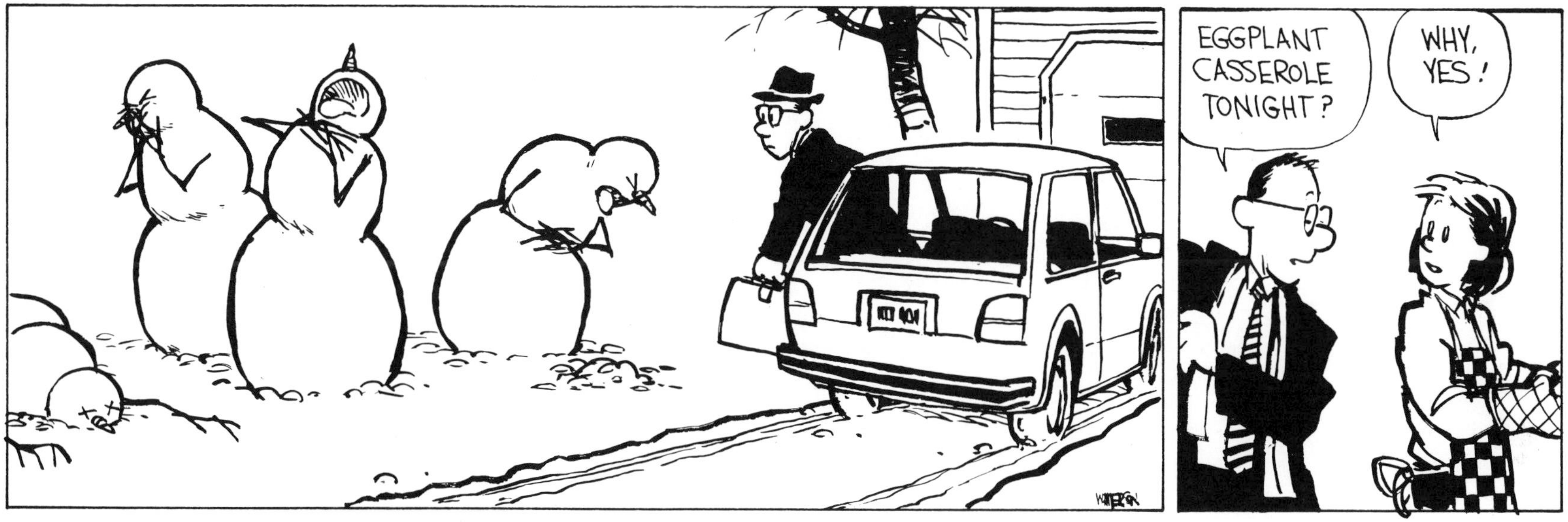
EGGPLANT CASSEROLE TONIGHT?
WHY, YES!

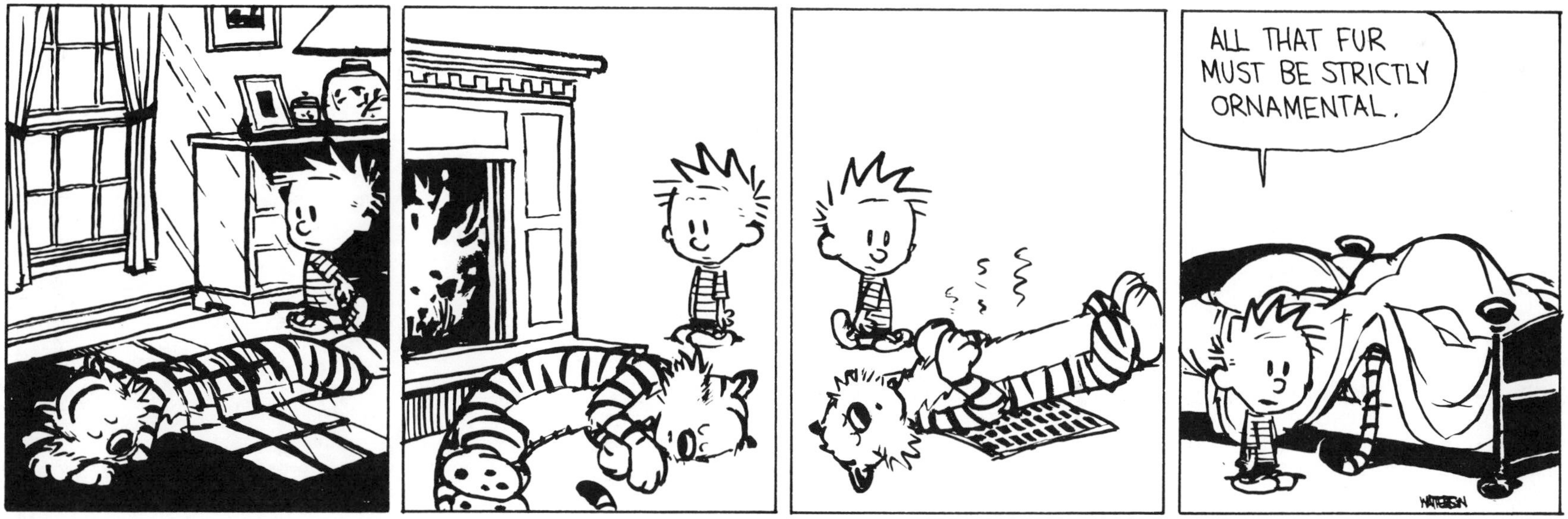
ALL THAT FUR MUST BE STRICTLY ORNAMENTAL.

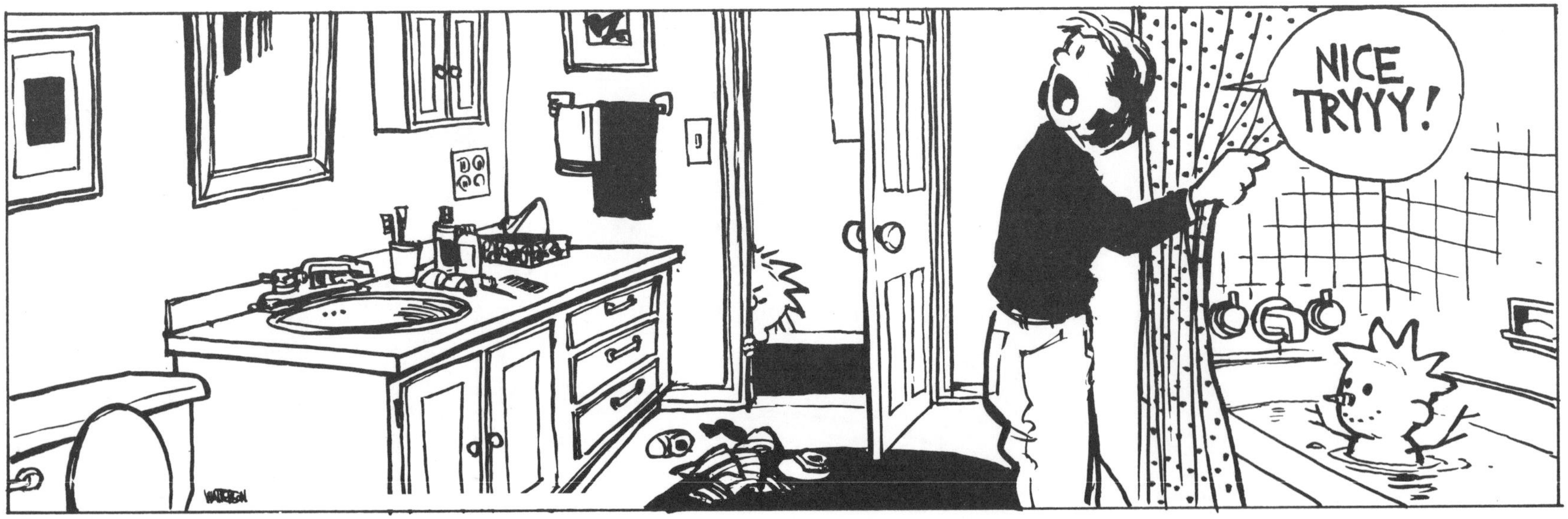
NICE TRYYY!

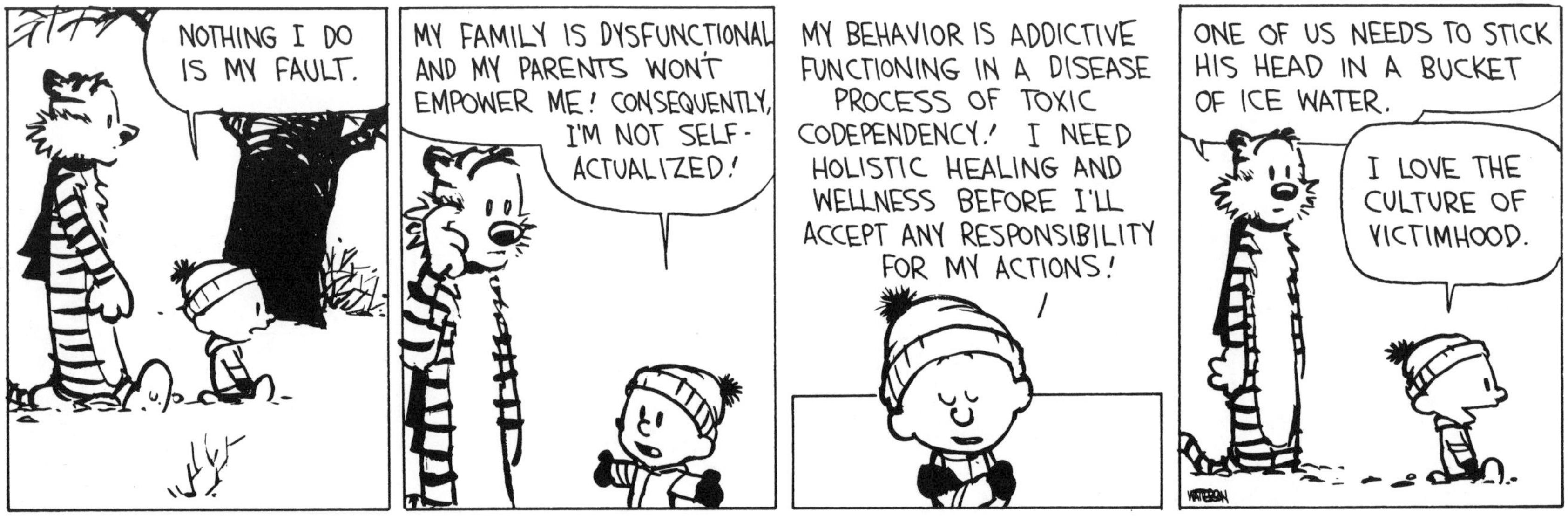
NOTHING I DO IS MY FAULT.
MY FAMILY IS DYSFUNCTIONAL AND MY PARENTS WON'T EMPOWER ME! CONSEQUENTLY, I'M NOT SELF-ACTUALIZED!
MY BEHAVIOR IS ADDICTIVE FUNCTIONING IN A DISEASE PROCESS OF TOXIC CODEPENDENCY! I NEED HOLISTIC HEALING AND WELLNESS BEFORE I'LL ACCEPT ANY RESPONSIBILITY FOR MY ACTIONS!
ONE OF US NEEDS TO STICK HIS HEAD IN A BUCKET OF ICE WATER.
I LOVE THE CULTURE OF VICTIMHOOD.

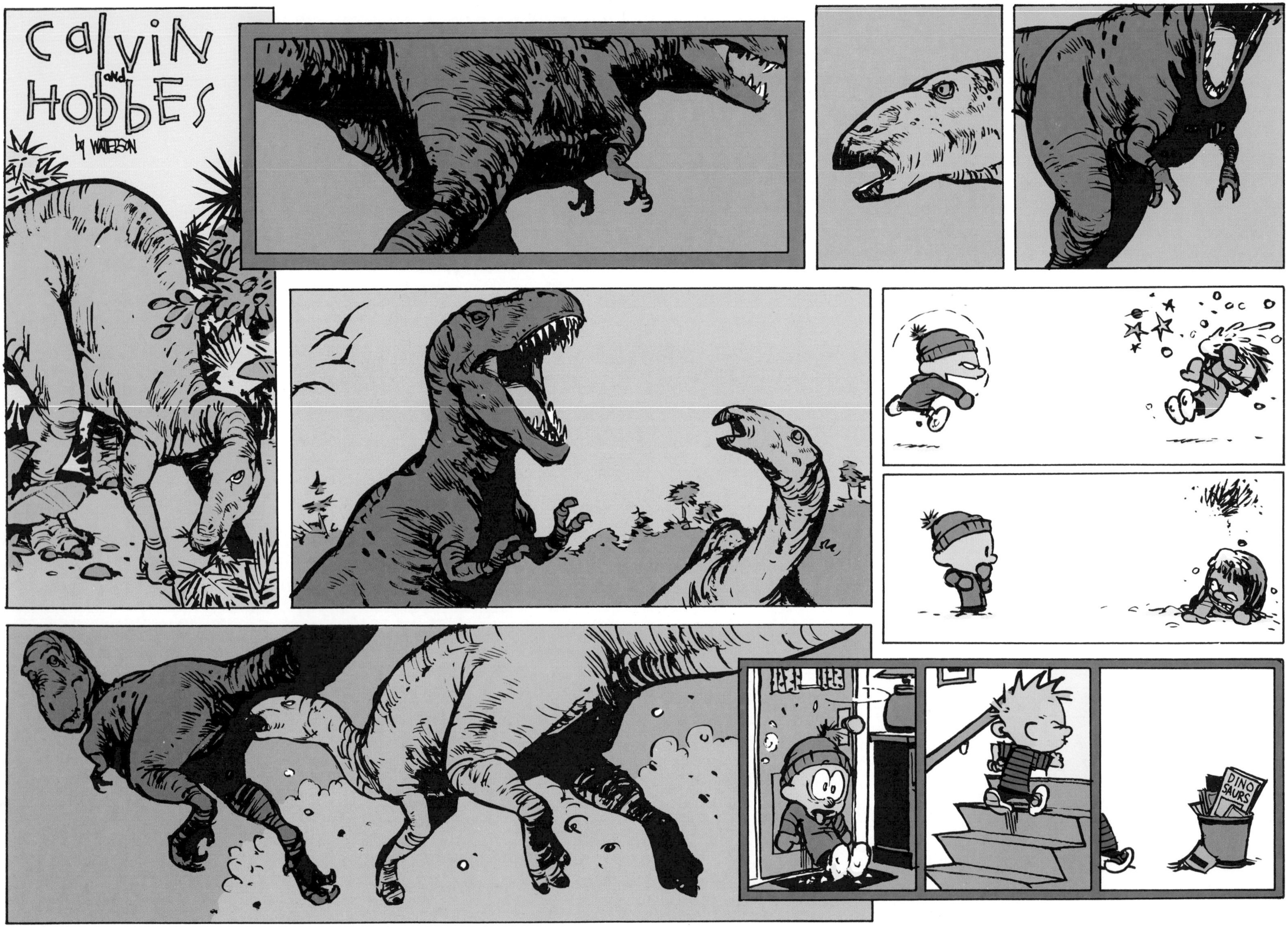
Calvin and Hobbes
by WATTERSON
DINO SAURS

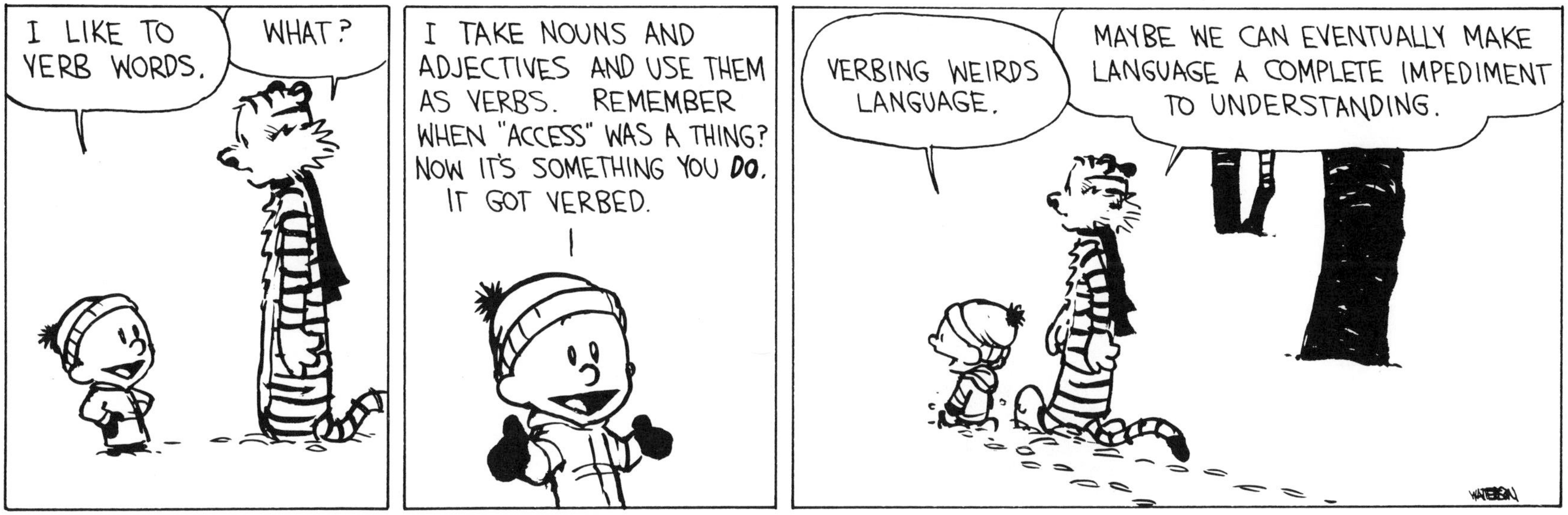
I LIKE TO VERB WORDS.
WHAT?
I TAKE NOUNS AND ADJECTIVES AND USE THEM AS VERBS. REMEMBER WHEN "ACCESS" WAS A THING? NOW IT'S SOMETHING YOU **DO.** IT GOT VERBED.
VERBING WEIRDS LANGUAGE.
MAYBE WE CAN EVENTUALLY MAKE LANGUAGE A COMPLETE IMPEDIMENT TO UNDERSTANDING.

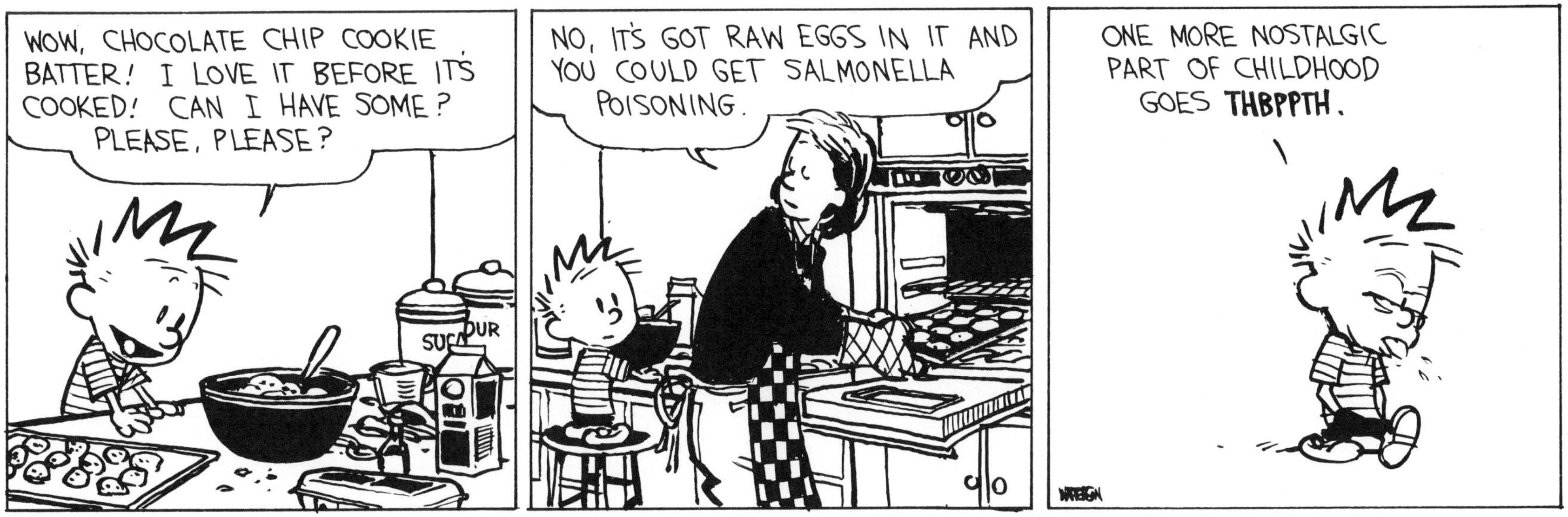
WOW, CHOCOLATE CHIP COOKIE BATTER! I LOVE IT BEFORE IT'S COOKED! CAN I HAVE SOME? PLEASE, PLEASE?
NO, IT'S GOT RAW EGGS IN IT AND YOU COULD GET SALMONELLA POISONING.
ONE MORE NOSTALGIC PART OF CHILDHOOD GOES **THBPPTH**.

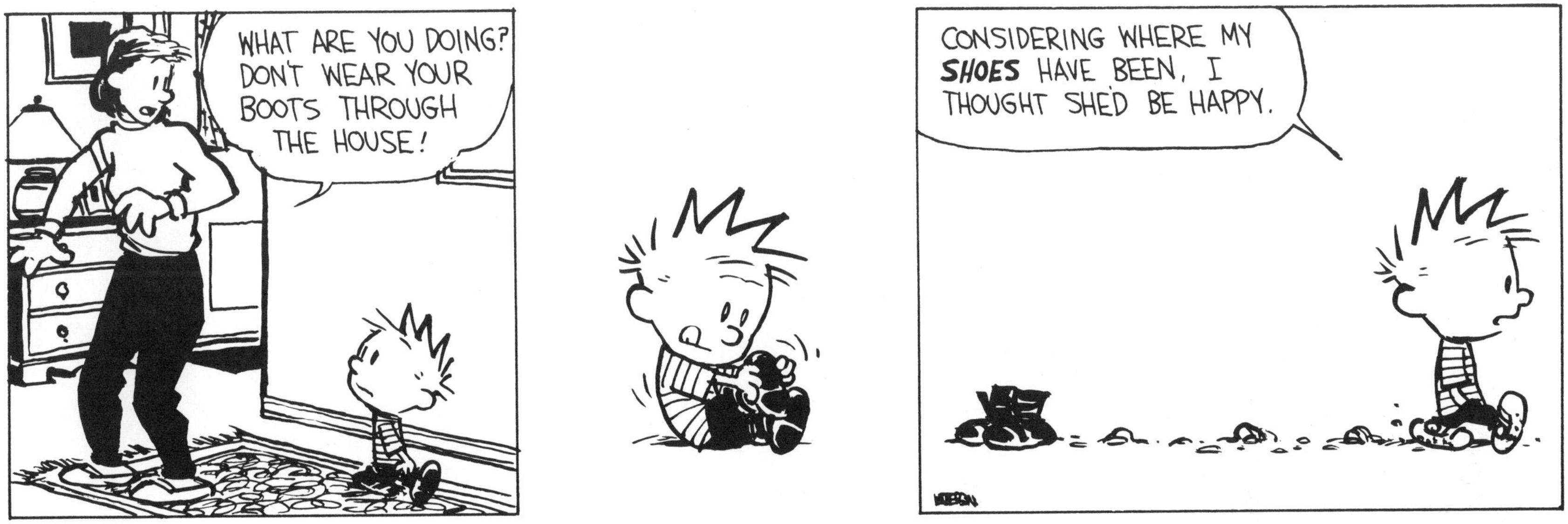
WHAT ARE YOU DOING? DON'T WEAR YOUR BOOTS THROUGH THE HOUSE!
CONSIDERING WHERE MY **SHOES** HAVE BEEN, I THOUGHT SHE'D BE HAPPY.

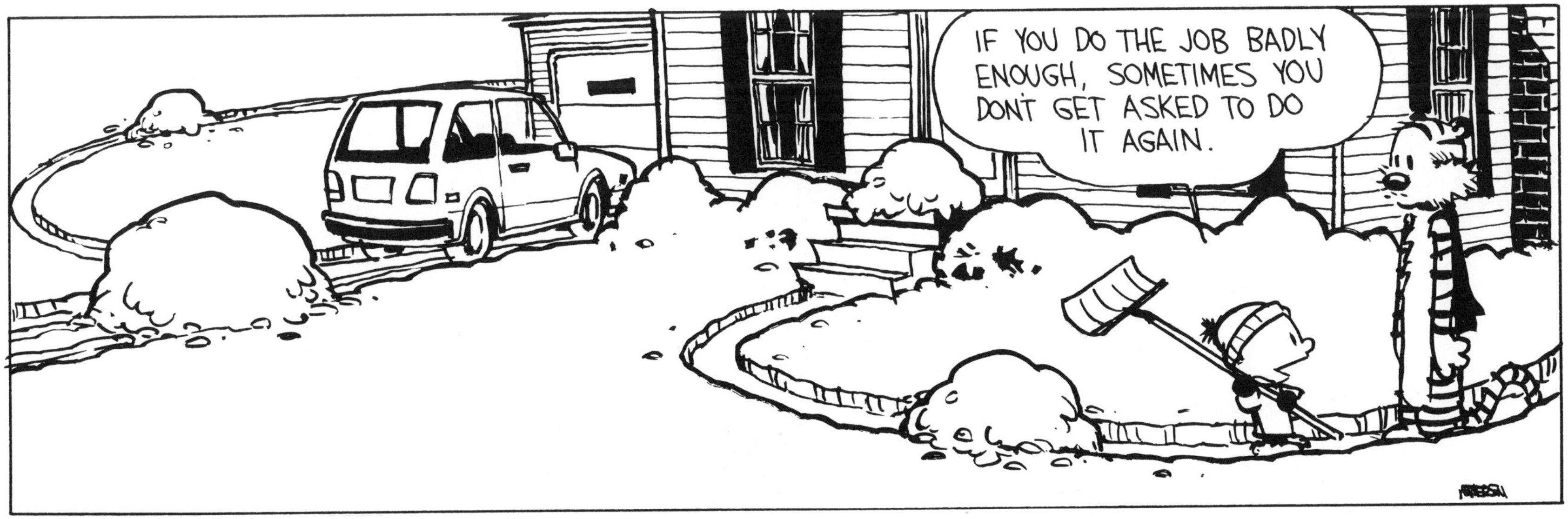
IF YOU DO THE JOB BADLY ENOUGH, SOMETIMES YOU DON'T GET ASKED TO DO IT AGAIN.

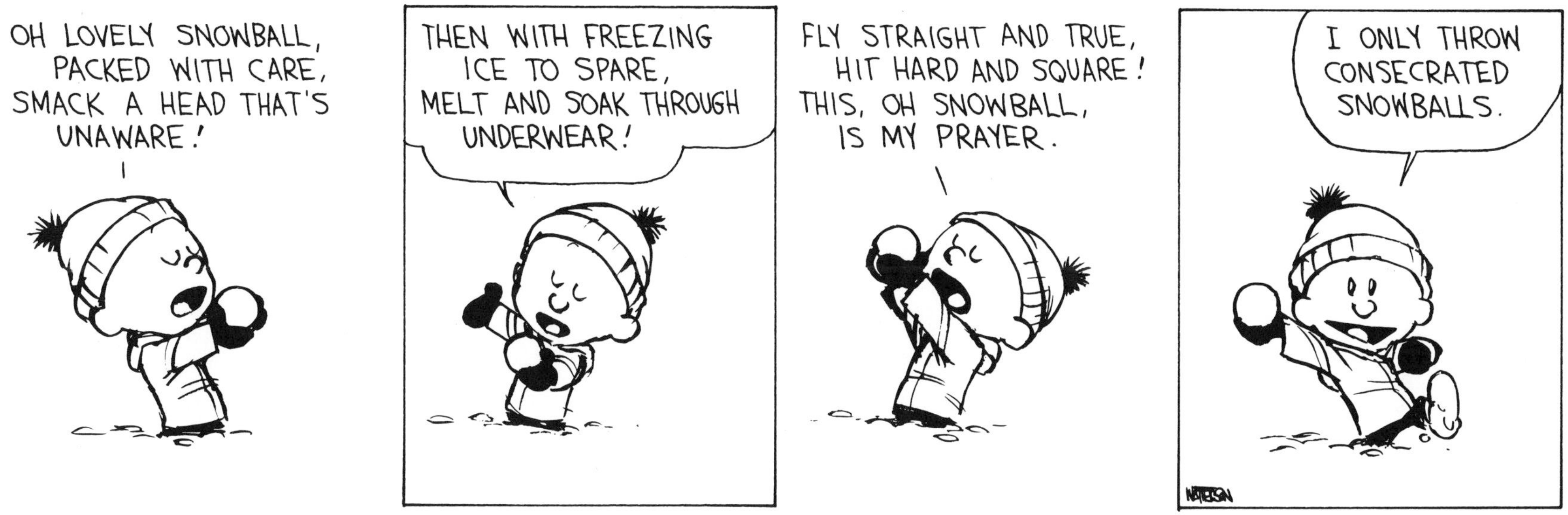
OH LOVELY SNOWBALL, PACKED WITH CARE, SMACK A HEAD THAT'S UNAWARE!
THEN WITH FREEZING ICE TO SPARE, MELT AND SOAK THROUGH UNDERWEAR!
FLY STRAIGHT AND TRUE, HIT HARD AND SQUARE! THIS, OH SNOWBALL, IS MY PRAYER.
I ONLY THROW CONSECRATED SNOWBALLS.

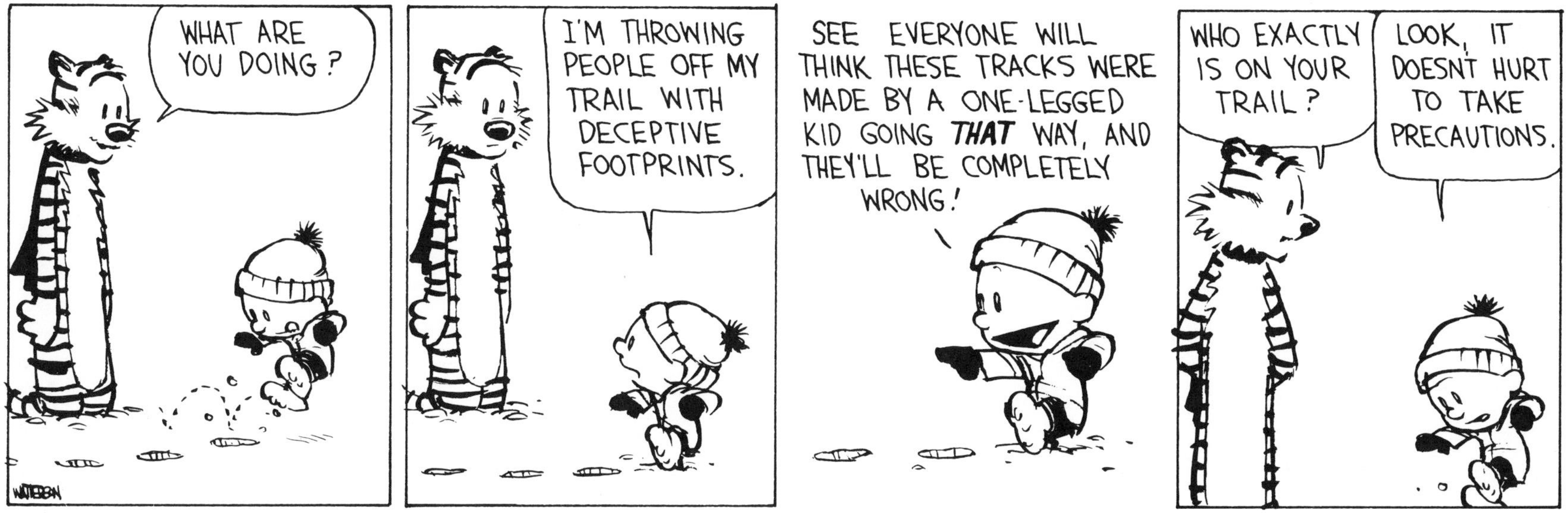
WHAT ARE YOU DOING?
I'M THROWING PEOPLE OFF MY TRAIL WITH DECEPTIVE FOOTPRINTS.
SEE EVERYONE WILL THINK THESE TRACKS WERE MADE BY A ONE-LEGGED KID GOING **THAT** WAY, AND THEY'LL BE COMPLETELY WRONG!
WHO EXACTLY IS ON YOUR TRAIL?
LOOK, IT DOESN'T HURT TO TAKE PRECAUTIONS.

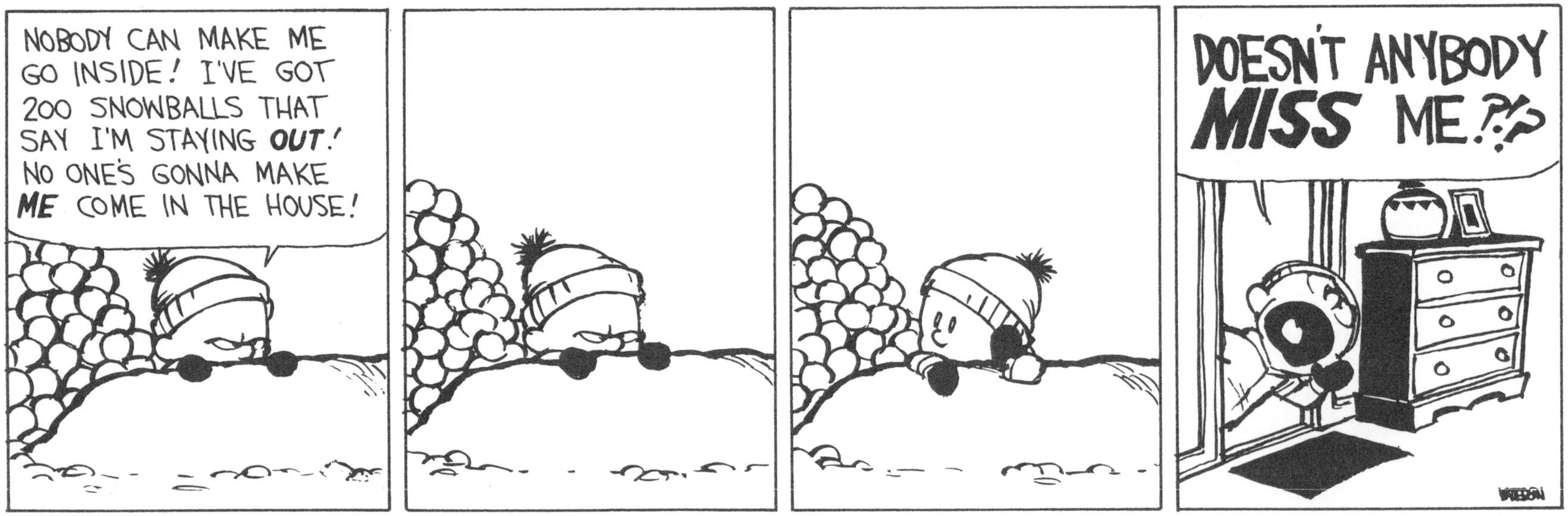
NOBODY CAN MAKE ME GO INSIDE! I'VE GOT 200 SNOWBALLS THAT SAY I'M STAYING **OUT**! NO ONE'S GONNA MAKE **ME** COME IN THE HOUSE!
DOESN'T ANYBODY **MISS** ME?!?
WATTERSON

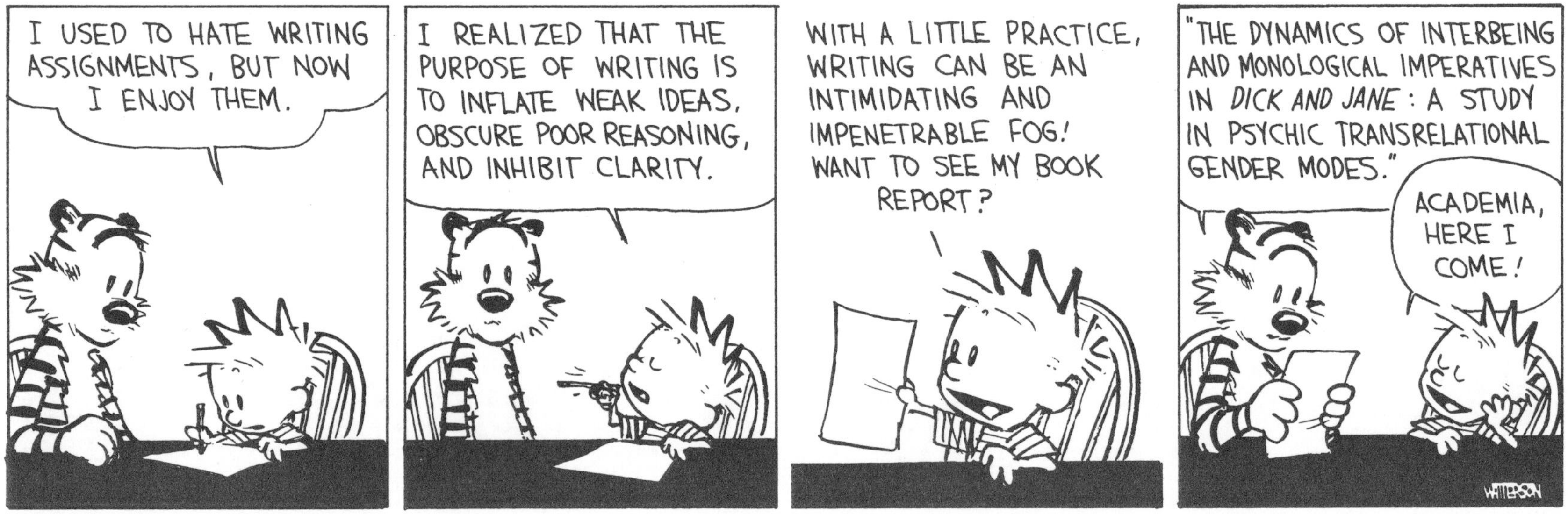
I USED TO HATE WRITING ASSIGNMENTS, BUT NOW I ENJOY THEM.
I REALIZED THAT THE PURPOSE OF WRITING IS TO INFLATE WEAK IDEAS, OBSCURE POOR REASONING, AND INHIBIT CLARITY.
WITH A LITTLE PRACTICE, WRITING CAN BE AN INTIMIDATING AND IMPENETRABLE FOG! WANT TO SEE MY BOOK REPORT?
"THE DYNAMICS OF INTERBEING AND MONOLOGICAL IMPERATIVES IN *DICK AND JANE*: A STUDY IN PSYCHIC TRANSRELATIONAL GENDER MODES."
ACADEMIA, HERE I COME!
WATTERSON

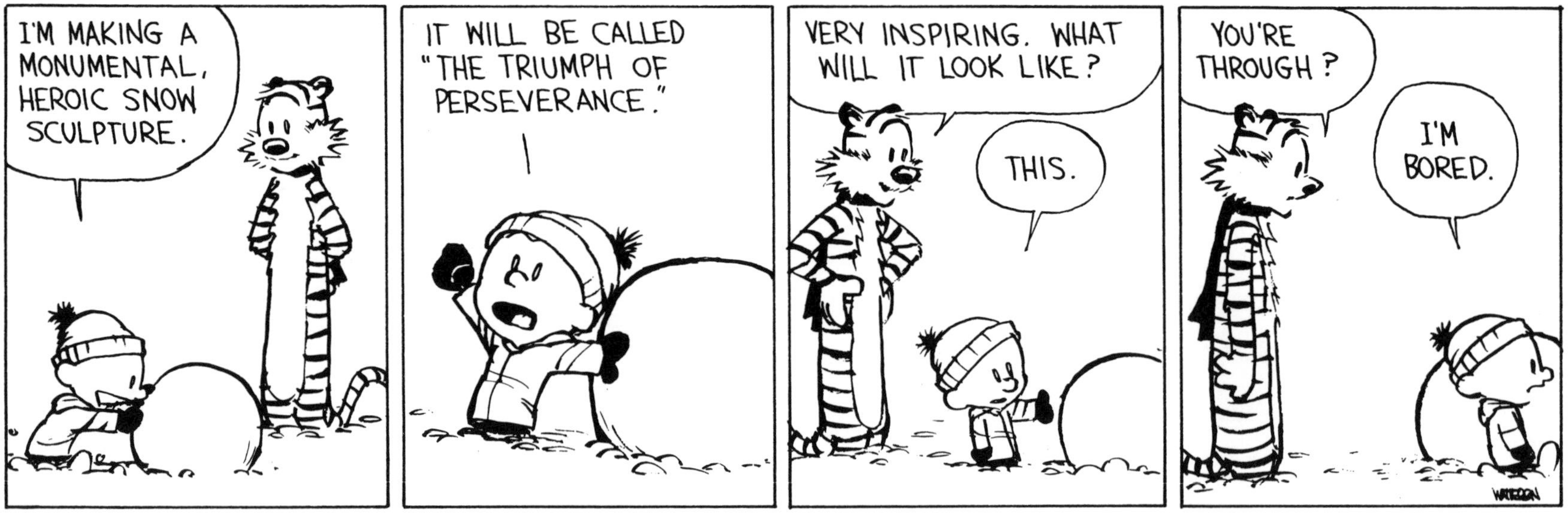
I'M MAKING A MONUMENTAL, HEROIC SNOW SCULPTURE.
IT WILL BE CALLED "THE TRIUMPH OF PERSEVERANCE."
VERY INSPIRING. WHAT WILL IT LOOK LIKE?
THIS.
YOU'RE THROUGH?
I'M BORED.

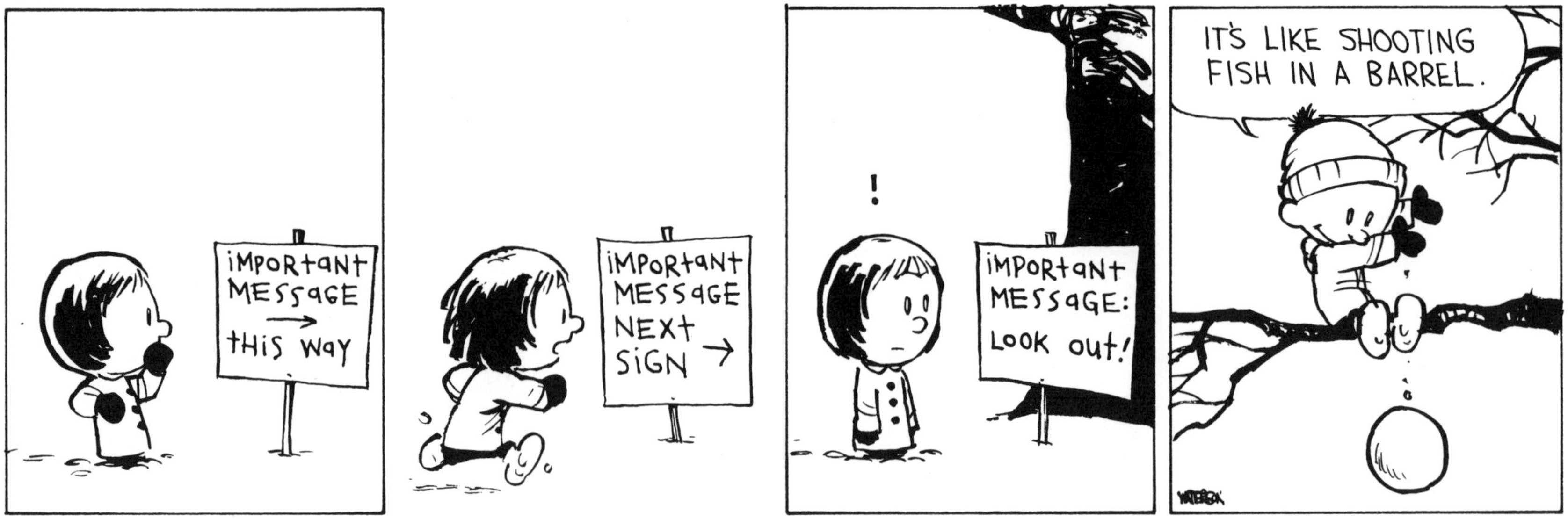
IMPORTANT MESSAGE → THIS WAY
IMPORTANT MESSAGE NEXT SIGN →
!
IMPORTANT MESSAGE: LOOK OUT!
IT'S LIKE SHOOTING FISH IN A BARREL.

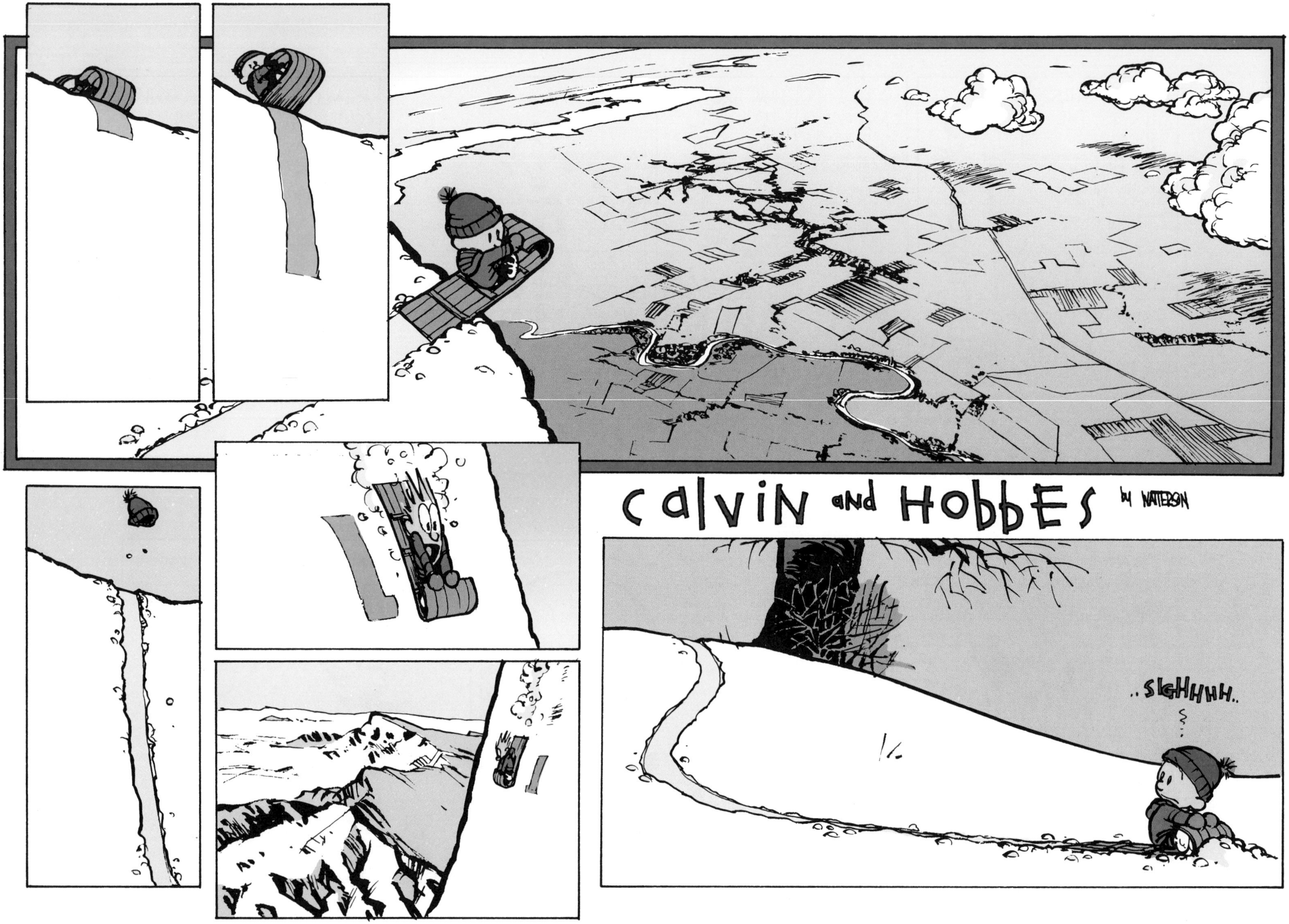

Calvin and HOBBES by WATTERSON
..SIGHHHH..

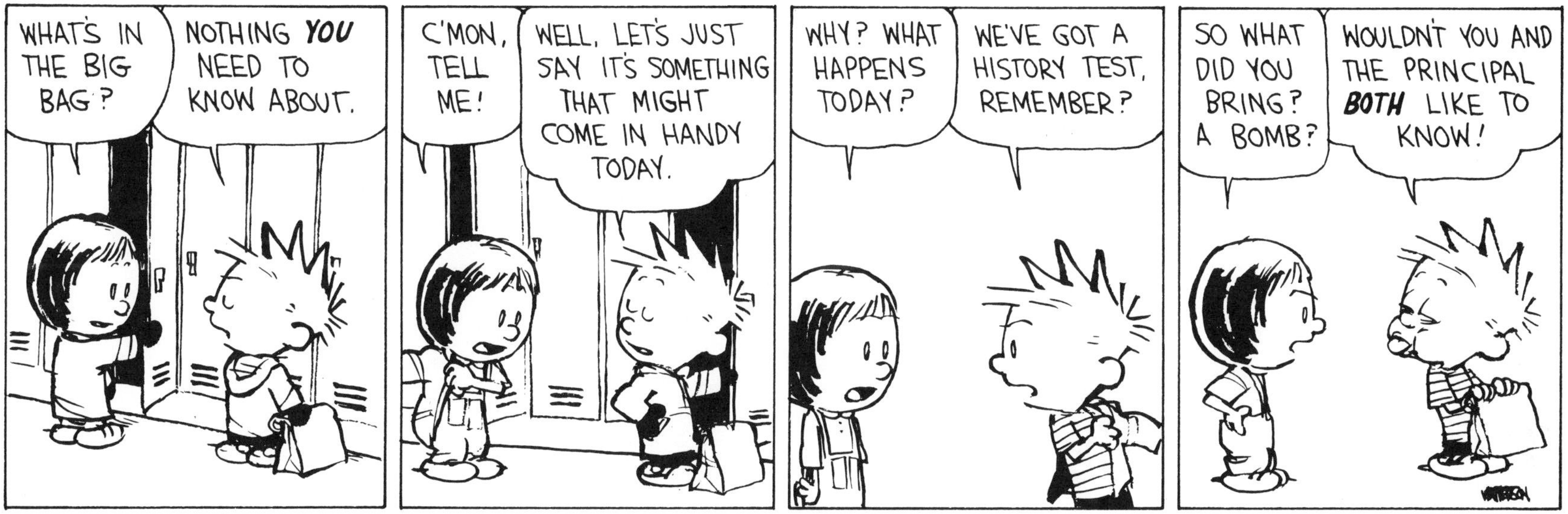
WHAT'S IN THE BIG BAG?
NOTHING **YOU** NEED TO KNOW ABOUT.
C'MON, TELL ME!
WELL, LET'S JUST SAY IT'S SOMETHING THAT MIGHT COME IN HANDY TODAY.
WHY? WHAT HAPPENS TODAY?
WE'VE GOT A HISTORY TEST, REMEMBER?
SO WHAT DID YOU BRING? A BOMB?
WOULDN'T YOU AND THE PRINCIPAL **BOTH** LIKE TO KNOW!

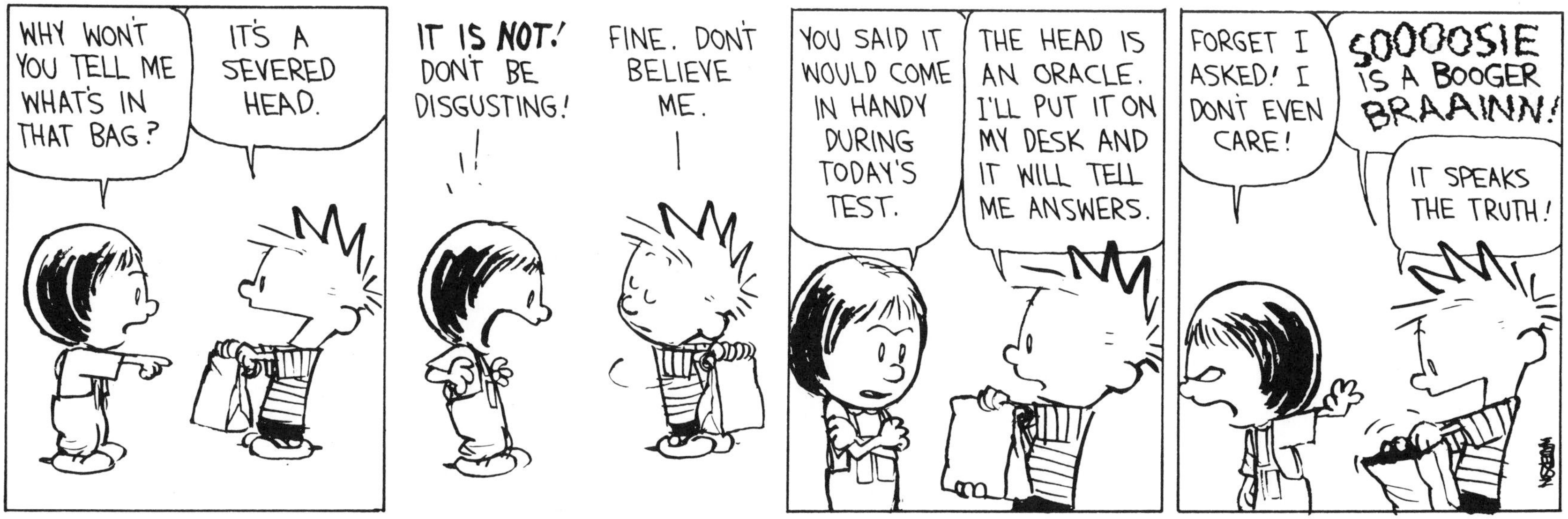
WHY WON'T YOU TELL ME WHAT'S IN THAT BAG?
IT'S A SEVERED HEAD.
IT IS NOT! DON'T BE DISGUSTING!
FINE. DON'T BELIEVE ME.
YOU SAID IT WOULD COME IN HANDY DURING TODAY'S TEST.
THE HEAD IS AN ORACLE. I'LL PUT IT ON MY DESK AND IT WILL TELL ME ANSWERS.
FORGET I ASKED! I DON'T EVEN CARE!
SOOOOSIE IS A BOOGER BRAAINN!
IT SPEAKS THE TRUTH!

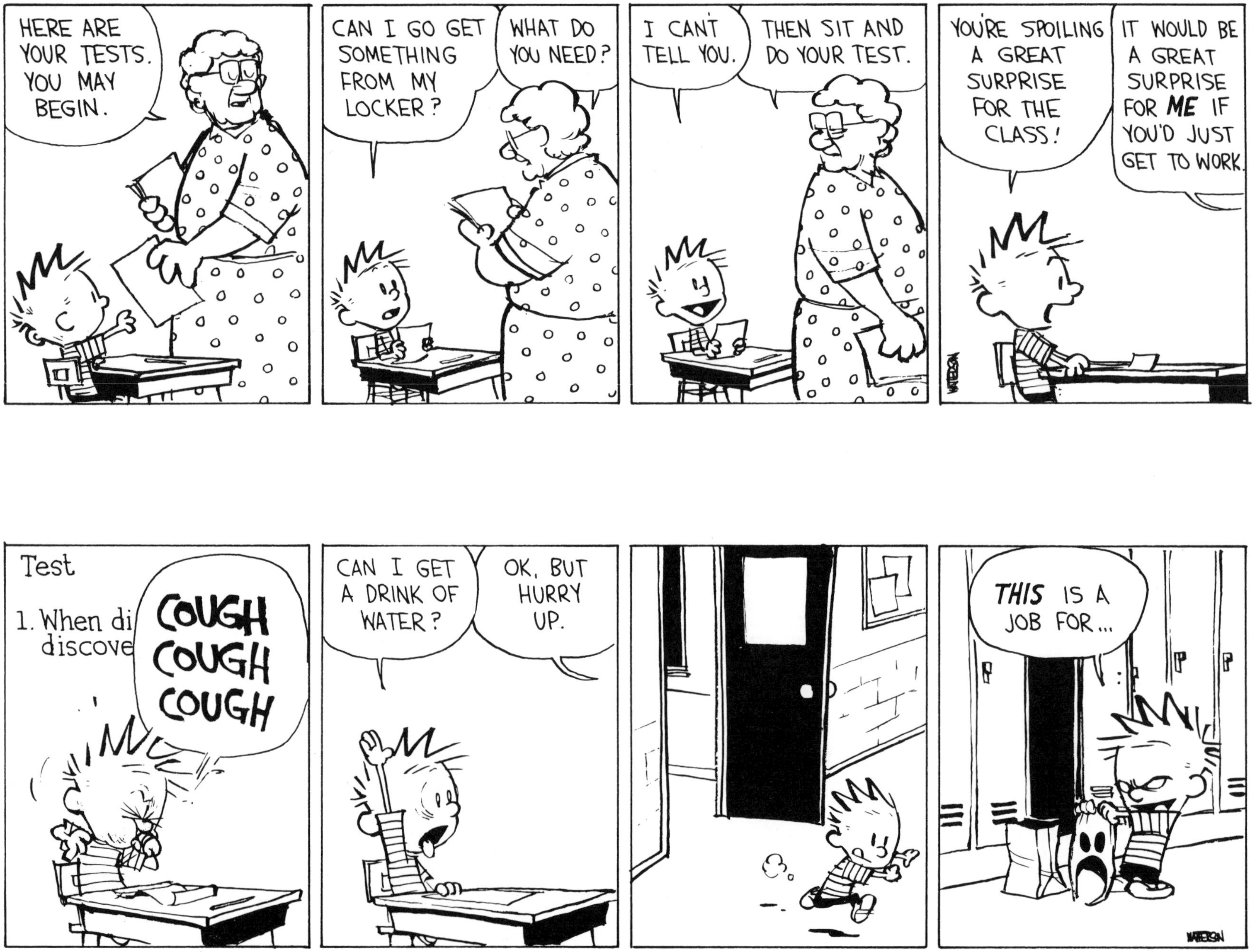
HERE ARE YOUR TESTS. YOU MAY BEGIN.
CAN I GO GET SOMETHING FROM MY LOCKER?
WHAT DO YOU NEED?
I CAN'T TELL YOU.
THEN SIT AND DO YOUR TEST.
YOU'RE SPOILING A GREAT SURPRISE FOR THE CLASS!
IT WOULD BE A GREAT SURPRISE FOR ME IF YOU'D JUST GET TO WORK.
Test
1. When di
discove
COUGH COUGH COUGH
CAN I GET A DRINK OF WATER?
OK, BUT HURRY UP.
THIS IS A JOB FOR...

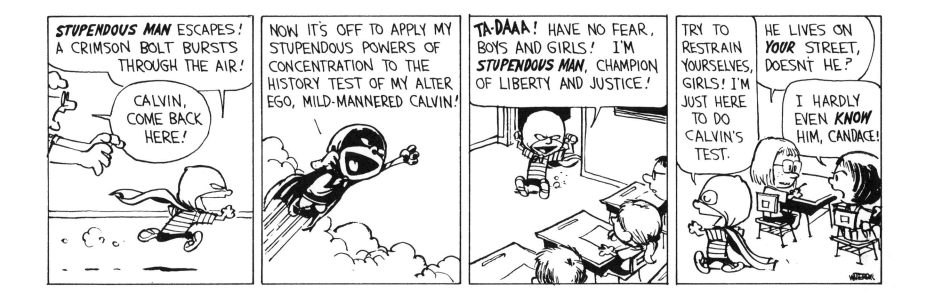

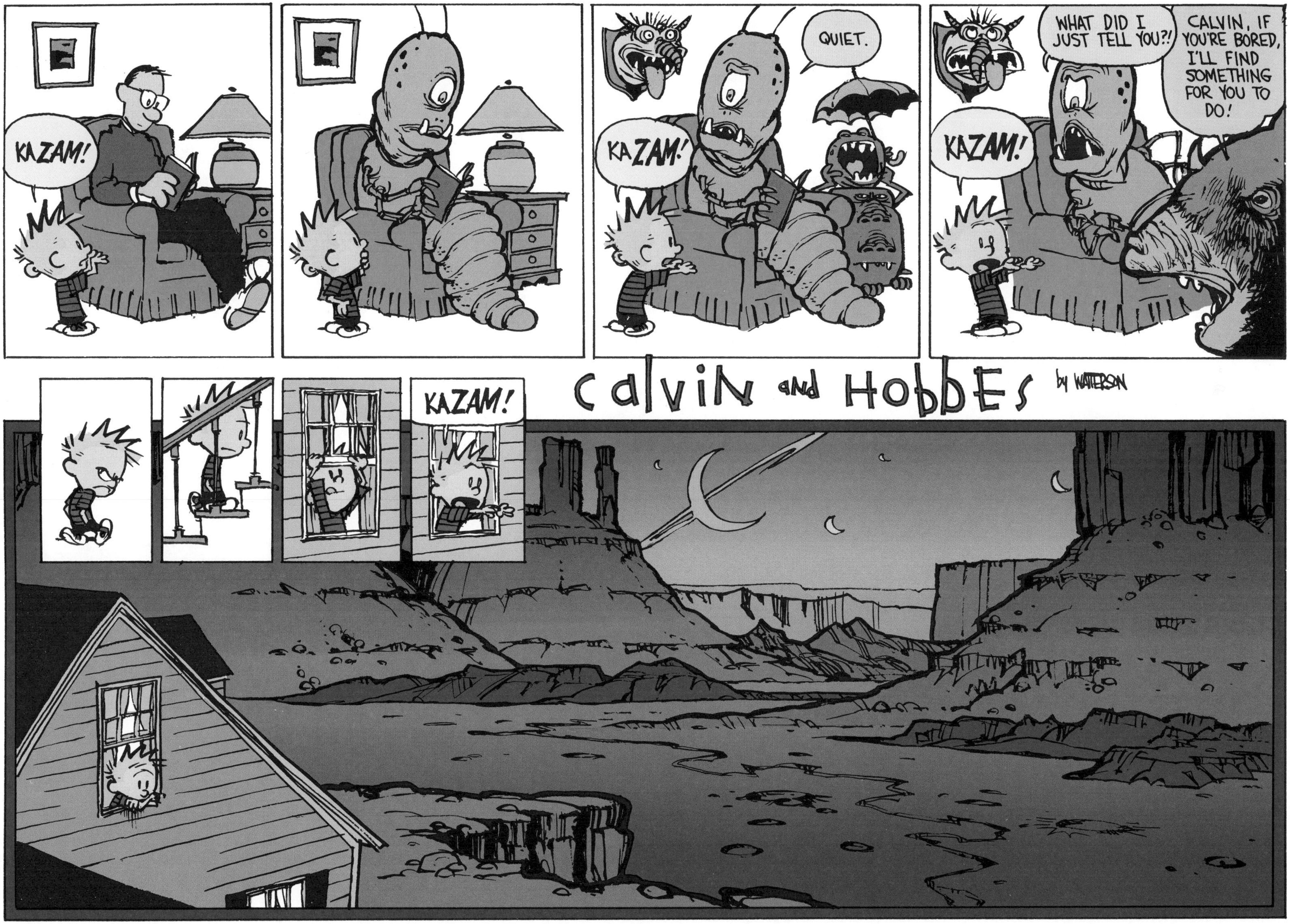
KAZAM!
KAZAM!
QUIET.
KAZAM!
WHAT DID I JUST TELL YOU?!
CALVIN, IF YOU'RE BORED, I'LL FIND SOMETHING FOR YOU TO DO!
Calvin and HOBBES
by WATTERSON
KAZAM!

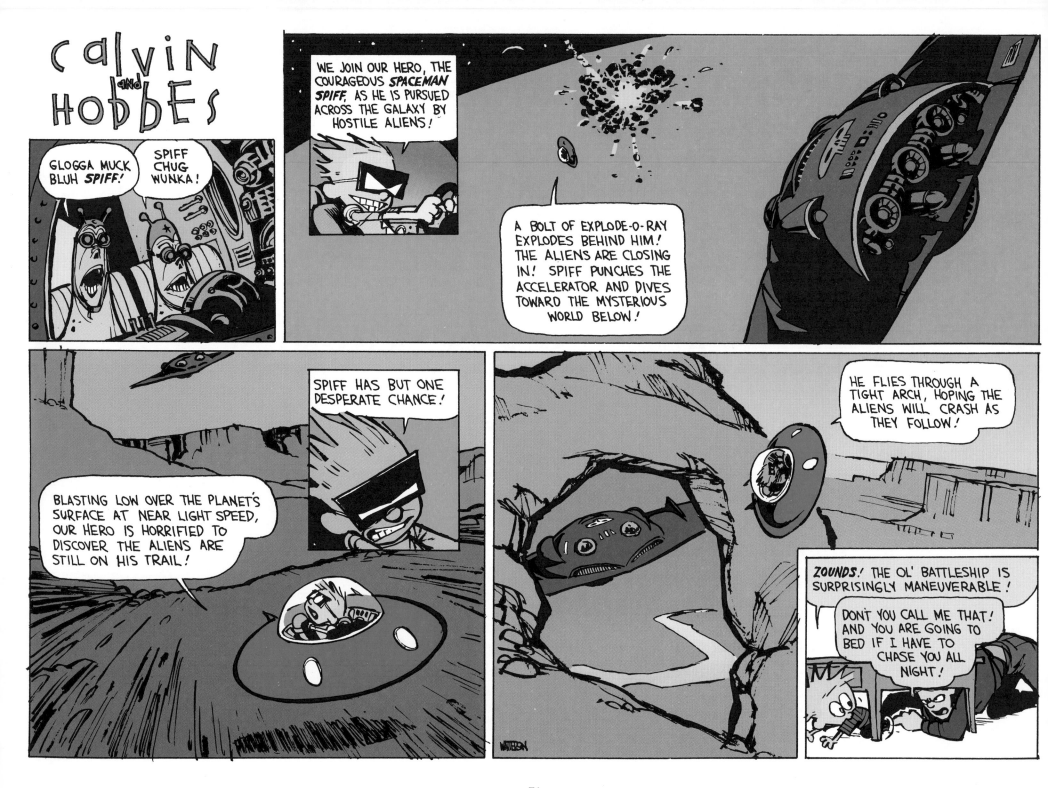

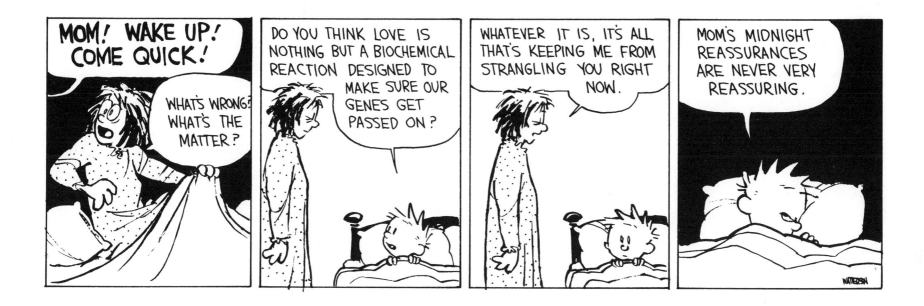

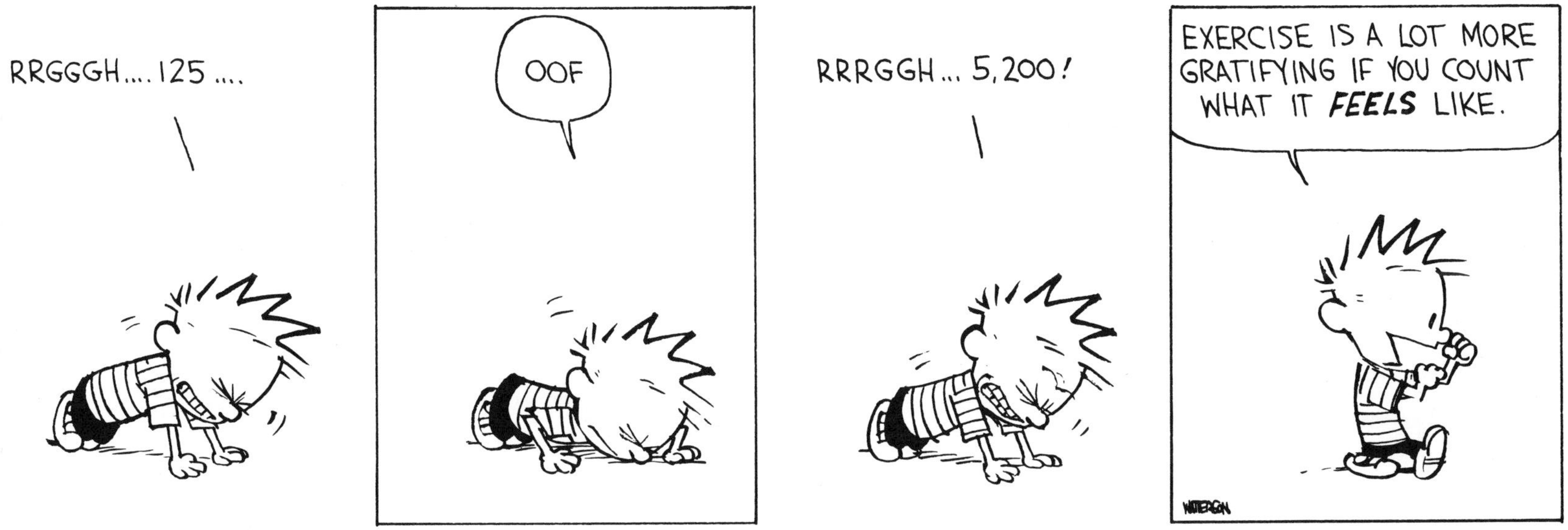
RRGGGH.... 125 ....
OOF
RRRGGH... 5,200!
EXERCISE IS A LOT MORE GRATIFYING IF YOU COUNT WHAT IT FEELS LIKE.

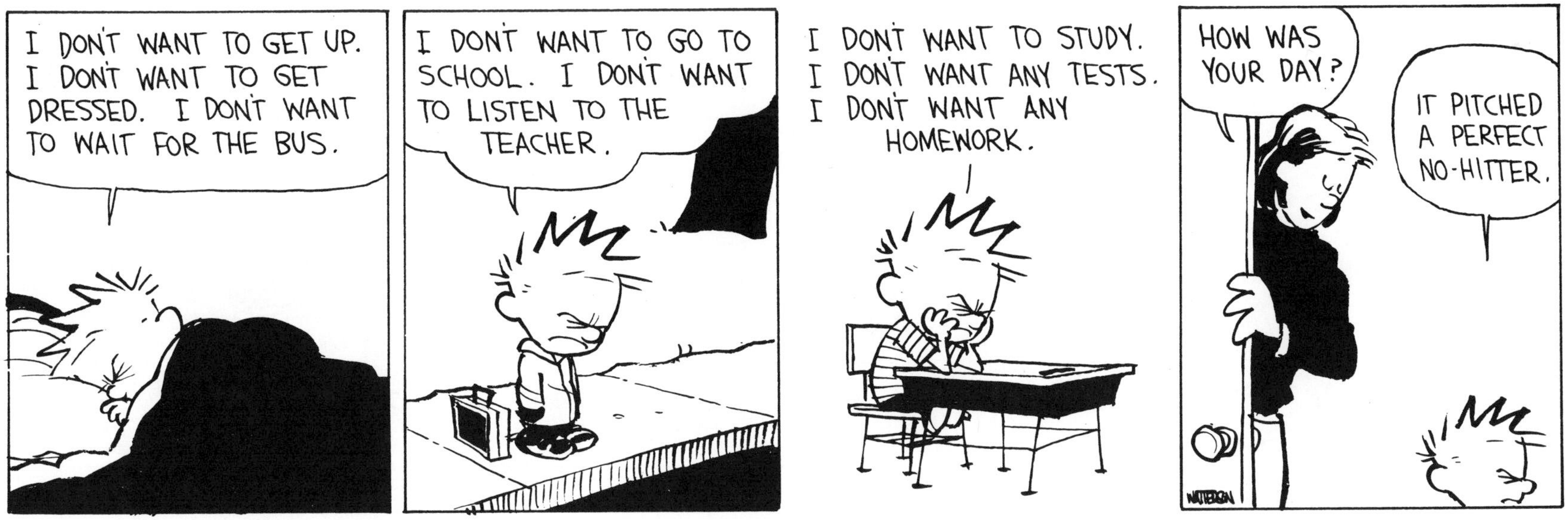
I DON'T WANT TO GET UP. I DON'T WANT TO GET DRESSED. I DON'T WANT TO WAIT FOR THE BUS.
I DON'T WANT TO GO TO SCHOOL. I DON'T WANT TO LISTEN TO THE TEACHER.
I DON'T WANT TO STUDY. I DON'T WANT ANY TESTS. I DON'T WANT ANY HOMEWORK.
HOW WAS YOUR DAY?
IT PITCHED A PERFECT NO-HITTER.

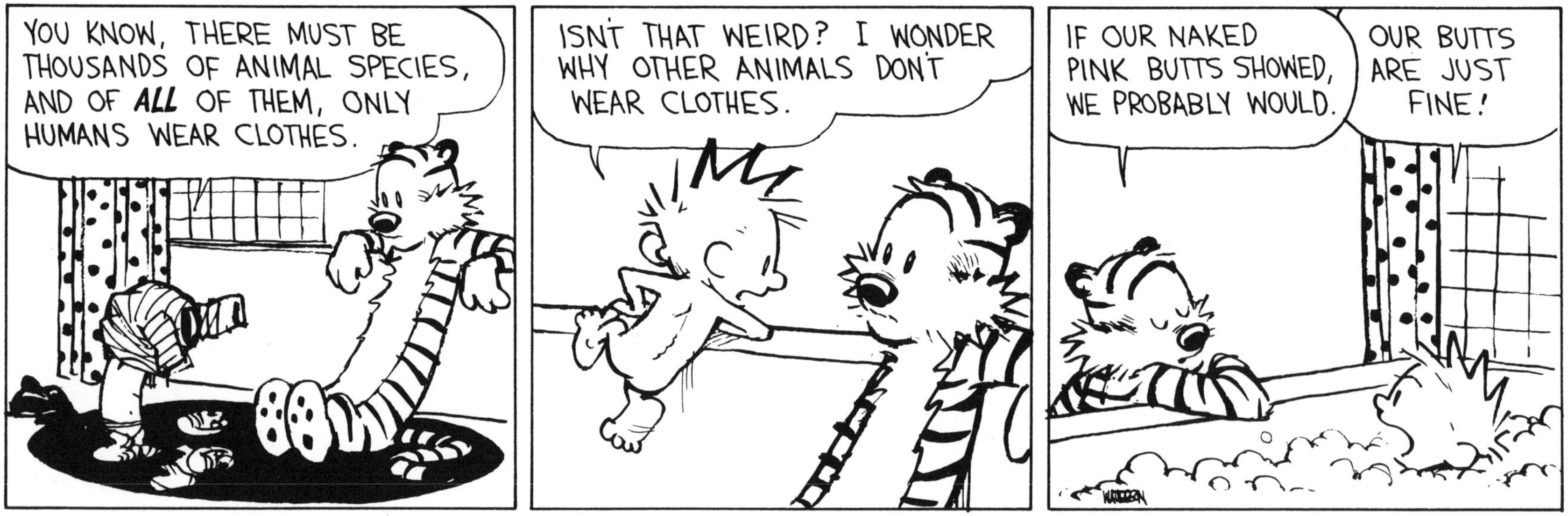
YOU KNOW, THERE MUST BE THOUSANDS OF ANIMAL SPECIES, AND OF **ALL** OF THEM, ONLY HUMANS WEAR CLOTHES.
ISN'T THAT WEIRD? I WONDER WHY OTHER ANIMALS DON'T WEAR CLOTHES.
IF OUR NAKED PINK BUTTS SHOWED, WE PROBABLY WOULD.
OUR BUTTS ARE JUST FINE!
WATTERSON

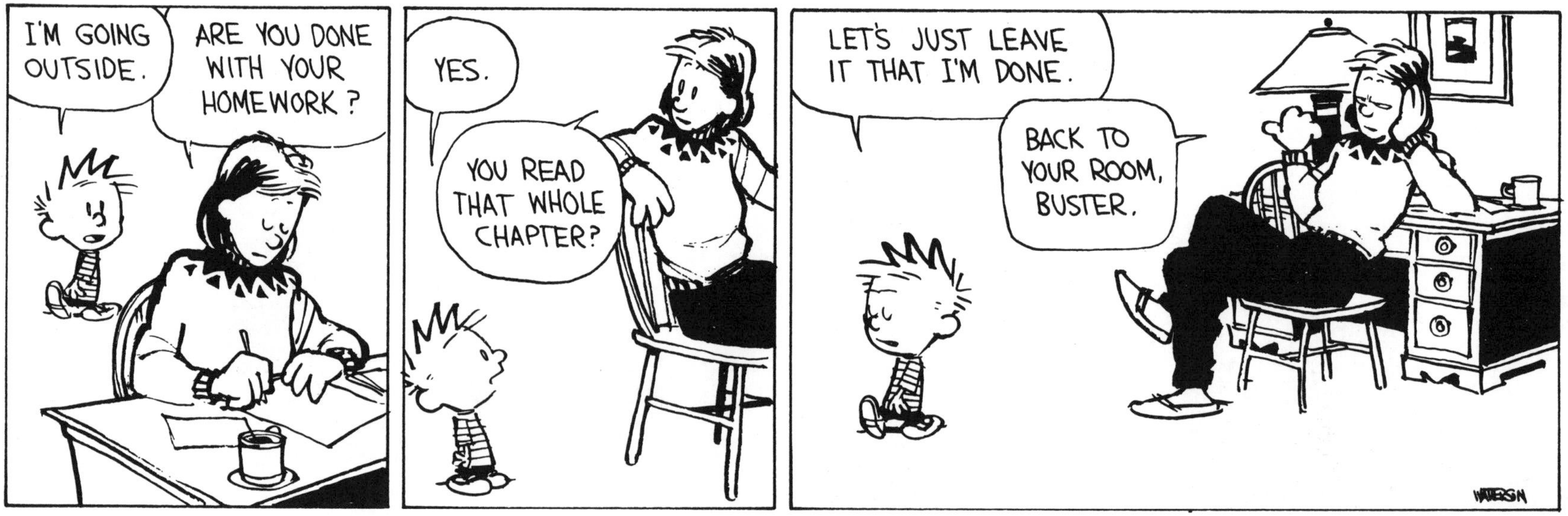
I'M GOING OUTSIDE.
ARE YOU DONE WITH YOUR HOMEWORK?
YES.
YOU READ THAT WHOLE CHAPTER?
LET'S JUST LEAVE IT THAT I'M DONE.
BACK TO YOUR ROOM, BUSTER.
WATTERSON

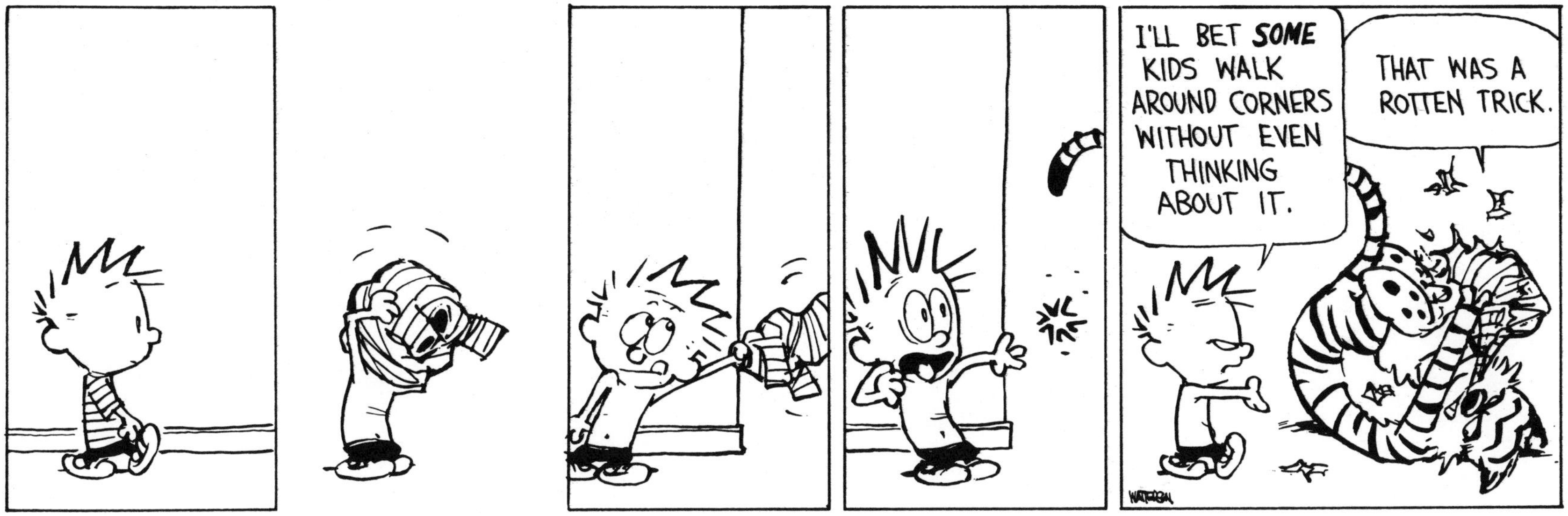
I'LL BET **SOME** KIDS WALK AROUND CORNERS WITHOUT EVEN THINKING ABOUT IT.
THAT WAS A ROTTEN TRICK.

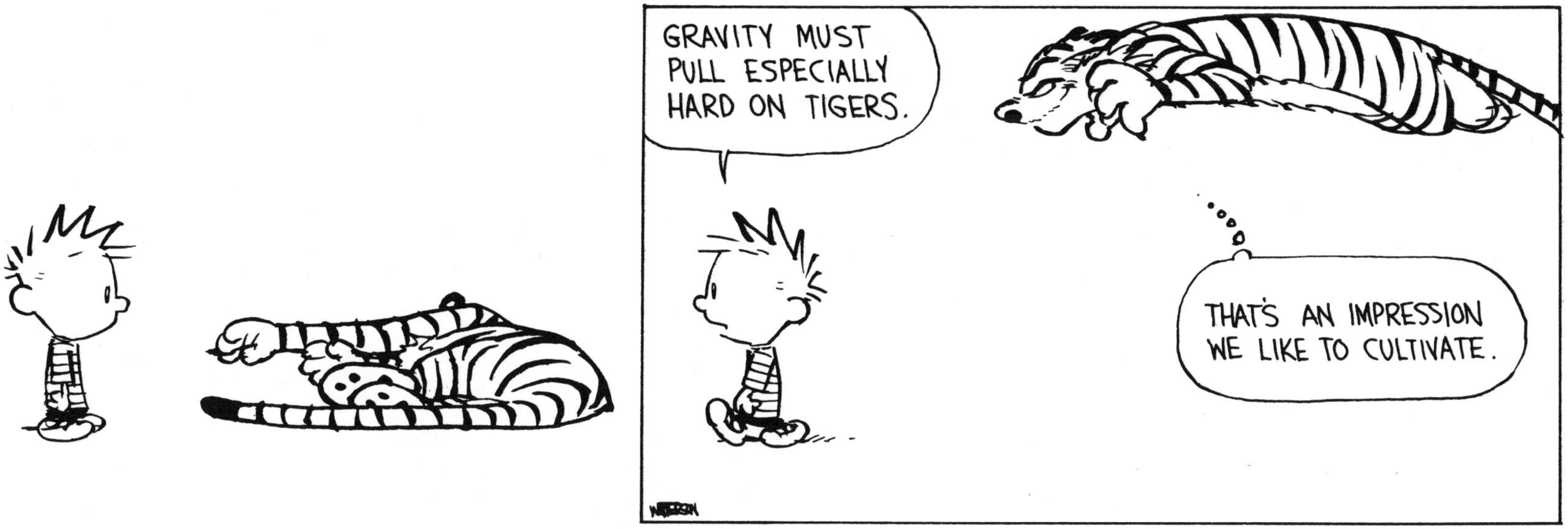
GRAVITY MUST PULL ESPECIALLY HARD ON TIGERS.
THAT'S AN IMPRESSION WE LIKE TO CULTIVATE.

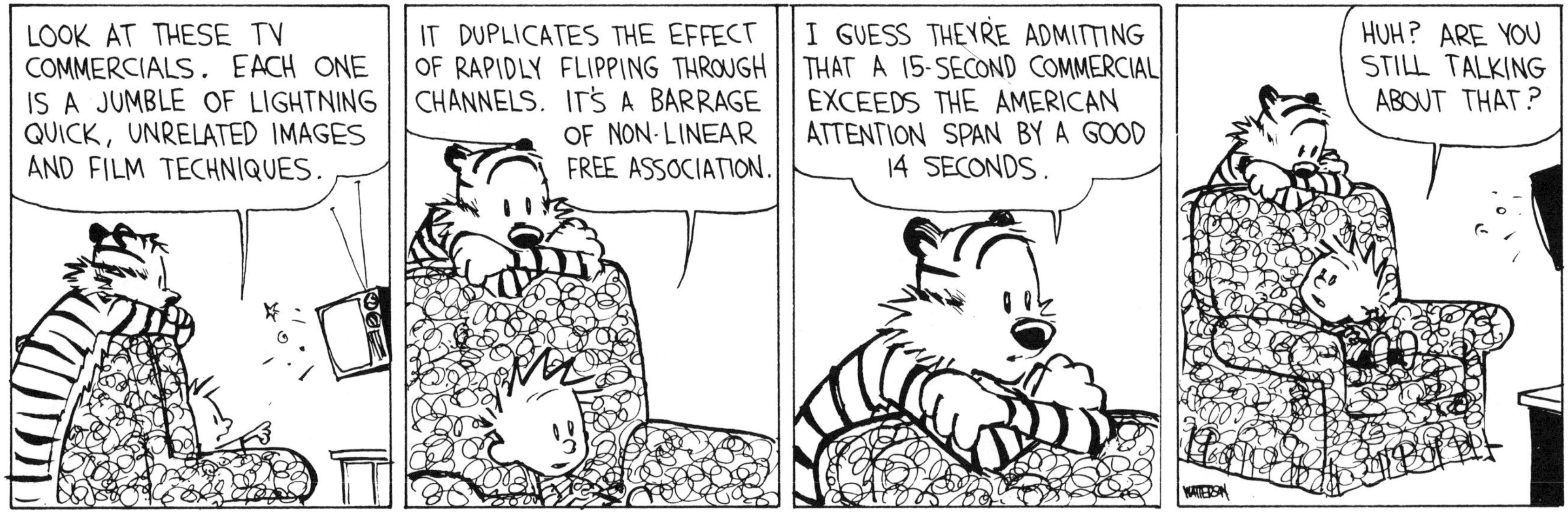
LOOK AT THESE TV COMMERCIALS. EACH ONE IS A JUMBLE OF LIGHTNING QUICK, UNRELATED IMAGES AND FILM TECHNIQUES.
IT DUPLICATES THE EFFECT OF RAPIDLY FLIPPING THROUGH CHANNELS. IT'S A BARRAGE OF NON-LINEAR FREE ASSOCIATION.
I GUESS THEY'RE ADMITTING THAT A 15-SECOND COMMERCIAL EXCEEDS THE AMERICAN ATTENTION SPAN BY A GOOD 14 SECONDS.
HUH? ARE YOU STILL TALKING ABOUT THAT?

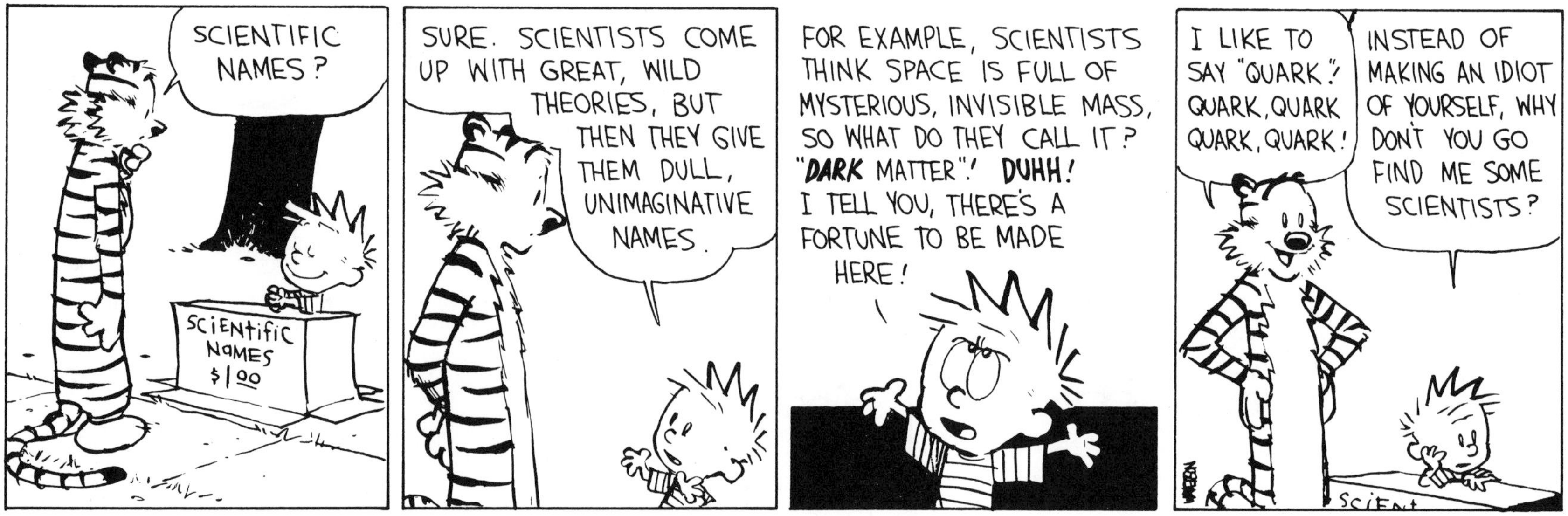
SCIENTIFIC NAMES?
SCIENTIFIC NAMES $1.00
SURE. SCIENTISTS COME UP WITH GREAT, WILD THEORIES, BUT THEN THEY GIVE THEM DULL, UNIMAGINATIVE NAMES.
FOR EXAMPLE, SCIENTISTS THINK SPACE IS FULL OF MYSTERIOUS, INVISIBLE MASS, SO WHAT DO THEY CALL IT? "DARK MATTER"! DUHH! I TELL YOU, THERE'S A FORTUNE TO BE MADE HERE!
I LIKE TO SAY "QUARK"! QUARK, QUARK QUARK, QUARK!
INSTEAD OF MAKING AN IDIOT OF YOURSELF, WHY DON'T YOU GO FIND ME SOME SCIENTISTS?

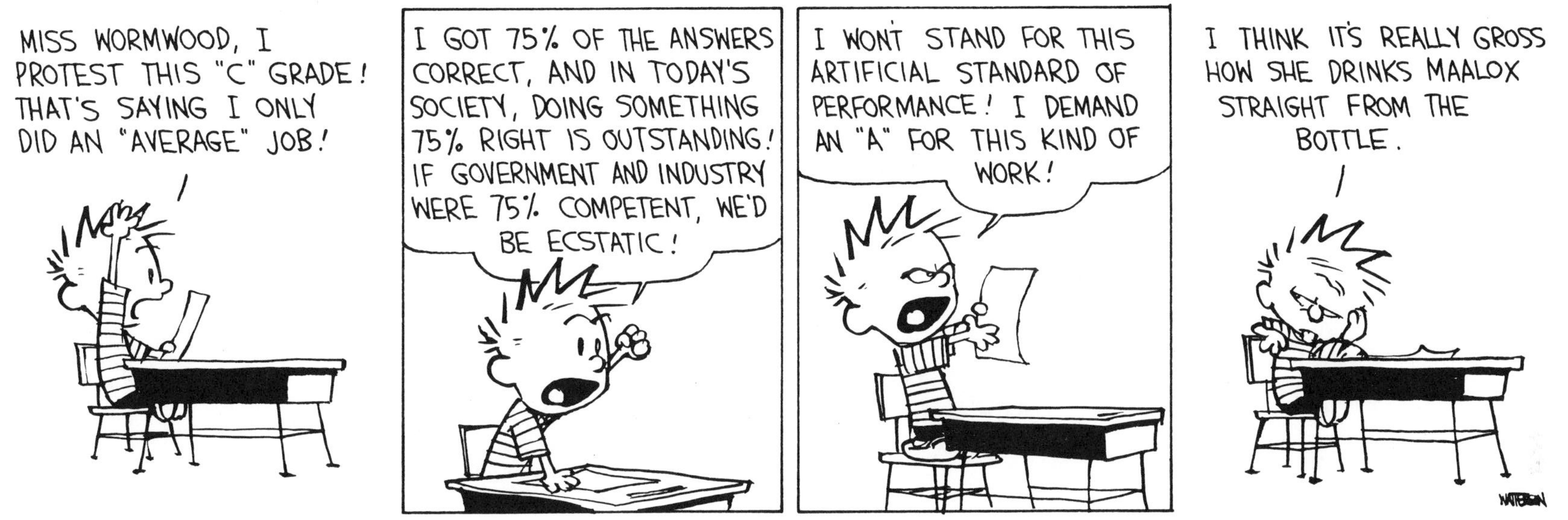
MISS WORMWOOD, I PROTEST THIS "C" GRADE! THAT'S SAYING I ONLY DID AN "AVERAGE" JOB!
I GOT 75% OF THE ANSWERS CORRECT, AND IN TODAY'S SOCIETY, DOING SOMETHING 75% RIGHT IS OUTSTANDING! IF GOVERNMENT AND INDUSTRY WERE 75% COMPETENT, WE'D BE ECSTATIC!
I WON'T STAND FOR THIS ARTIFICIAL STANDARD OF PERFORMANCE! I DEMAND AN "A" FOR THIS KIND OF WORK!
I THINK IT'S REALLY GROSS HOW SHE DRINKS MAALOX STRAIGHT FROM THE BOTTLE.

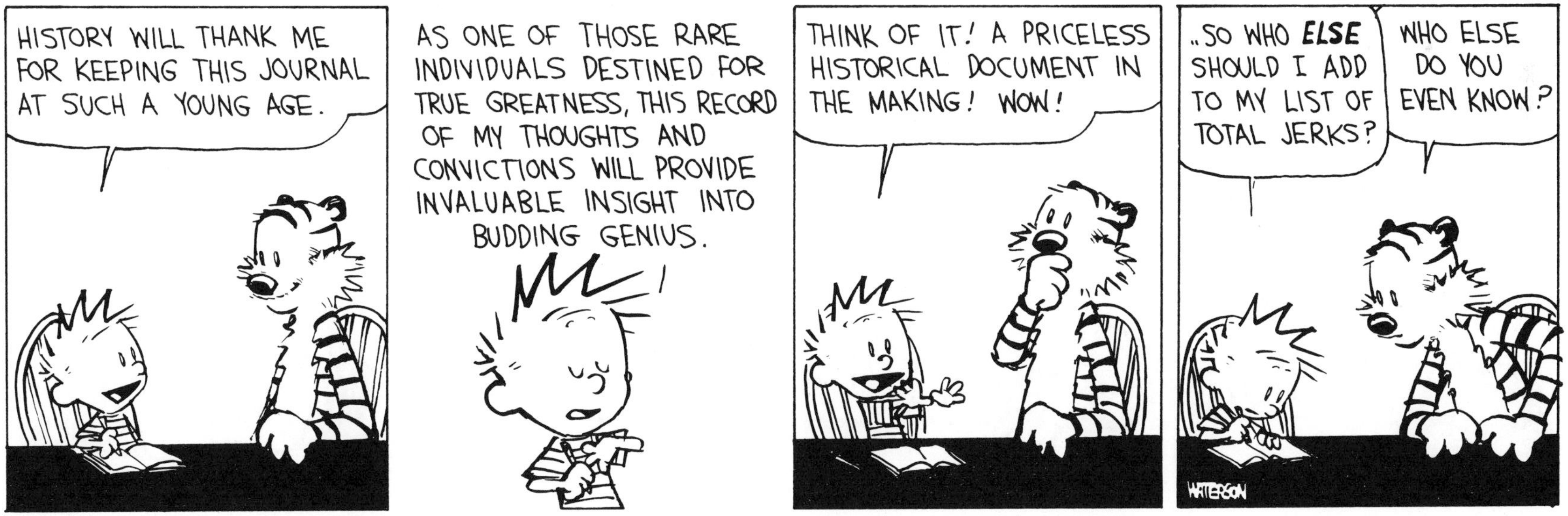
HISTORY WILL THANK ME FOR KEEPING THIS JOURNAL AT SUCH A YOUNG AGE.
AS ONE OF THOSE RARE INDIVIDUALS DESTINED FOR TRUE GREATNESS, THIS RECORD OF MY THOUGHTS AND CONVICTIONS WILL PROVIDE INVALUABLE INSIGHT INTO BUDDING GENIUS.
THINK OF IT! A PRICELESS HISTORICAL DOCUMENT IN THE MAKING! WOW!
..SO WHO **ELSE** SHOULD I ADD TO MY LIST OF TOTAL JERKS?
WHO ELSE DO YOU EVEN KNOW?

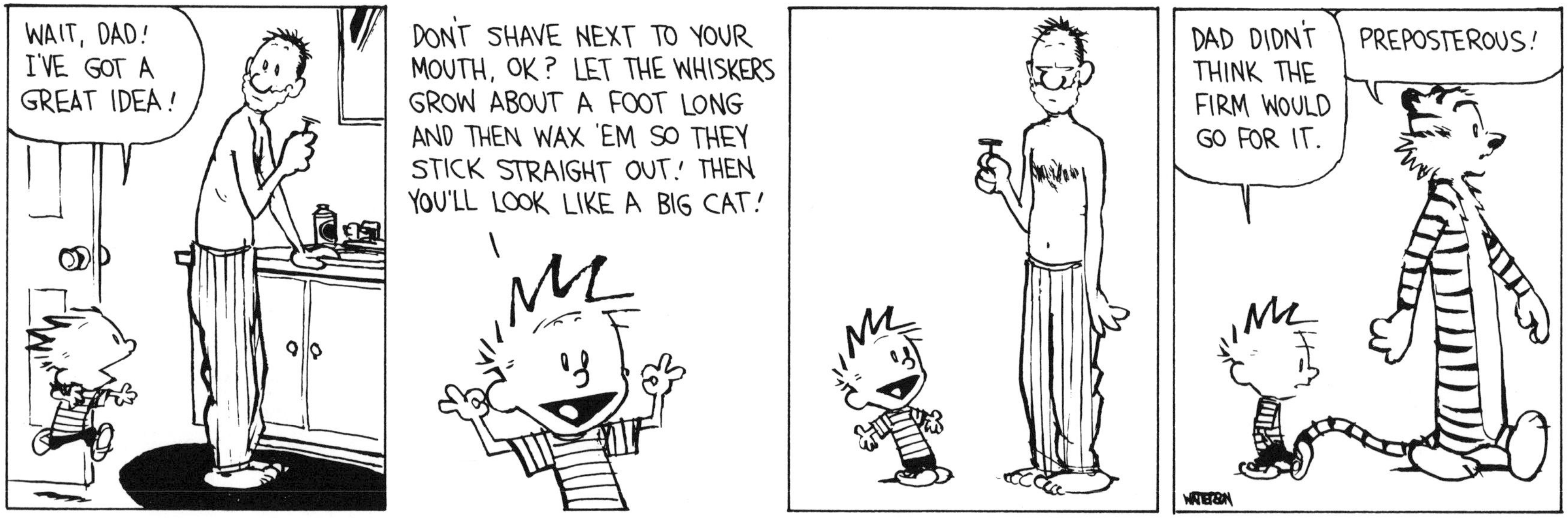
WAIT, DAD! I'VE GOT A GREAT IDEA!
DON'T SHAVE NEXT TO YOUR MOUTH, OK? LET THE WHISKERS GROW ABOUT A FOOT LONG AND THEN WAX 'EM SO THEY STICK STRAIGHT OUT! THEN YOU'LL LOOK LIKE A BIG CAT!
DAD DIDN'T THINK THE FIRM WOULD GO FOR IT.
PREPOSTEROUS!

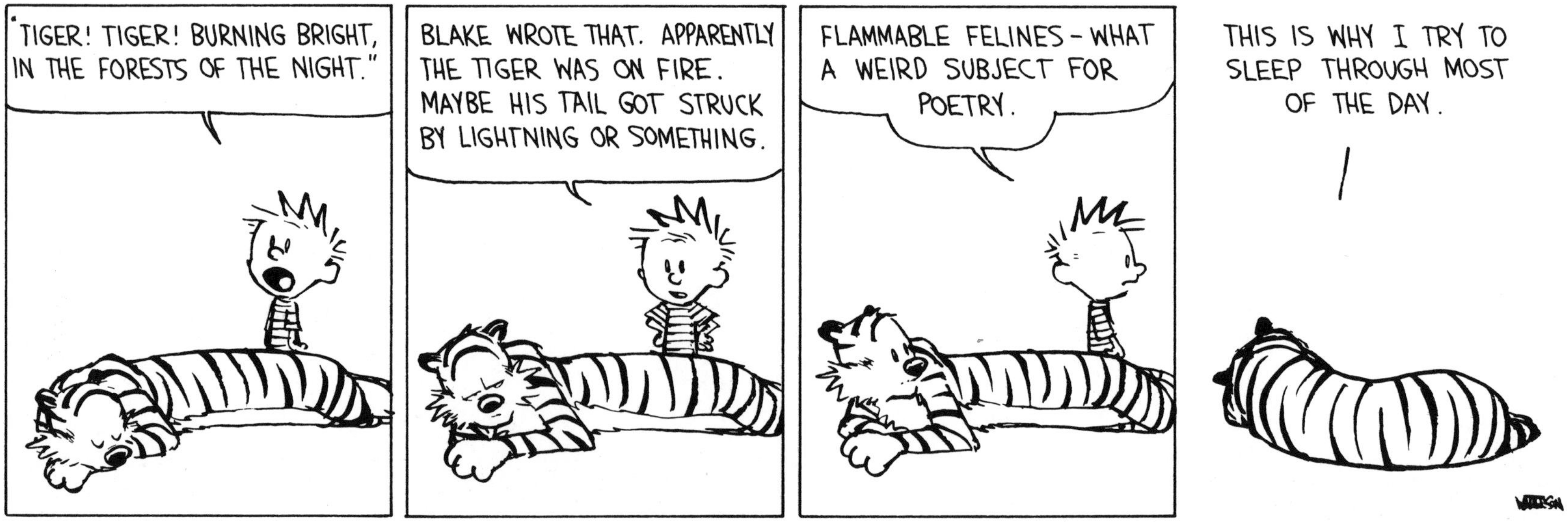
"TIGER! TIGER! BURNING BRIGHT, IN THE FORESTS OF THE NIGHT."
BLAKE WROTE THAT. APPARENTLY THE TIGER WAS ON FIRE. MAYBE HIS TAIL GOT STRUCK BY LIGHTNING OR SOMETHING.
FLAMMABLE FELINES - WHAT A WEIRD SUBJECT FOR POETRY.
THIS IS WHY I TRY TO SLEEP THROUGH MOST OF THE DAY.

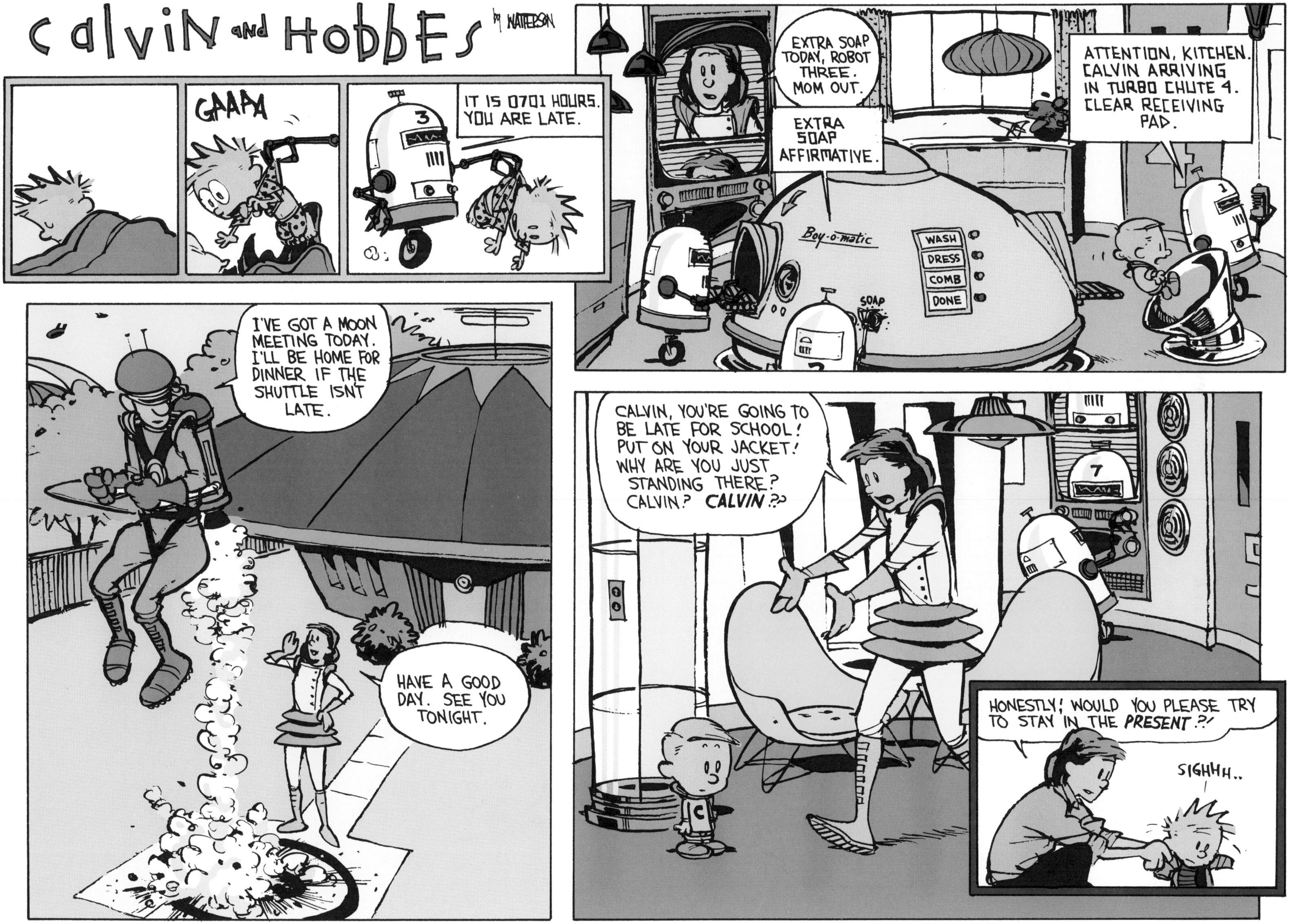
Calvin and Hobbes
by WATTERSON
GAAAA
IT IS 0701 HOURS. YOU ARE LATE.
EXTRA SOAP TODAY, ROBOT THREE. MOM OUT.
EXTRA SOAP AFFIRMATIVE.
ATTENTION, KITCHEN. CALVIN ARRIVING IN TURBO CHUTE 4. CLEAR RECEIVING PAD.
Boy-o-matic
WASH
DRESS
COMB
DONE
SOAP
I'VE GOT A MOON MEETING TODAY. I'LL BE HOME FOR DINNER IF THE SHUTTLE ISN'T LATE.
HAVE A GOOD DAY. SEE YOU TONIGHT.
CALVIN, YOU'RE GOING TO BE LATE FOR SCHOOL! PUT ON YOUR JACKET! WHY ARE YOU JUST STANDING THERE? CALVIN? CALVIN?!
HONESTLY! WOULD YOU PLEASE TRY TO STAY IN THE PRESENT?!
SIGHHH..

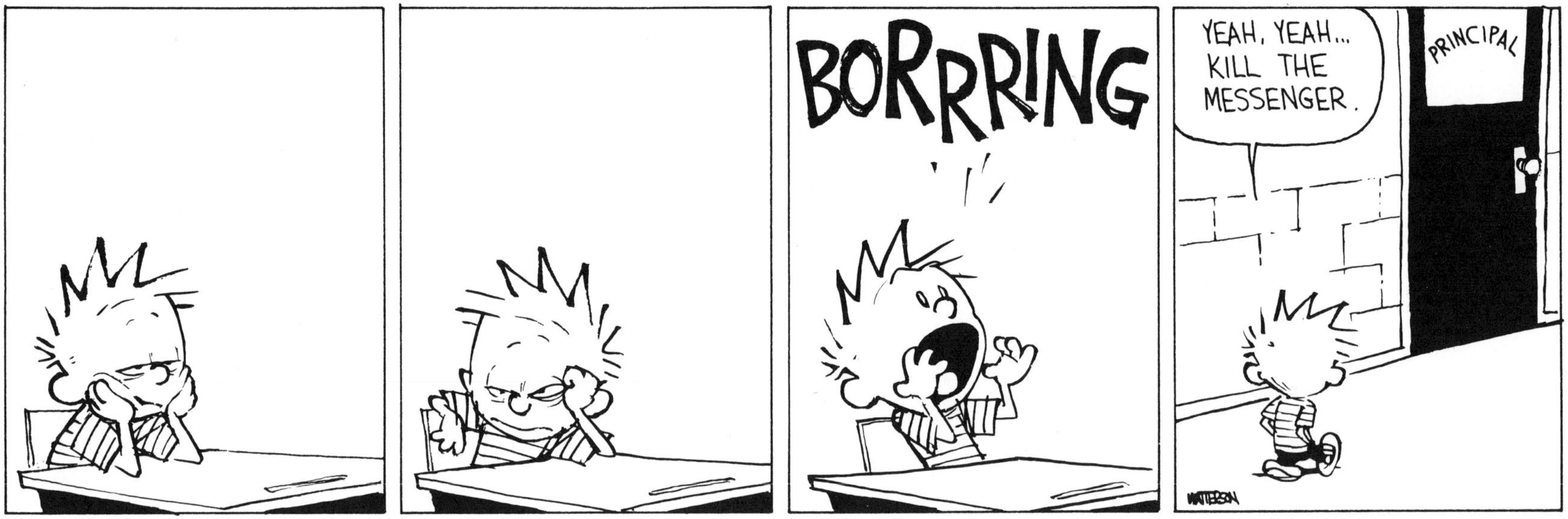
BORRRING
YEAH, YEAH... KILL THE MESSENGER.
PRINCIPAL
WATTERSON

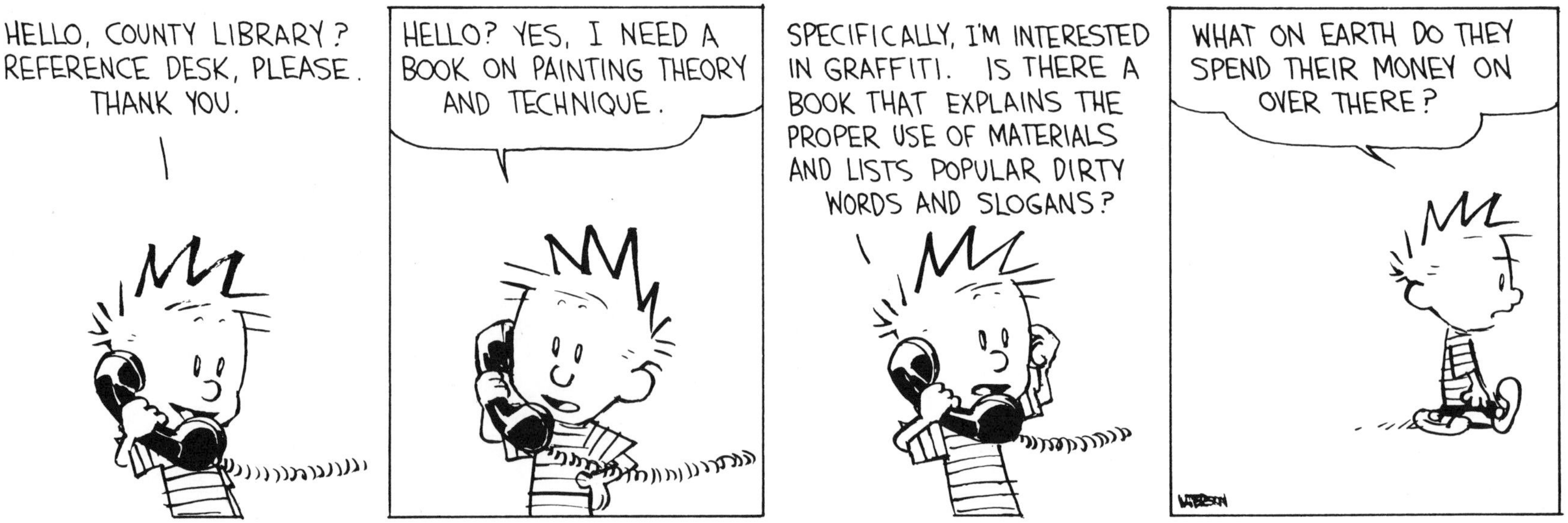
HELLO, COUNTY LIBRARY? REFERENCE DESK, PLEASE. THANK YOU.
HELLO? YES, I NEED A BOOK ON PAINTING THEORY AND TECHNIQUE.
SPECIFICALLY, I'M INTERESTED IN GRAFFITI. IS THERE A BOOK THAT EXPLAINS THE PROPER USE OF MATERIALS AND LISTS POPULAR DIRTY WORDS AND SLOGANS?
WHAT ON EARTH DO THEY SPEND THEIR MONEY ON OVER THERE?
WATTERSON

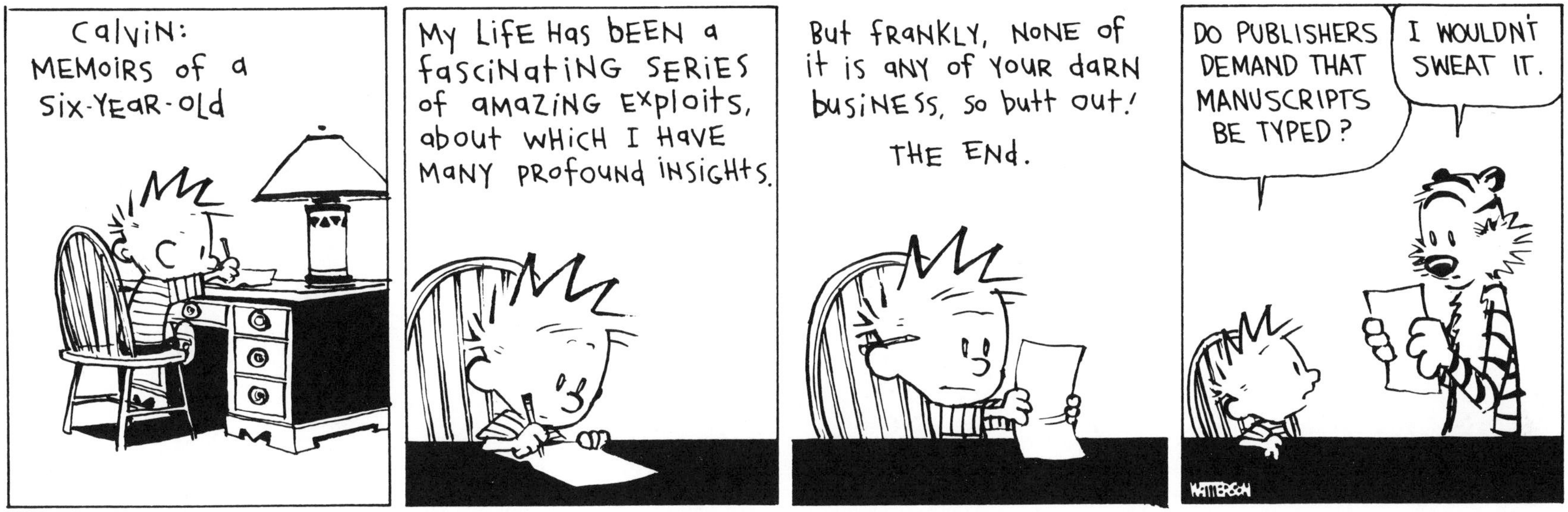
CALVIN: MEMOIRS OF A SIX-YEAR-OLD
MY LIFE HAS BEEN A FASCINATING SERIES OF AMAZING EXPLOITS, ABOUT WHICH I HAVE MANY PROFOUND INSIGHTS.
BUT FRANKLY, NONE OF IT IS ANY OF YOUR DARN BUSINESS, SO BUTT OUT!
THE END.
DO PUBLISHERS DEMAND THAT MANUSCRIPTS BE TYPED?
I WOULDN'T SWEAT IT.
WATTERSON

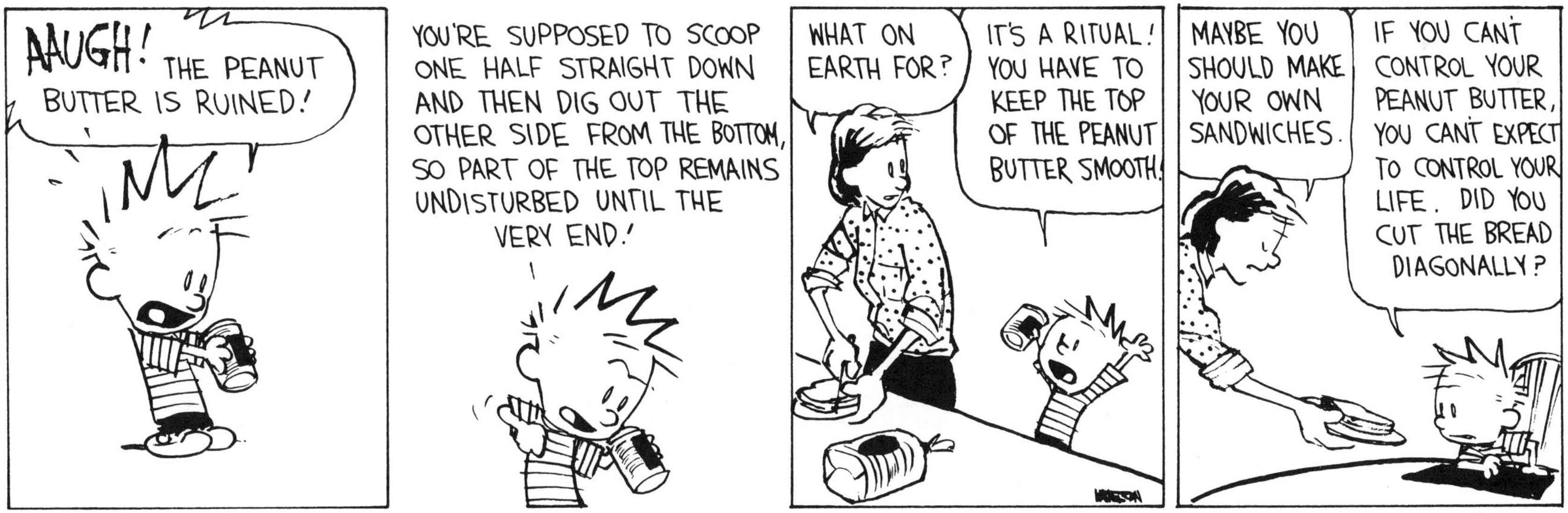
AAUGH! THE PEANUT BUTTER IS RUINED!
YOU'RE SUPPOSED TO SCOOP ONE HALF STRAIGHT DOWN AND THEN DIG OUT THE OTHER SIDE FROM THE BOTTOM, SO PART OF THE TOP REMAINS UNDISTURBED UNTIL THE VERY END!
WHAT ON EARTH FOR?
IT'S A RITUAL! YOU HAVE TO KEEP THE TOP OF THE PEANUT BUTTER SMOOTH!
MAYBE YOU SHOULD MAKE YOUR OWN SANDWICHES.
IF YOU CAN'T CONTROL YOUR PEANUT BUTTER, YOU CAN'T EXPECT TO CONTROL YOUR LIFE. DID YOU CUT THE BREAD DIAGONALLY?

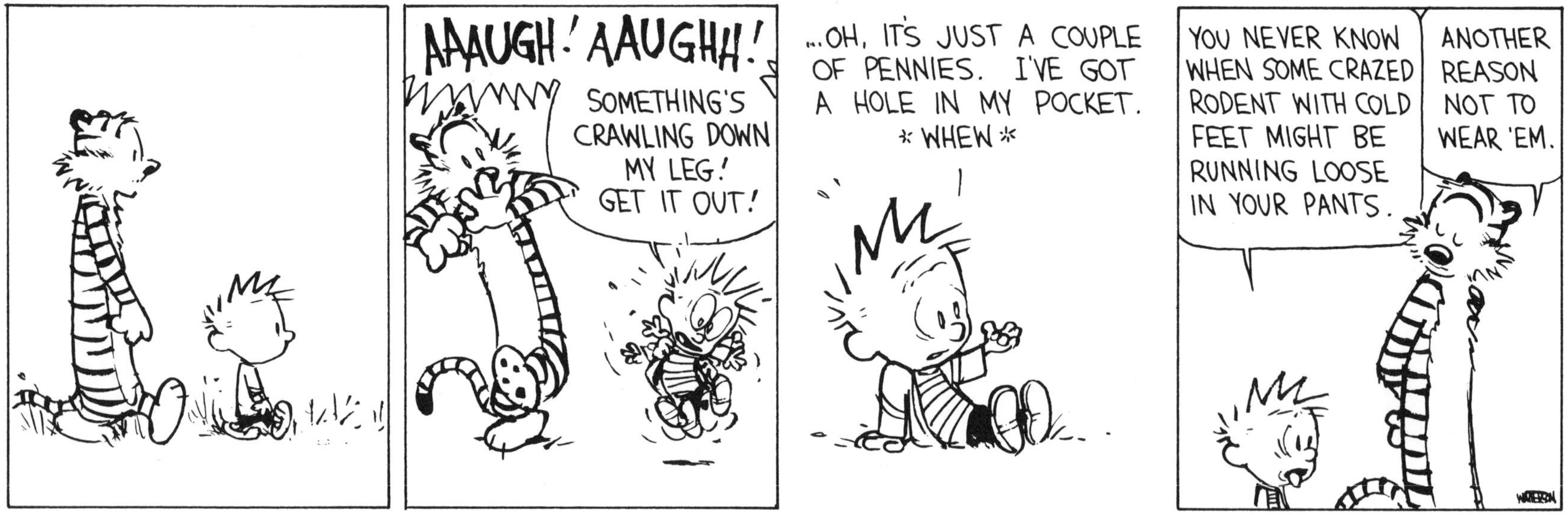
AAAUGH! AAUGHH!
SOMETHING'S CRAWLING DOWN MY LEG! GET IT OUT!
...OH, IT'S JUST A COUPLE OF PENNIES. I'VE GOT A HOLE IN MY POCKET. *WHEW*
YOU NEVER KNOW WHEN SOME CRAZED RODENT WITH COLD FEET MIGHT BE RUNNING LOOSE IN YOUR PANTS.
ANOTHER REASON NOT TO WEAR 'EM.

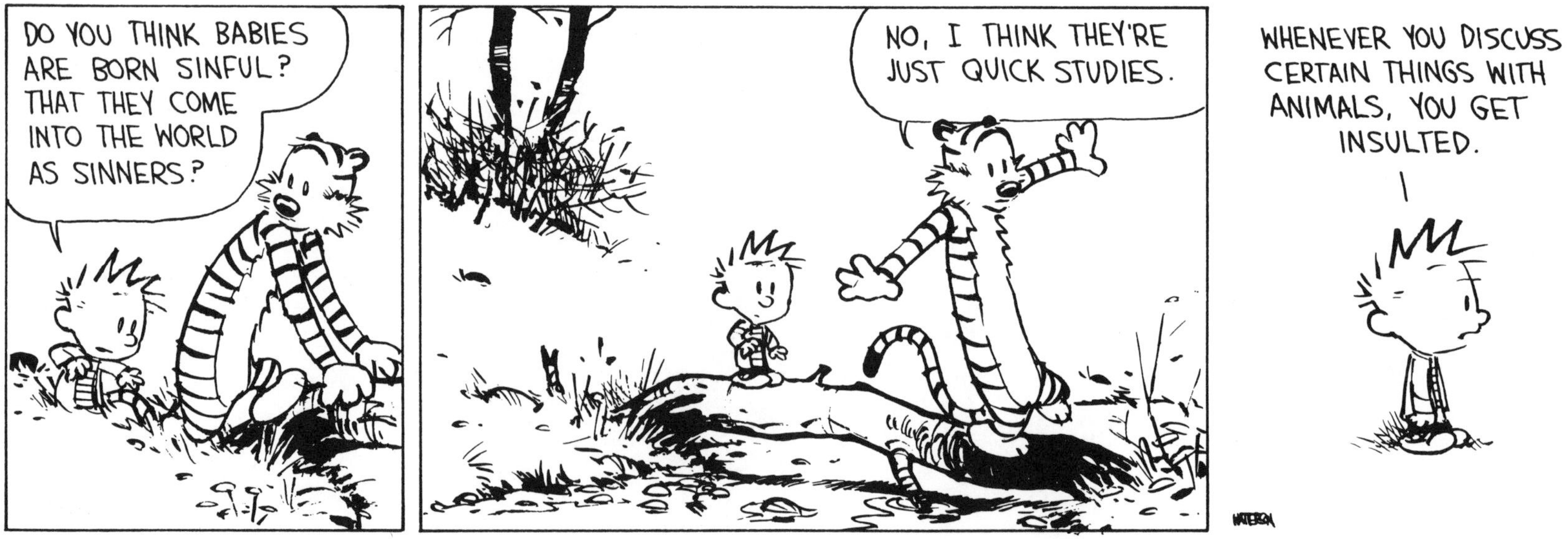
DO YOU THINK BABIES ARE BORN SINFUL? THAT THEY COME INTO THE WORLD AS SINNERS?
NO, I THINK THEY'RE JUST QUICK STUDIES.
WHENEVER YOU DISCUSS CERTAIN THINGS WITH ANIMALS, YOU GET INSULTED.

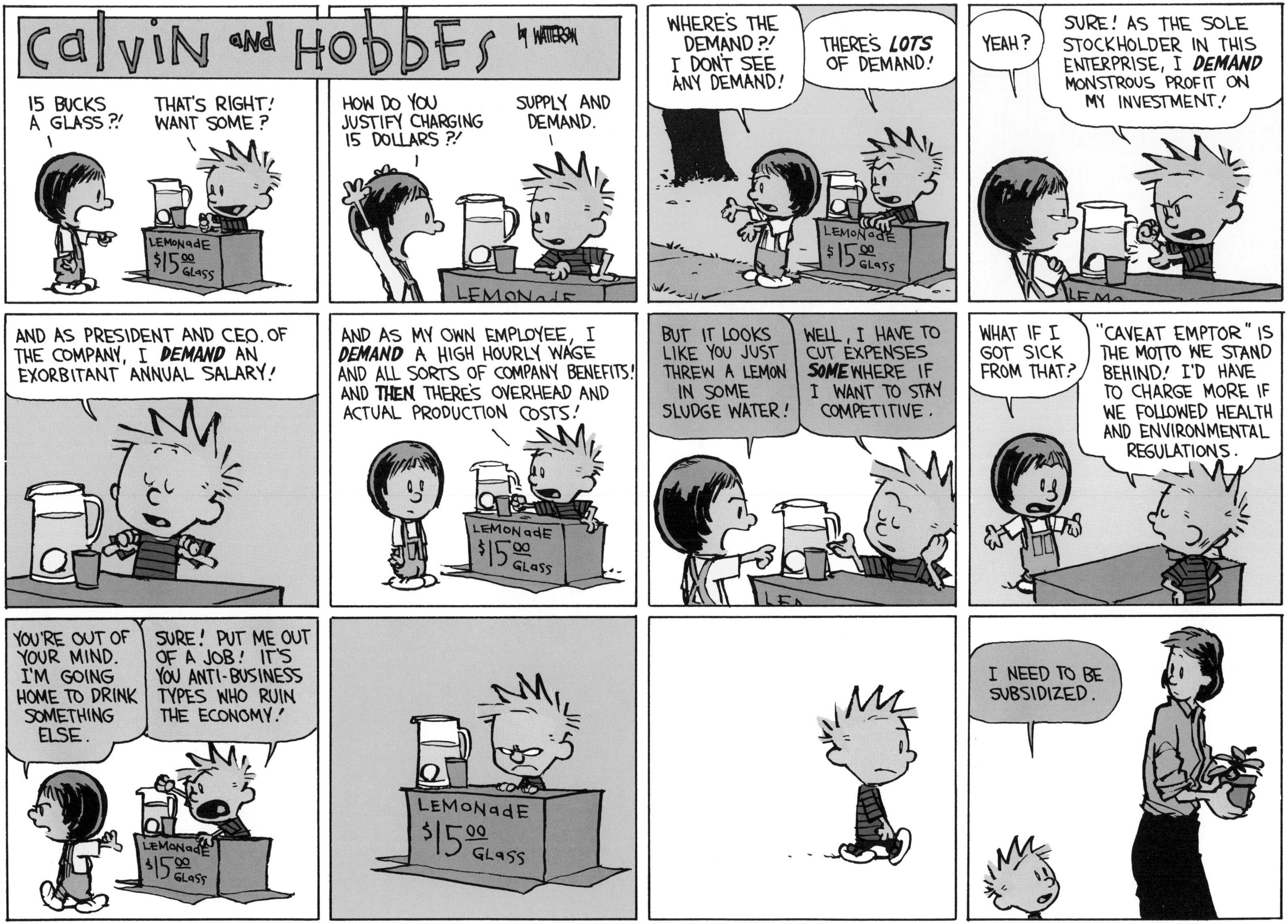
Calvin and Hobbes
by WATTERSON
15 BUCKS A GLASS ?!
THAT'S RIGHT! WANT SOME ?
LEMONadE $15.00 GLass
HOW DO YOU JUSTIFY CHARGING 15 DOLLARS ?!
SUPPLY AND DEMAND.
WHERE'S THE DEMAND ?! I DON'T SEE ANY DEMAND!
THERE'S LOTS OF DEMAND!
YEAH ?
SURE! AS THE SOLE STOCKHOLDER IN THIS ENTERPRISE, I DEMAND MONSTROUS PROFIT ON MY INVESTMENT!
AND AS PRESIDENT AND C.E.O. OF THE COMPANY, I DEMAND AN EXORBITANT ANNUAL SALARY!
AND AS MY OWN EMPLOYEE, I DEMAND A HIGH HOURLY WAGE AND ALL SORTS OF COMPANY BENEFITS! AND THEN THERE'S OVERHEAD AND ACTUAL PRODUCTION COSTS!
BUT IT LOOKS LIKE YOU JUST THREW A LEMON IN SOME SLUDGE WATER!
WELL, I HAVE TO CUT EXPENSES SOMEWHERE IF I WANT TO STAY COMPETITIVE.
WHAT IF I GOT SICK FROM THAT?
"CAVEAT EMPTOR" IS THE MOTTO WE STAND BEHIND! I'D HAVE TO CHARGE MORE IF WE FOLLOWED HEALTH AND ENVIRONMENTAL REGULATIONS.
YOU'RE OUT OF YOUR MIND. I'M GOING HOME TO DRINK SOMETHING ELSE.
SURE! PUT ME OUT OF A JOB! IT'S YOU ANTI-BUSINESS TYPES WHO RUIN THE ECONOMY!
I NEED TO BE SUBSIDIZED.

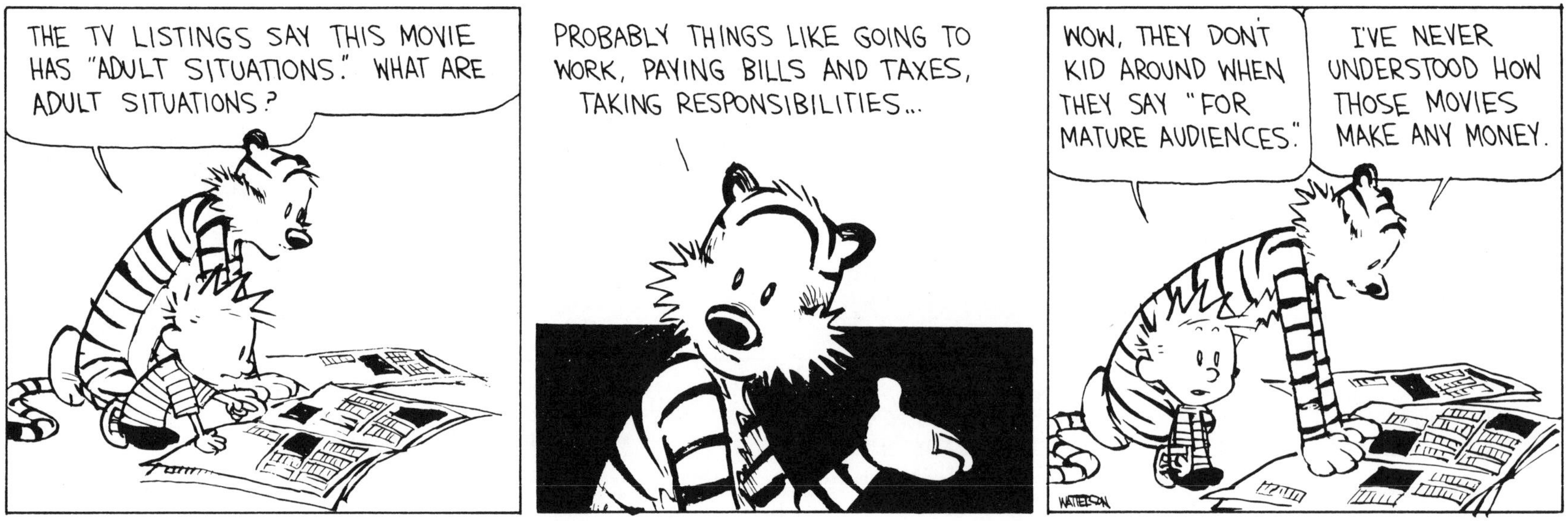
THE TV LISTINGS SAY THIS MOVIE HAS "ADULT SITUATIONS." WHAT ARE ADULT SITUATIONS?
PROBABLY THINGS LIKE GOING TO WORK, PAYING BILLS AND TAXES, TAKING RESPONSIBILITIES...
WOW, THEY DON'T KID AROUND WHEN THEY SAY "FOR MATURE AUDIENCES."
I'VE NEVER UNDERSTOOD HOW THOSE MOVIES MAKE ANY MONEY.
WATTERSON

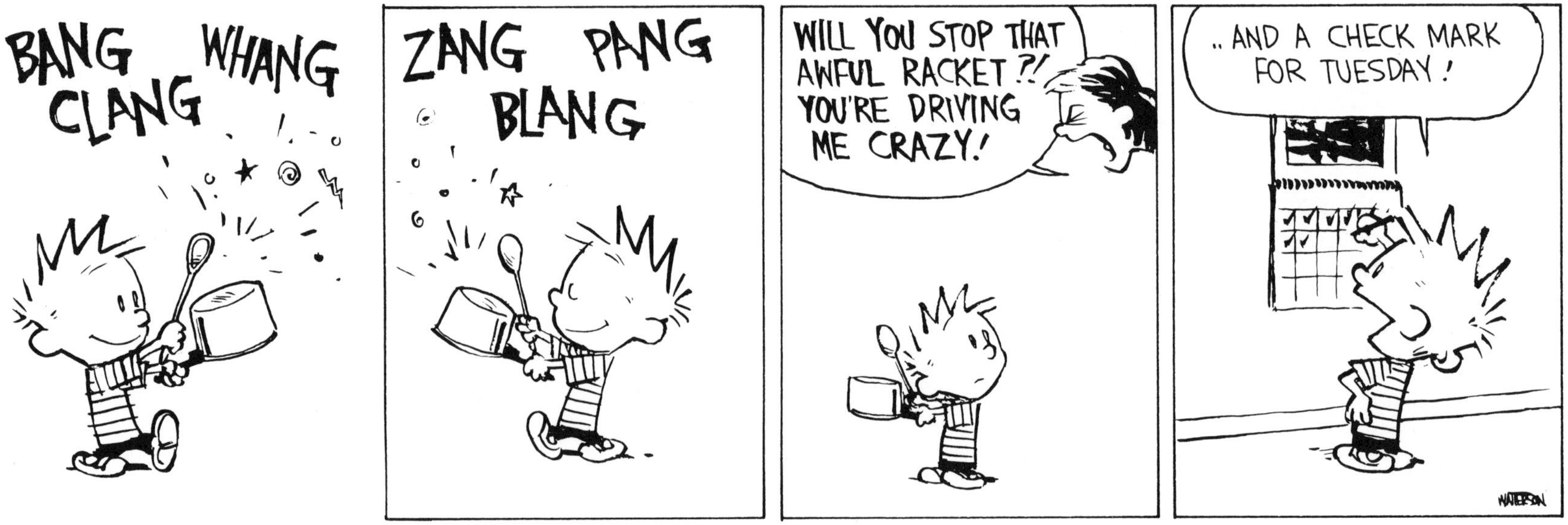
BANG
WHANG
CLANG
ZANG
PANG
BLANG
WILL YOU STOP THAT AWFUL RACKET?! YOU'RE DRIVING ME CRAZY!
..AND A CHECK MARK FOR TUESDAY!
WATTERSON

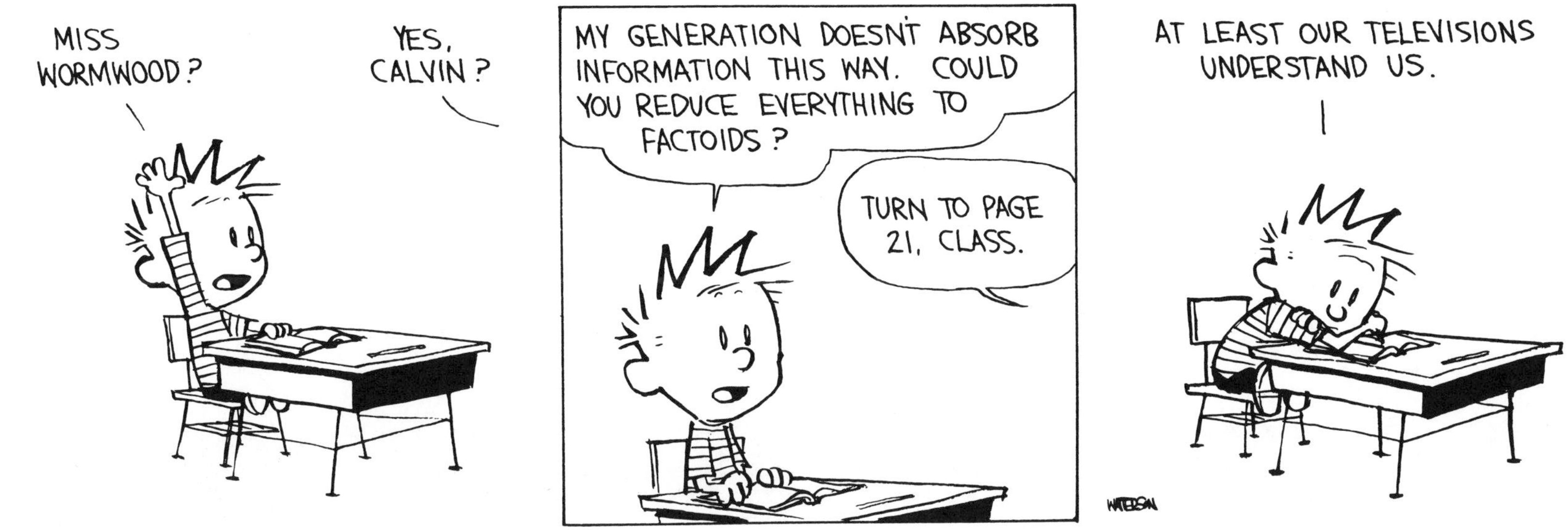
MISS WORMWOOD?
YES, CALVIN?
MY GENERATION DOESN'T ABSORB INFORMATION THIS WAY. COULD YOU REDUCE EVERYTHING TO FACTOIDS?
TURN TO PAGE 21, CLASS.
AT LEAST OUR TELEVISIONS UNDERSTAND US.

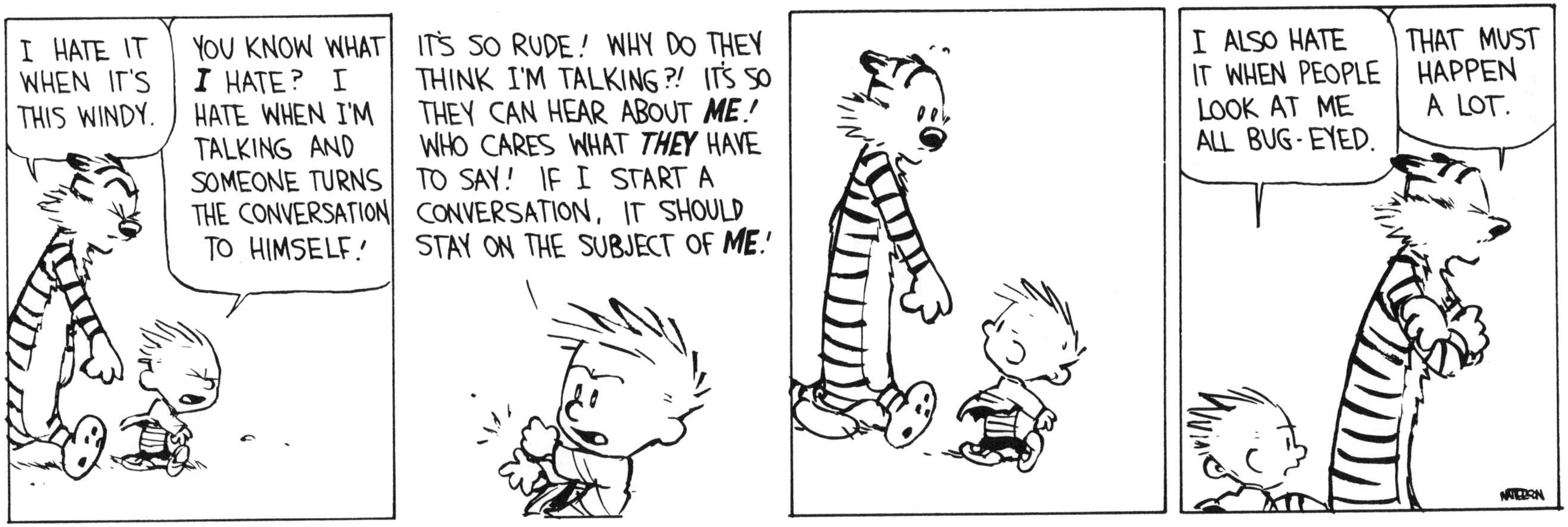
I HATE IT WHEN IT'S THIS WINDY.
YOU KNOW WHAT I HATE? I HATE WHEN I'M TALKING AND SOMEONE TURNS THE CONVERSATION TO HIMSELF!
IT'S SO RUDE! WHY DO THEY THINK I'M TALKING?! IT'S SO THEY CAN HEAR ABOUT ME! WHO CARES WHAT THEY HAVE TO SAY! IF I START A CONVERSATION, IT SHOULD STAY ON THE SUBJECT OF ME!
I ALSO HATE IT WHEN PEOPLE LOOK AT ME ALL BUG-EYED.
THAT MUST HAPPEN A LOT.

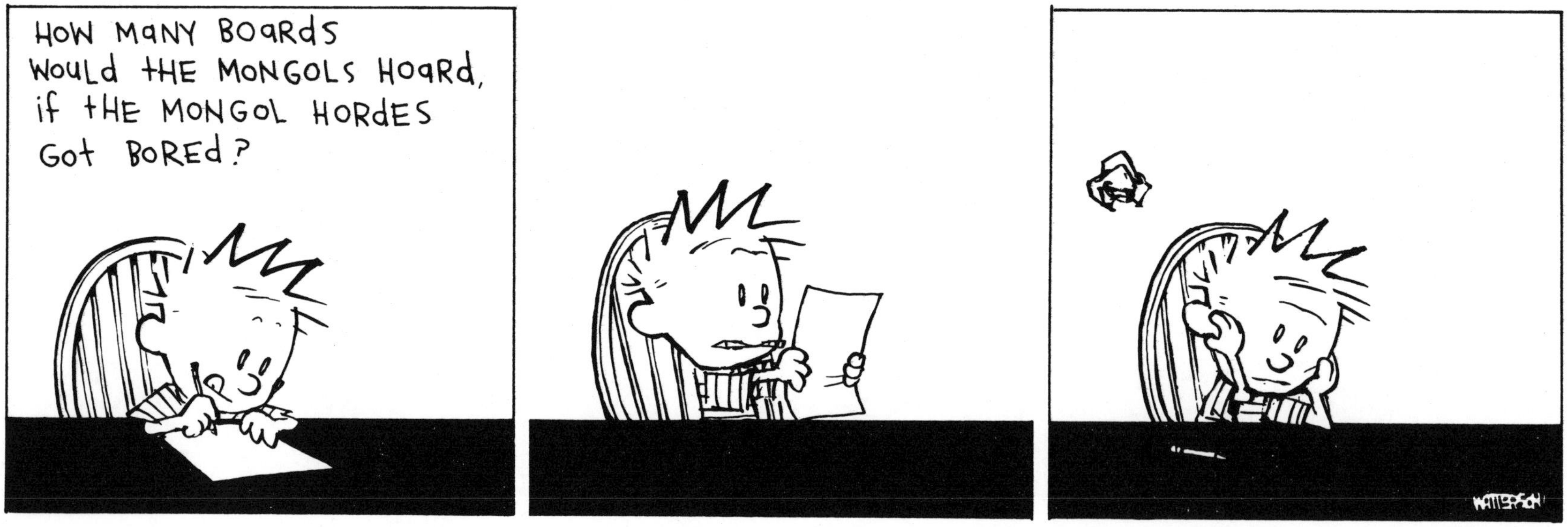
HOW MaNY BOaRdS
WOuLd tHE MONGOLS HOaRd,
if tHE MONGOL HORdES
Got BORED?

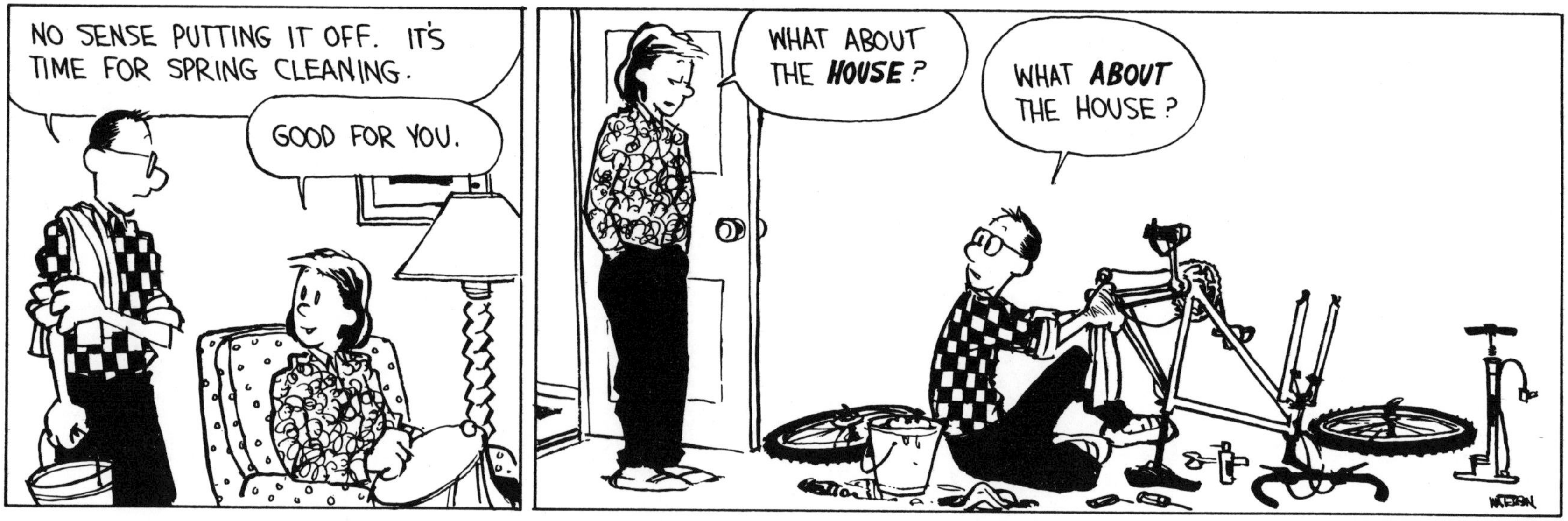
NO SENSE PUTTING IT OFF. IT'S TIME FOR SPRING CLEANING.
GOOD FOR YOU.
WHAT ABOUT THE HOUSE?
WHAT ABOUT THE HOUSE?

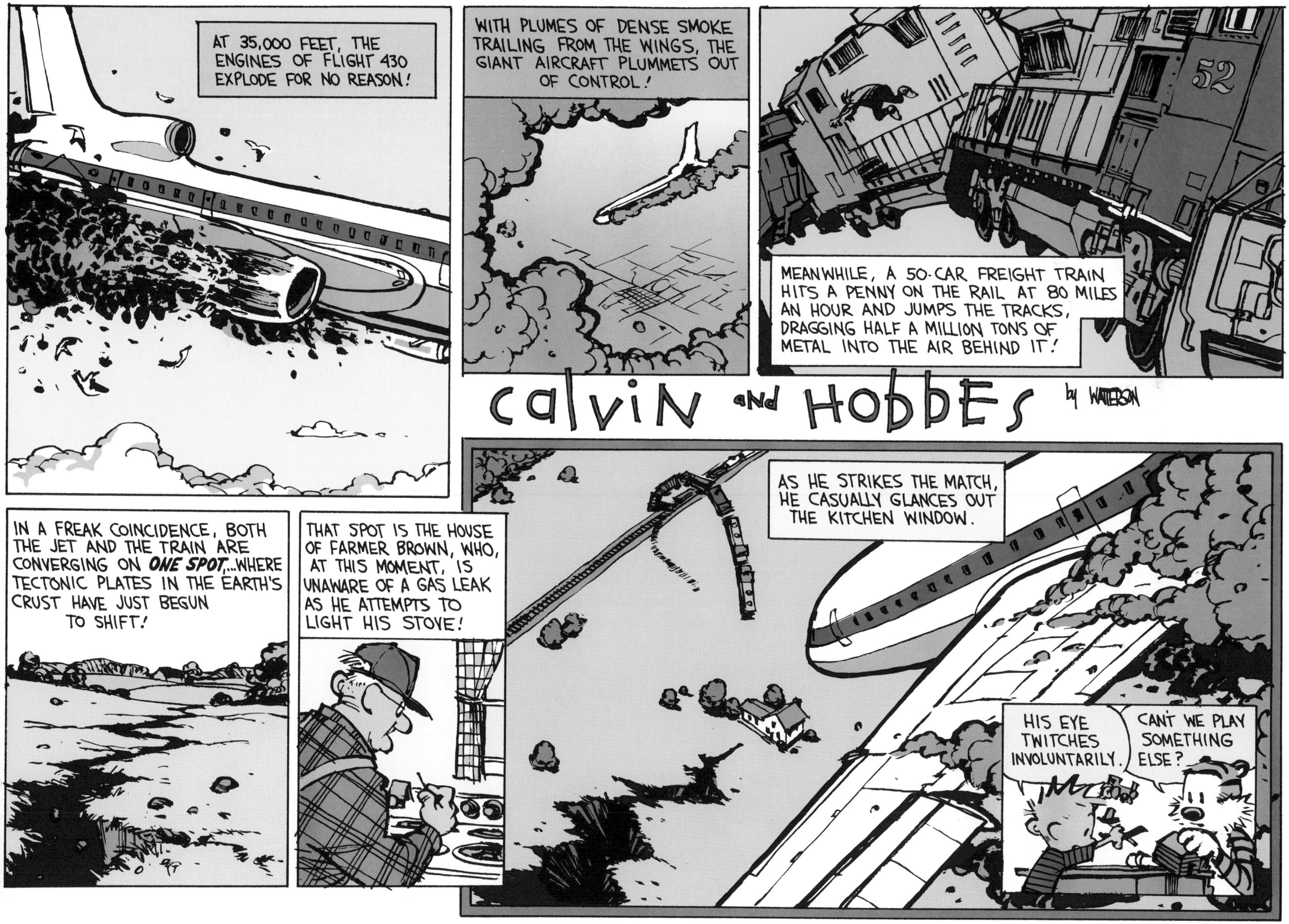
AT 35,000 FEET, THE ENGINES OF FLIGHT 430 EXPLODE FOR NO REASON!
WITH PLUMES OF DENSE SMOKE TRAILING FROM THE WINGS, THE GIANT AIRCRAFT PLUMMETS OUT OF CONTROL!
MEANWHILE, A 50-CAR FREIGHT TRAIN HITS A PENNY ON THE RAIL AT 80 MILES AN HOUR AND JUMPS THE TRACKS, DRAGGING HALF A MILLION TONS OF METAL INTO THE AIR BEHIND IT!
52
calvin and HOBBES by WATTERSON
IN A FREAK COINCIDENCE, BOTH THE JET AND THE TRAIN ARE CONVERGING ON ONE SPOT...WHERE TECTONIC PLATES IN THE EARTH'S CRUST HAVE JUST BEGUN TO SHIFT!
THAT SPOT IS THE HOUSE OF FARMER BROWN, WHO, AT THIS MOMENT, IS UNAWARE OF A GAS LEAK AS HE ATTEMPTS TO LIGHT HIS STOVE!
AS HE STRIKES THE MATCH, HE CASUALLY GLANCES OUT THE KITCHEN WINDOW.
HIS EYE TWITCHES INVOLUNTARILY.
CAN'T WE PLAY SOMETHING ELSE?

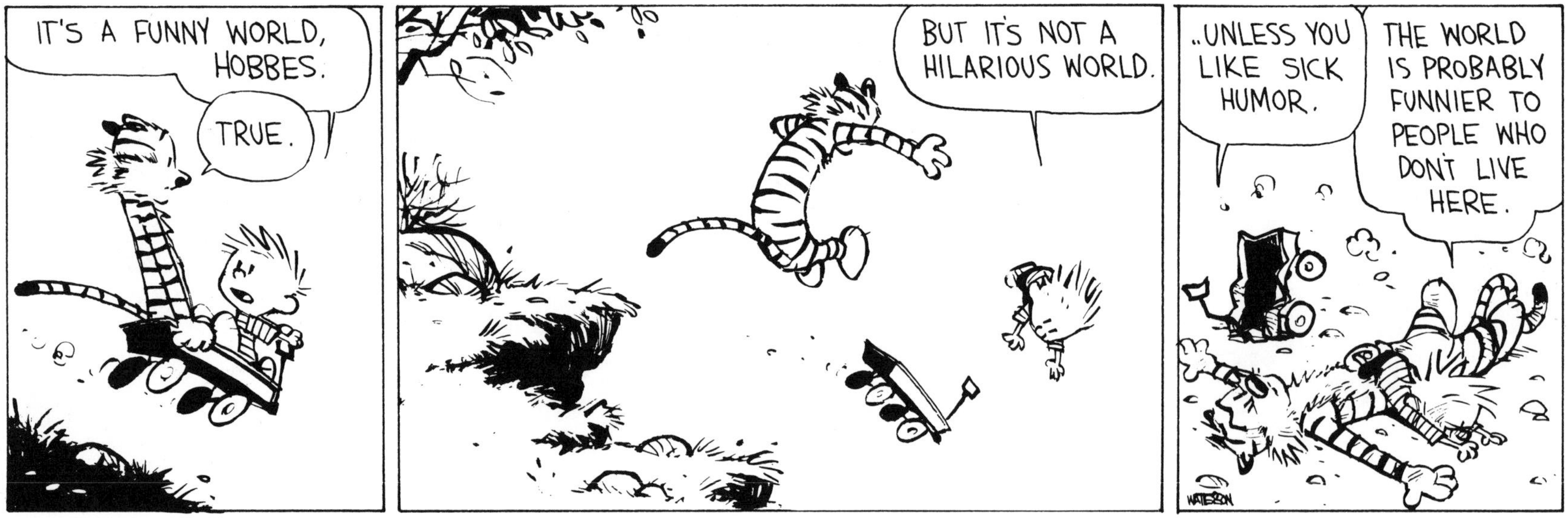
IT'S A FUNNY WORLD, HOBBES.
TRUE.
BUT IT'S NOT A HILARIOUS WORLD.
..UNLESS YOU LIKE SICK HUMOR.
THE WORLD IS PROBABLY FUNNIER TO PEOPLE WHO DON'T LIVE HERE.
WATTERSON

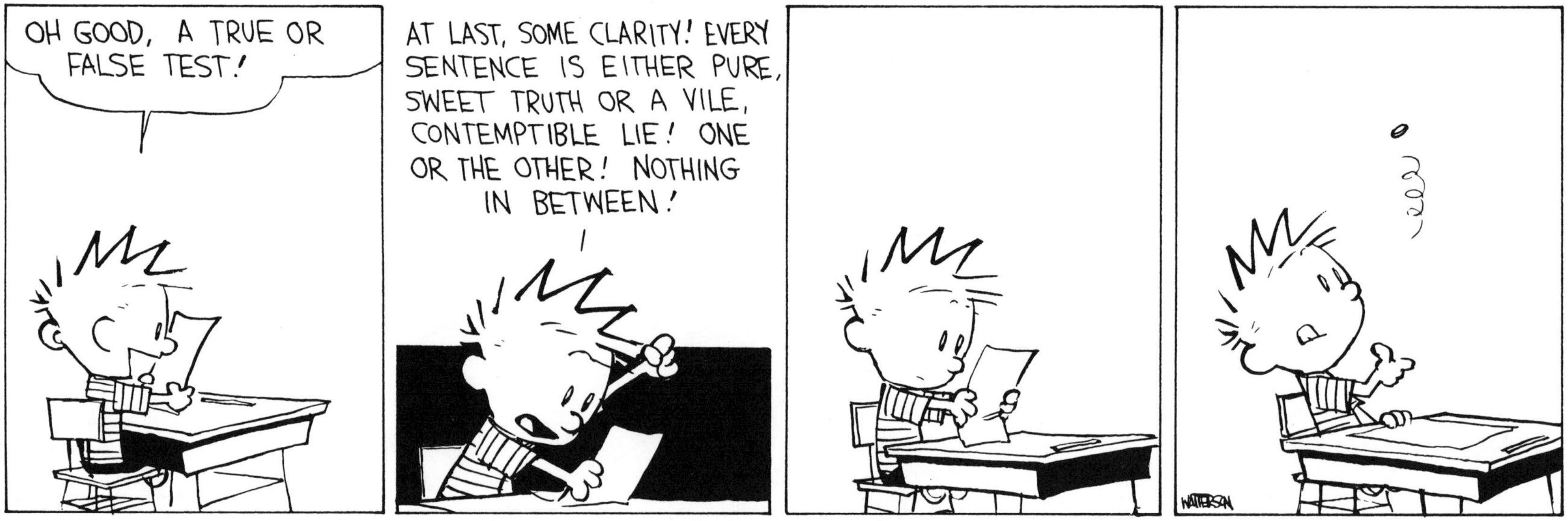
OH GOOD, A TRUE OR FALSE TEST!
AT LAST, SOME CLARITY! EVERY SENTENCE IS EITHER PURE, SWEET TRUTH OR A VILE, CONTEMPTIBLE LIE! ONE OR THE OTHER! NOTHING IN BETWEEN!
WATTERSON

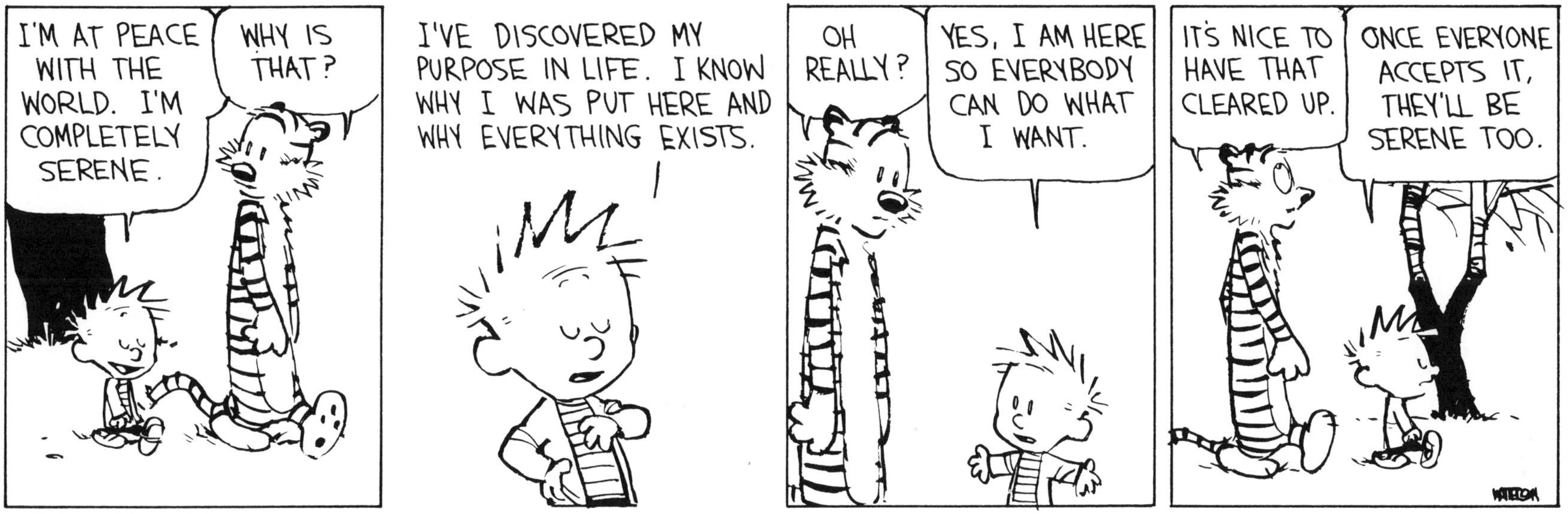
I'M AT PEACE WITH THE WORLD. I'M COMPLETELY SERENE.
WHY IS THAT?
I'VE DISCOVERED MY PURPOSE IN LIFE. I KNOW WHY I WAS PUT HERE AND WHY EVERYTHING EXISTS.
OH REALLY?
YES, I AM HERE SO EVERYBODY CAN DO WHAT I WANT.
IT'S NICE TO HAVE THAT CLEARED UP.
ONCE EVERYONE ACCEPTS IT, THEY'LL BE SERENE TOO.

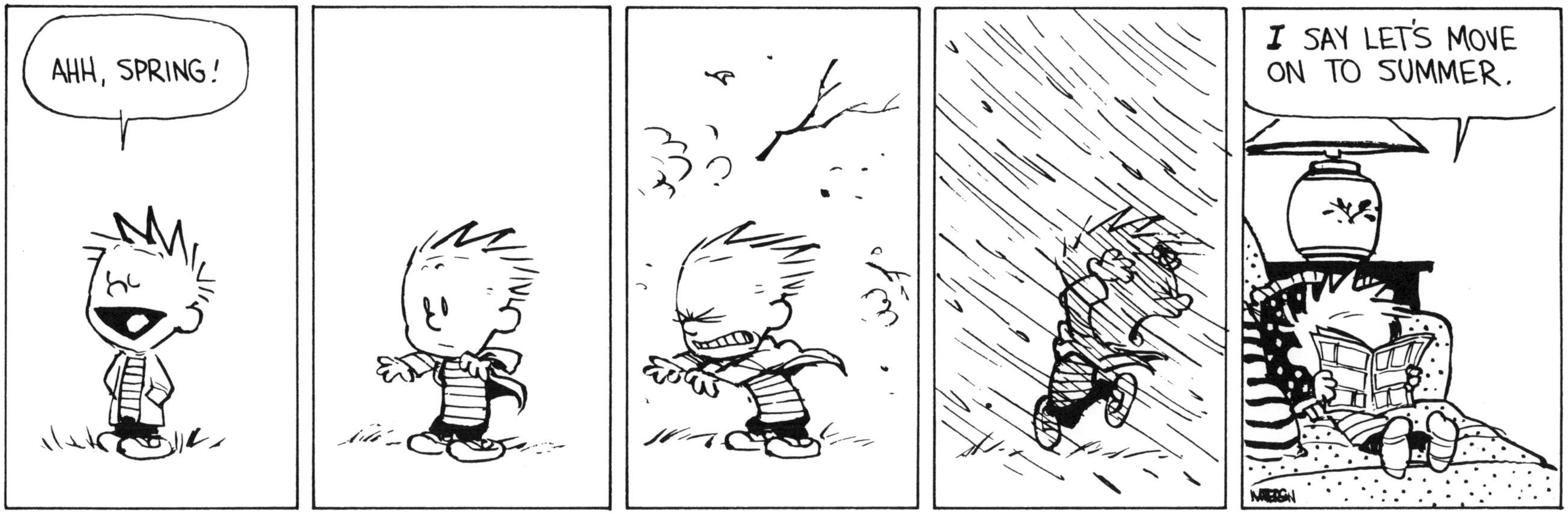
AHH, SPRING!
I SAY LET'S MOVE ON TO SUMMER.

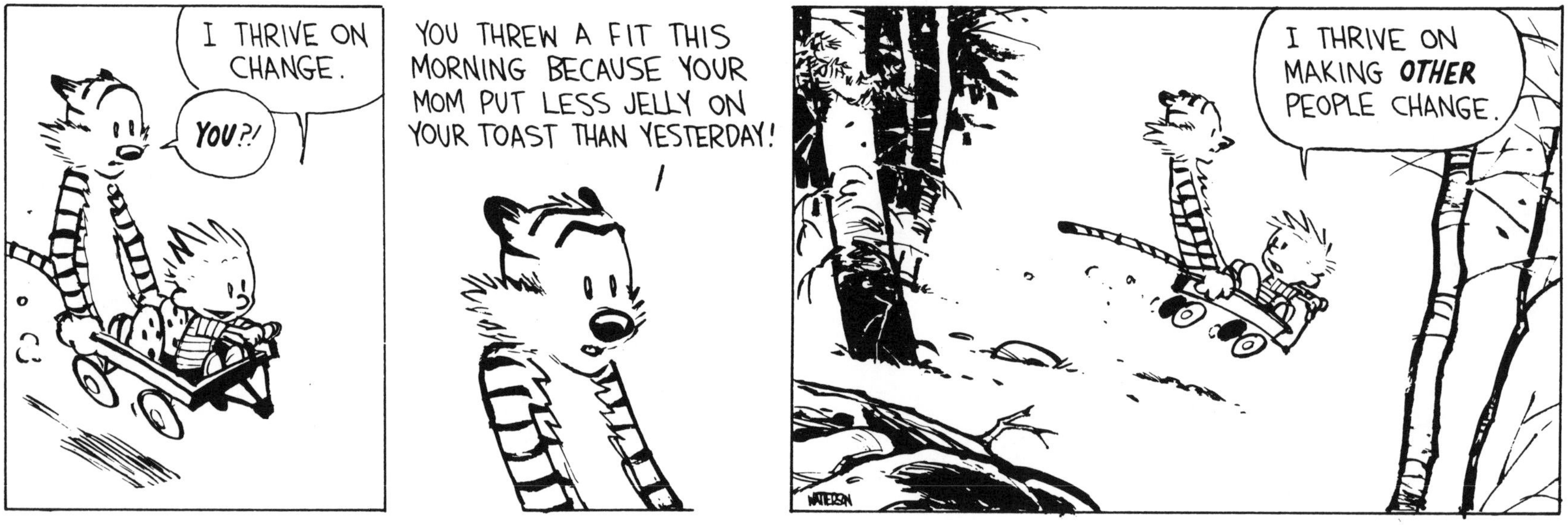
I THRIVE ON CHANGE.
YOU?!
YOU THREW A FIT THIS MORNING BECAUSE YOUR MOM PUT LESS JELLY ON YOUR TOAST THAN YESTERDAY!
I THRIVE ON MAKING OTHER PEOPLE CHANGE.

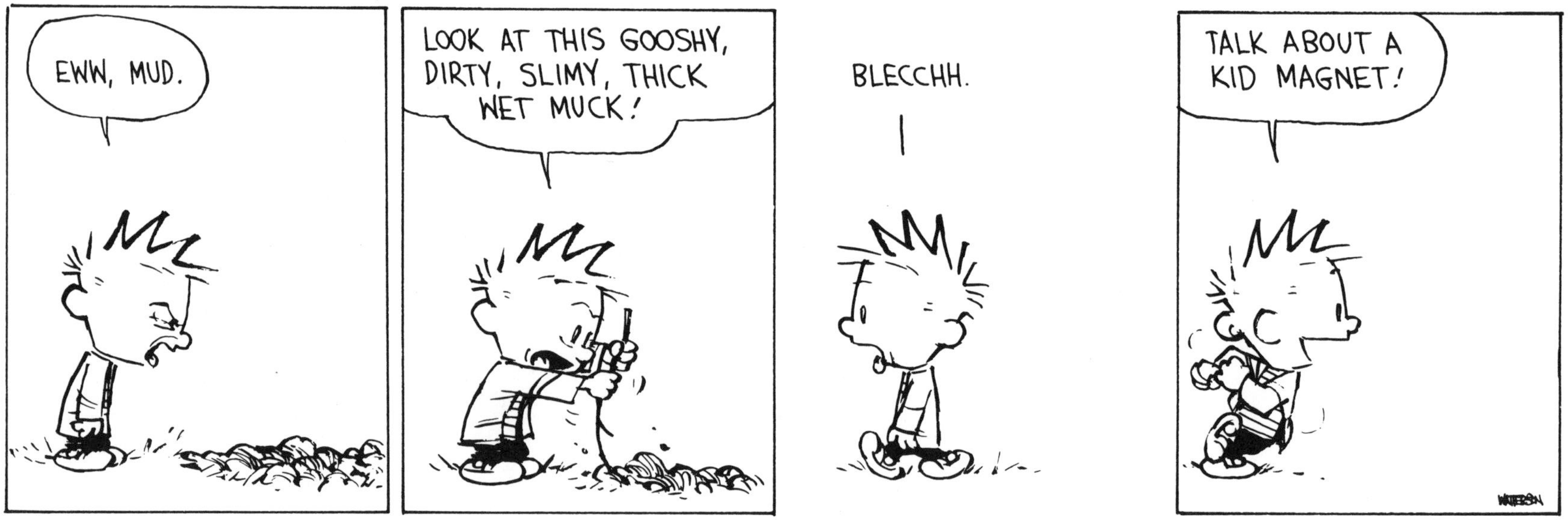
EWW, MUD.
LOOK AT THIS GOOSHY, DIRTY, SLIMY, THICK WET MUCK!
BLECCHH.
TALK ABOUT A KID MAGNET!

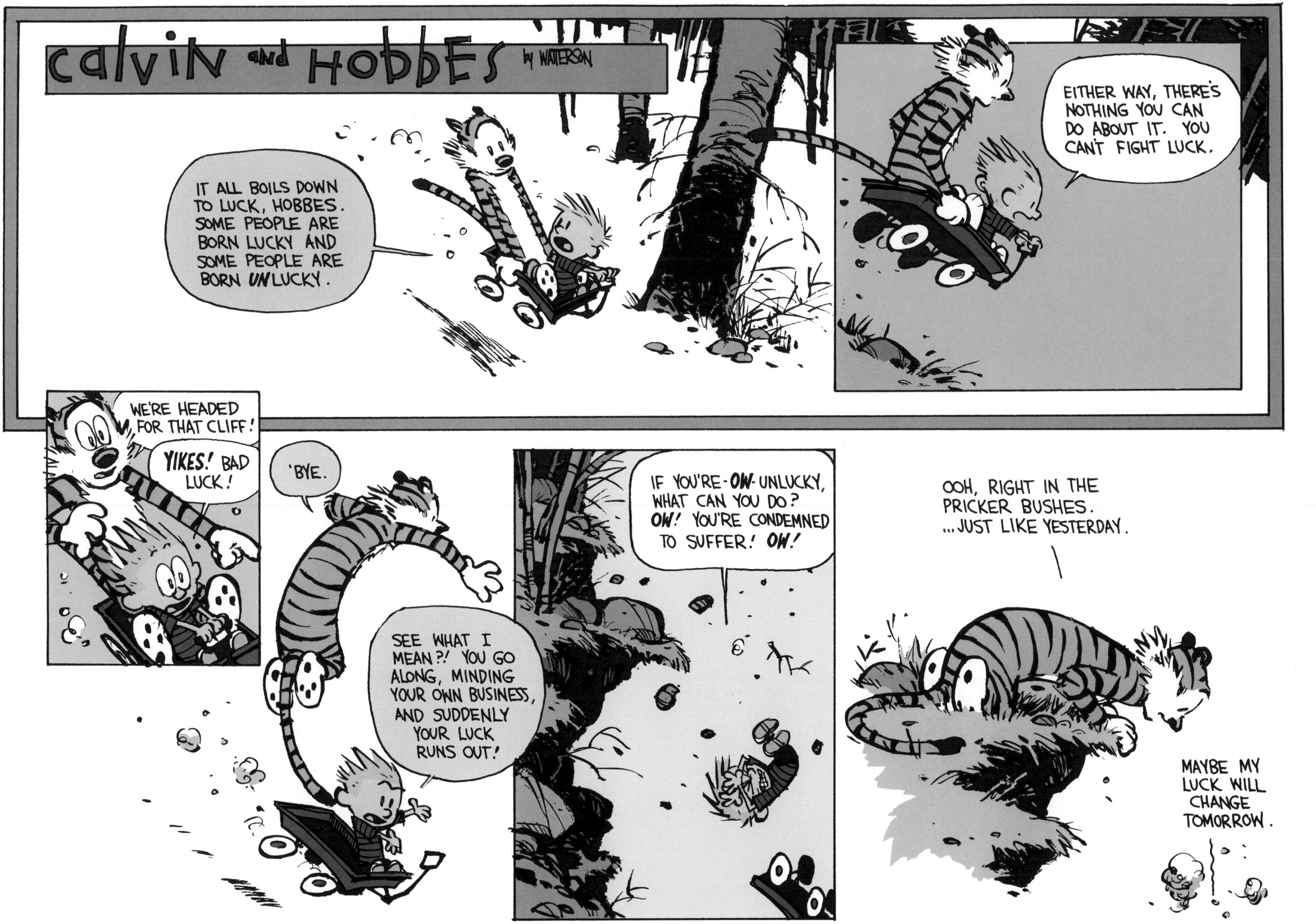
Calvin and HOBBES by WATTERSON
IT ALL BOILS DOWN TO LUCK, HOBBES. SOME PEOPLE ARE BORN LUCKY AND SOME PEOPLE ARE BORN **UN**LUCKY.
EITHER WAY, THERE'S NOTHING YOU CAN DO ABOUT IT. YOU CAN'T FIGHT LUCK.
WE'RE HEADED FOR THAT CLIFF!
YIKES! BAD LUCK!
'BYE.
SEE WHAT I MEAN?! YOU GO ALONG, MINDING YOUR OWN BUSINESS, AND SUDDENLY YOUR LUCK RUNS OUT!
IF YOU'RE-**OW**-UNLUCKY, WHAT CAN YOU DO? **OW!** YOU'RE CONDEMNED TO SUFFER! **OW!**
OOH, RIGHT IN THE PRICKER BUSHES. ...JUST LIKE YESTERDAY.
MAYBE MY LUCK WILL CHANGE TOMORROW.

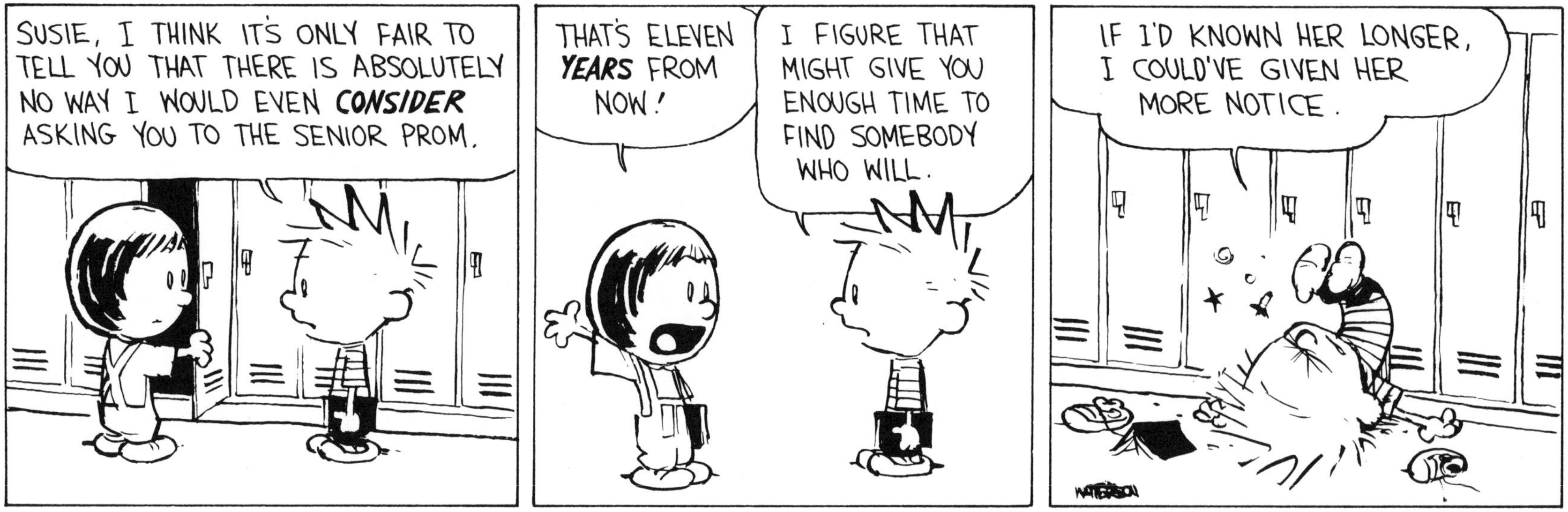
SUSIE, I THINK IT'S ONLY FAIR TO TELL YOU THAT THERE IS ABSOLUTELY NO WAY I WOULD EVEN **CONSIDER** ASKING YOU TO THE SENIOR PROM.
THAT'S ELEVEN **YEARS** FROM NOW!
I FIGURE THAT MIGHT GIVE YOU ENOUGH TIME TO FIND SOMEBODY WHO WILL.
IF I'D KNOWN HER LONGER, I COULD'VE GIVEN HER MORE NOTICE.

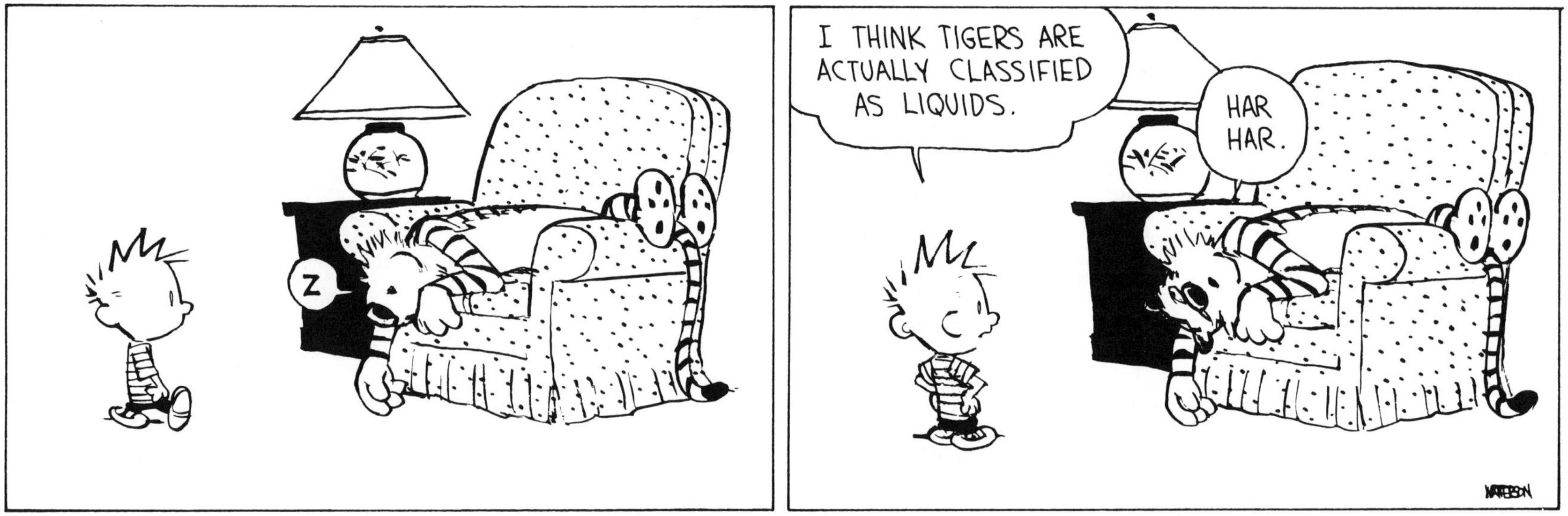
Z
I THINK TIGERS ARE ACTUALLY CLASSIFIED AS LIQUIDS.
HAR HAR.

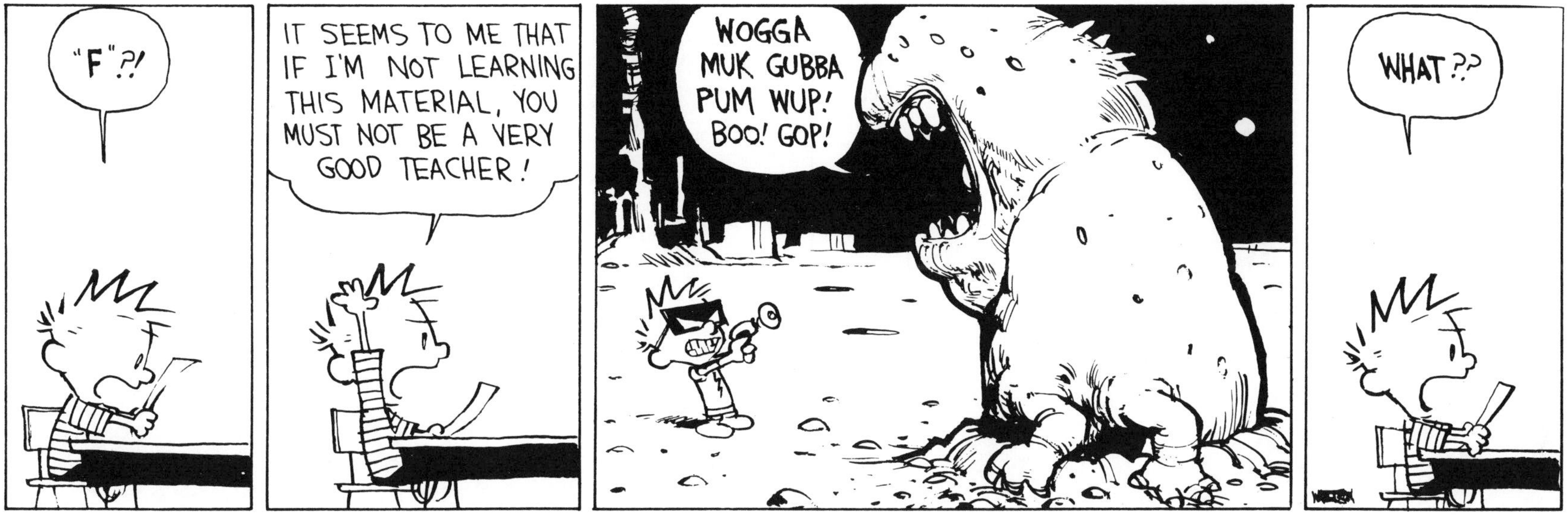
"F"?!
IT SEEMS TO ME THAT IF I'M NOT LEARNING THIS MATERIAL, YOU MUST NOT BE A VERY GOOD TEACHER!
WOGGA MUK GUBBA PUM WUP! BOO! GOP!
WHAT??
WATTERSON

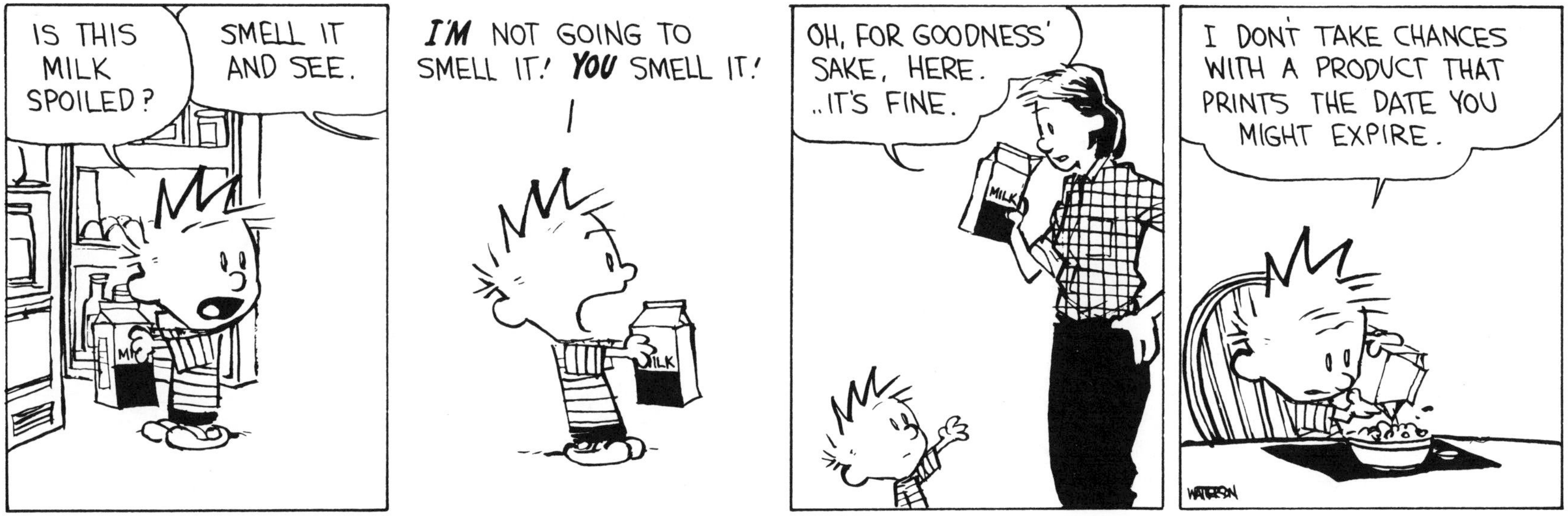
IS THIS MILK SPOILED?
SMELL IT AND SEE.
I'M NOT GOING TO SMELL IT! YOU SMELL IT!
OH, FOR GOODNESS' SAKE, HERE. ..IT'S FINE.
MILK
I DON'T TAKE CHANCES WITH A PRODUCT THAT PRINTS THE DATE YOU MIGHT EXPIRE.
WATTERSON

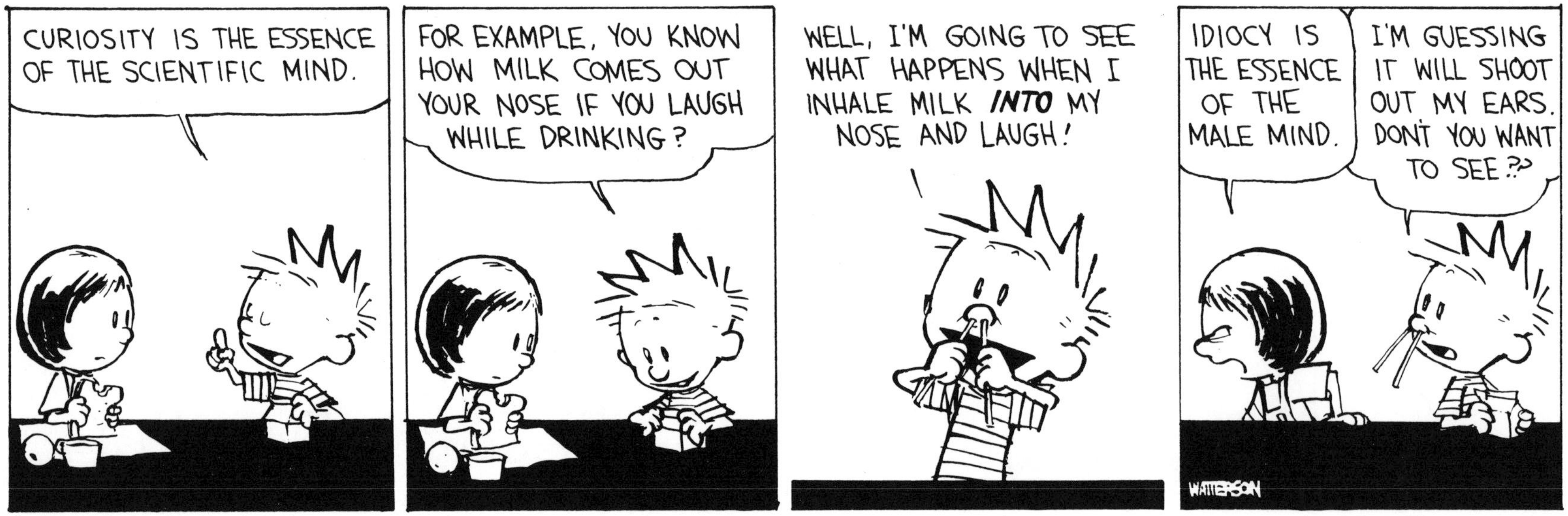
CURIOSITY IS THE ESSENCE OF THE SCIENTIFIC MIND.
FOR EXAMPLE, YOU KNOW HOW MILK COMES OUT YOUR NOSE IF YOU LAUGH WHILE DRINKING?
WELL, I'M GOING TO SEE WHAT HAPPENS WHEN I INHALE MILK **INTO** MY NOSE AND LAUGH!
IDIOCY IS THE ESSENCE OF THE MALE MIND.
I'M GUESSING IT WILL SHOOT OUT MY EARS. DON'T YOU WANT TO SEE?!?
WATTERSON

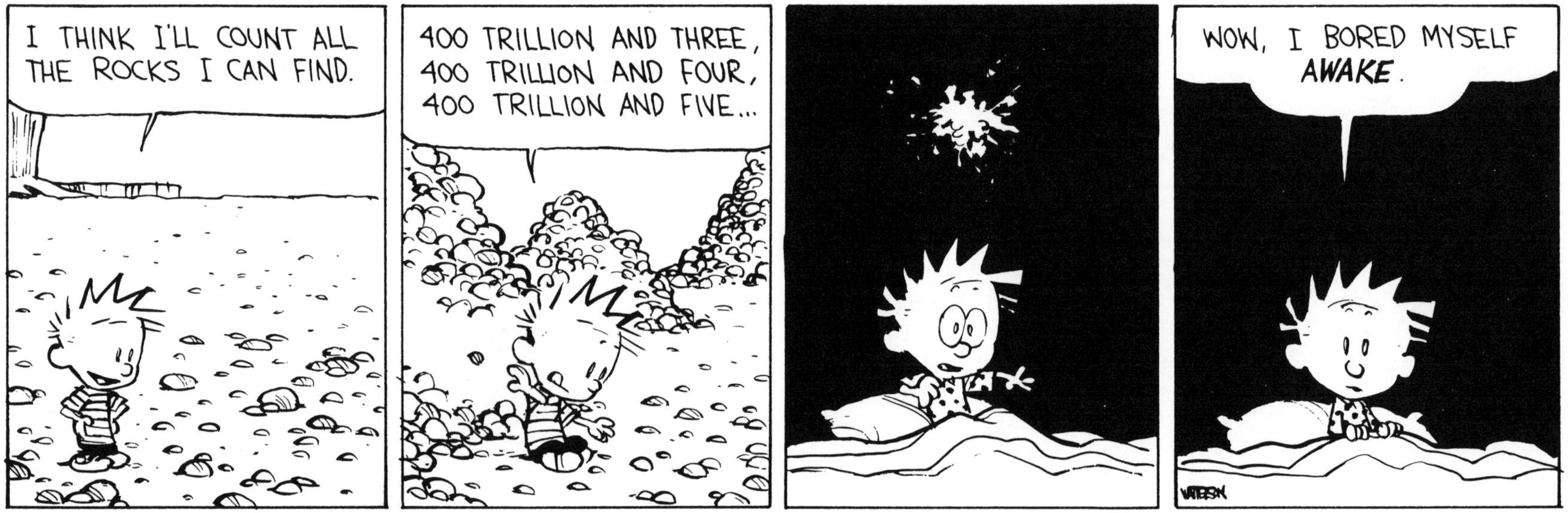
I THINK I'LL COUNT ALL THE ROCKS I CAN FIND.
400 TRILLION AND THREE, 400 TRILLION AND FOUR, 400 TRILLION AND FIVE...
WOW, I BORED MYSELF **AWAKE**.
WATTERSON

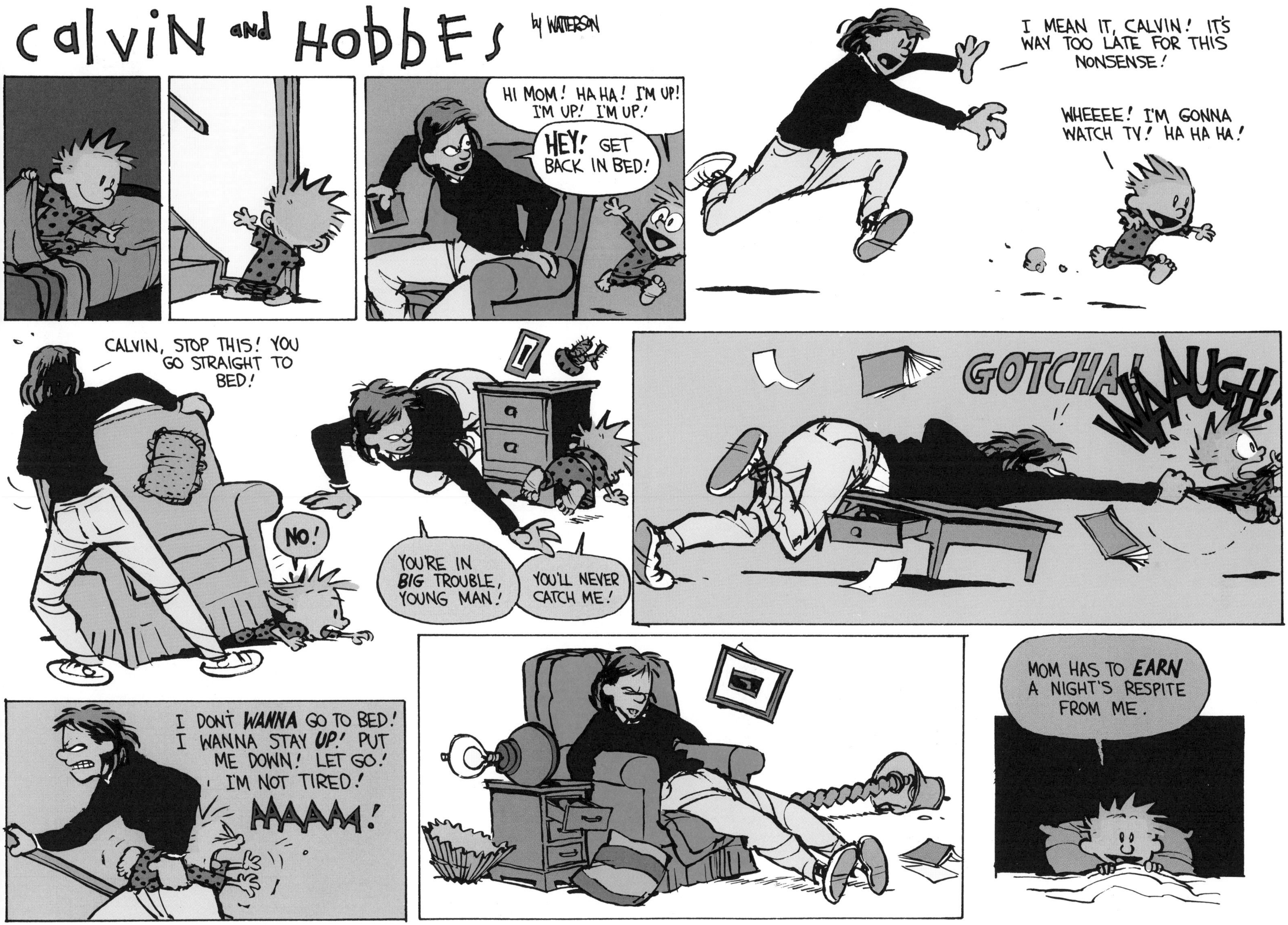
Calvin and Hobbes
by WATTERSON
HI MOM! HA HA! I'M UP! I'M UP! I'M UP!
HEY! GET BACK IN BED!
I MEAN IT, CALVIN! IT'S WAY TOO LATE FOR THIS NONSENSE!
WHEEEE! I'M GONNA WATCH TV! HA HA HA!
CALVIN, STOP THIS! YOU GO STRAIGHT TO BED!
NO!
YOU'RE IN BIG TROUBLE, YOUNG MAN!
YOU'LL NEVER CATCH ME!
GOTCHA!
WAAUGH!
I DON'T WANNA GO TO BED! I WANNA STAY UP! PUT ME DOWN! LET GO! I'M NOT TIRED!
AAAAA!
MOM HAS TO EARN A NIGHT'S RESPITE FROM ME.

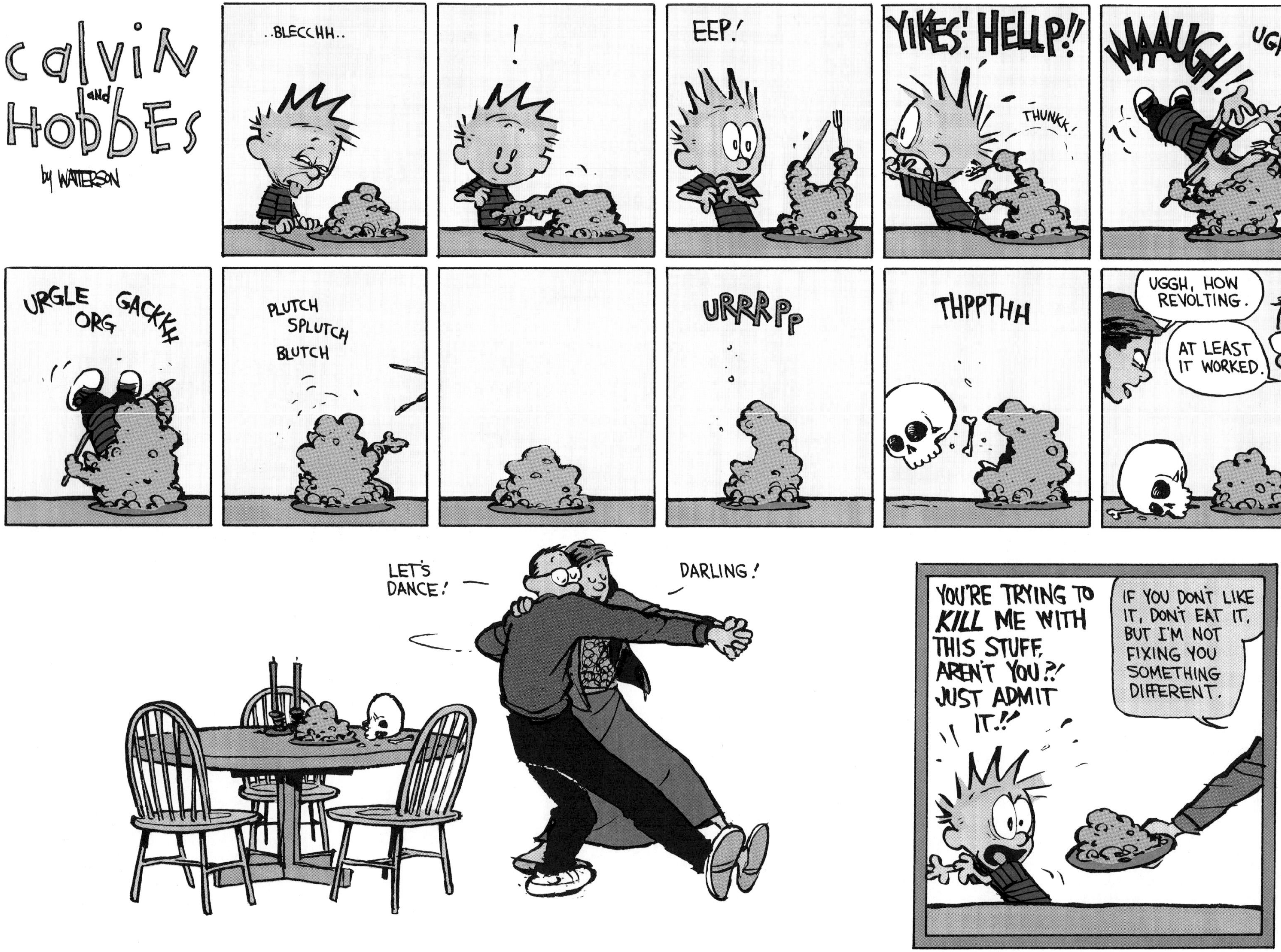
Calvin and Hobbes
by WATTERSON
..BLECCHH..
!
EEP!
YIKES! HELLP!!
THUNKK!
WAAUGH!!
UGHH
URGLE ORG GACKKH
PLUTCH SPLUTCH BLUTCH
URRRPP
THPPTHH
UGGH, HOW REVOLTING.
AT LEAST IT WORKED.
LET'S DANCE!
DARLING!
YOU'RE TRYING TO KILL ME WITH THIS STUFF, AREN'T YOU?! JUST ADMIT IT!!
IF YOU DON'T LIKE IT, DON'T EAT IT, BUT I'M NOT FIXING YOU SOMETHING DIFFERENT.

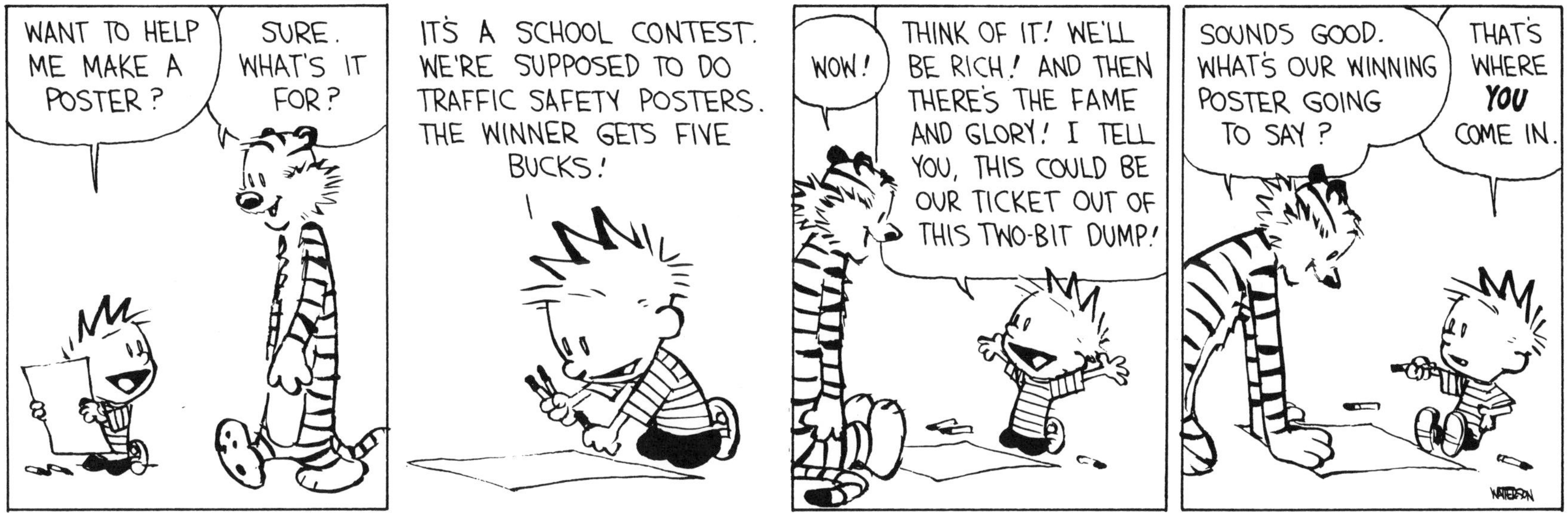
WANT TO HELP ME MAKE A POSTER?
SURE. WHAT'S IT FOR?
IT'S A SCHOOL CONTEST. WE'RE SUPPOSED TO DO TRAFFIC SAFETY POSTERS. THE WINNER GETS FIVE BUCKS!
WOW!
THINK OF IT! WE'LL BE RICH! AND THEN THERE'S THE FAME AND GLORY! I TELL YOU, THIS COULD BE OUR TICKET OUT OF THIS TWO-BIT DUMP!
SOUNDS GOOD. WHAT'S OUR WINNING POSTER GOING TO SAY?
THAT'S WHERE **YOU** COME IN.

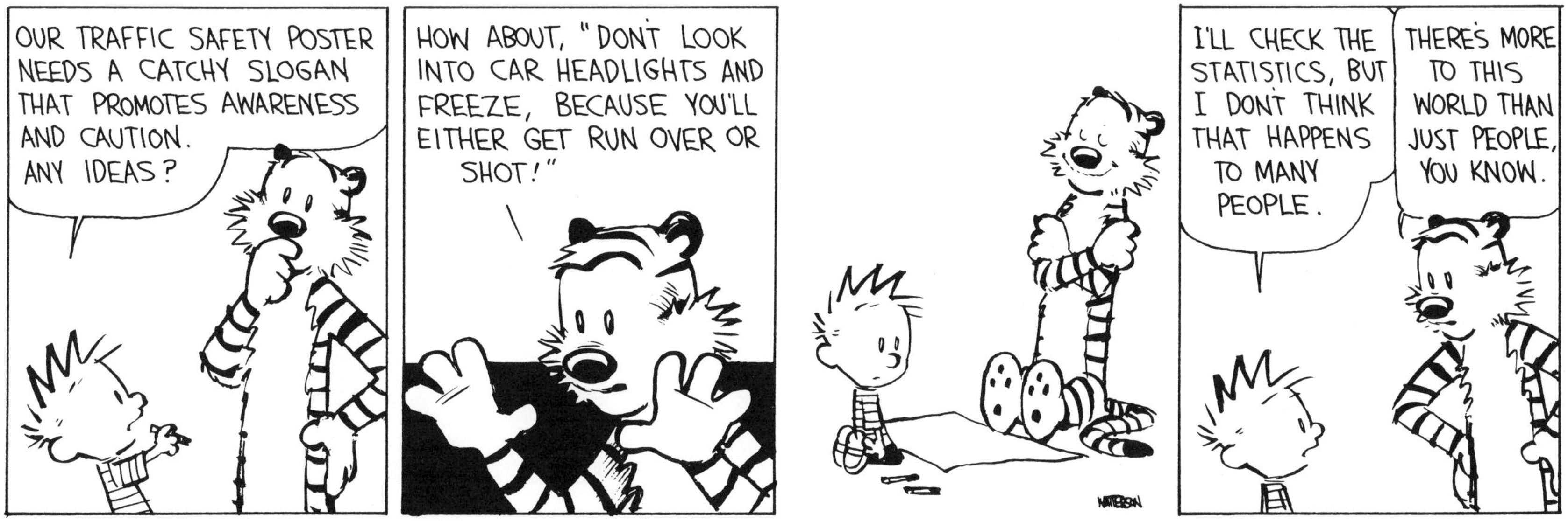
OUR TRAFFIC SAFETY POSTER NEEDS A CATCHY SLOGAN THAT PROMOTES AWARENESS AND CAUTION. ANY IDEAS?
HOW ABOUT, "DON'T LOOK INTO CAR HEADLIGHTS AND FREEZE, BECAUSE YOU'LL EITHER GET RUN OVER OR SHOT!"
I'LL CHECK THE STATISTICS, BUT I DON'T THINK THAT HAPPENS TO MANY PEOPLE.
THERE'S MORE TO THIS WORLD THAN JUST PEOPLE, YOU KNOW.

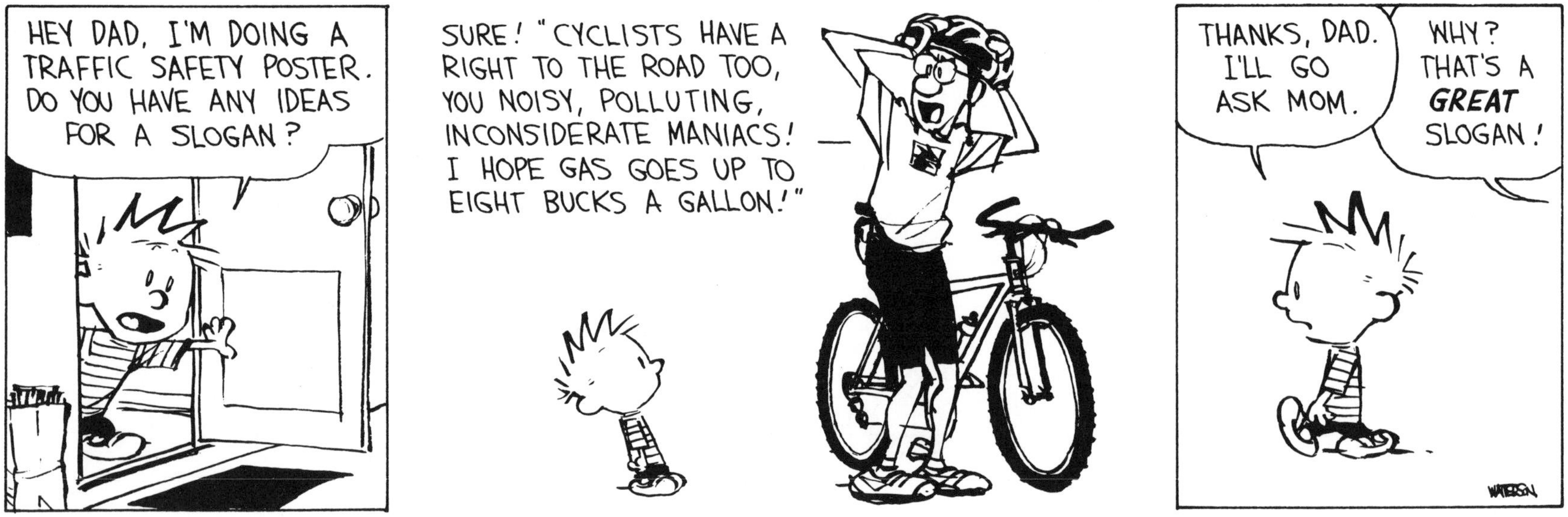
HEY DAD, I'M DOING A TRAFFIC SAFETY POSTER. DO YOU HAVE ANY IDEAS FOR A SLOGAN?
SURE! "CYCLISTS HAVE A RIGHT TO THE ROAD TOO, YOU NOISY, POLLUTING, INCONSIDERATE MANIACS! — I HOPE GAS GOES UP TO EIGHT BUCKS A GALLON!"
THANKS, DAD. I'LL GO ASK MOM.
WHY? THAT'S A **GREAT** SLOGAN!

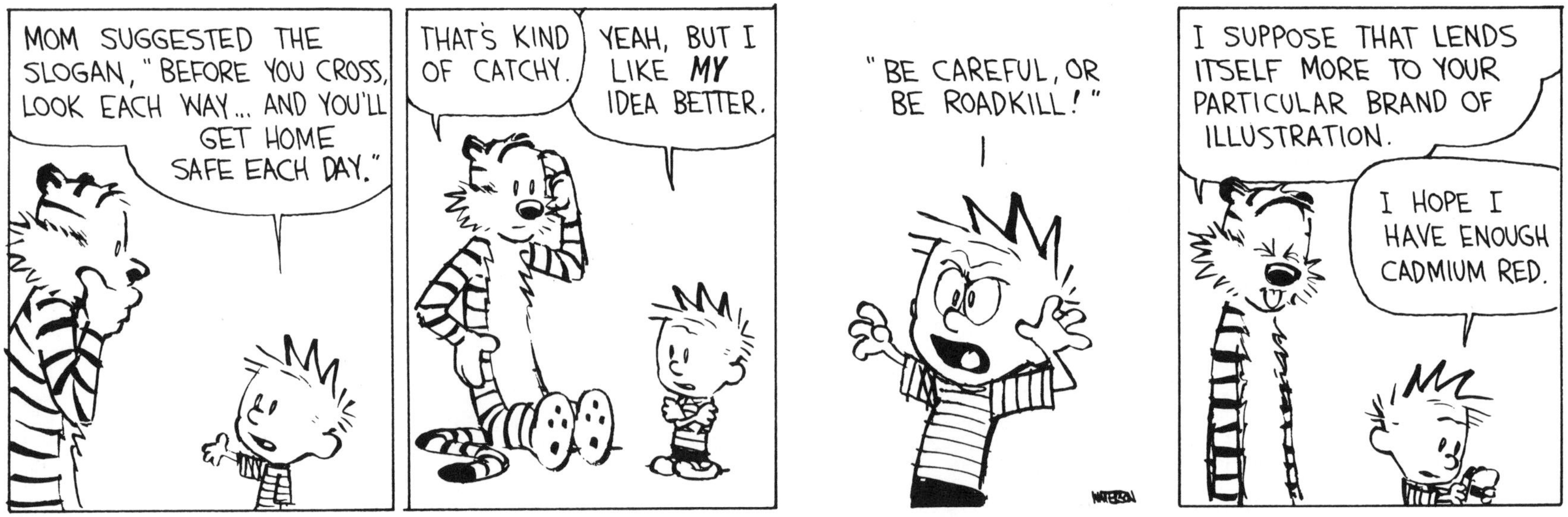
MOM SUGGESTED THE SLOGAN, "BEFORE YOU CROSS, LOOK EACH WAY... AND YOU'LL GET HOME SAFE EACH DAY."
THAT'S KIND OF CATCHY.
YEAH, BUT I LIKE **MY** IDEA BETTER.
"BE CAREFUL, OR BE ROADKILL!"
I SUPPOSE THAT LENDS ITSELF MORE TO YOUR PARTICULAR BRAND OF ILLUSTRATION.
I HOPE I HAVE ENOUGH CADMIUM RED.

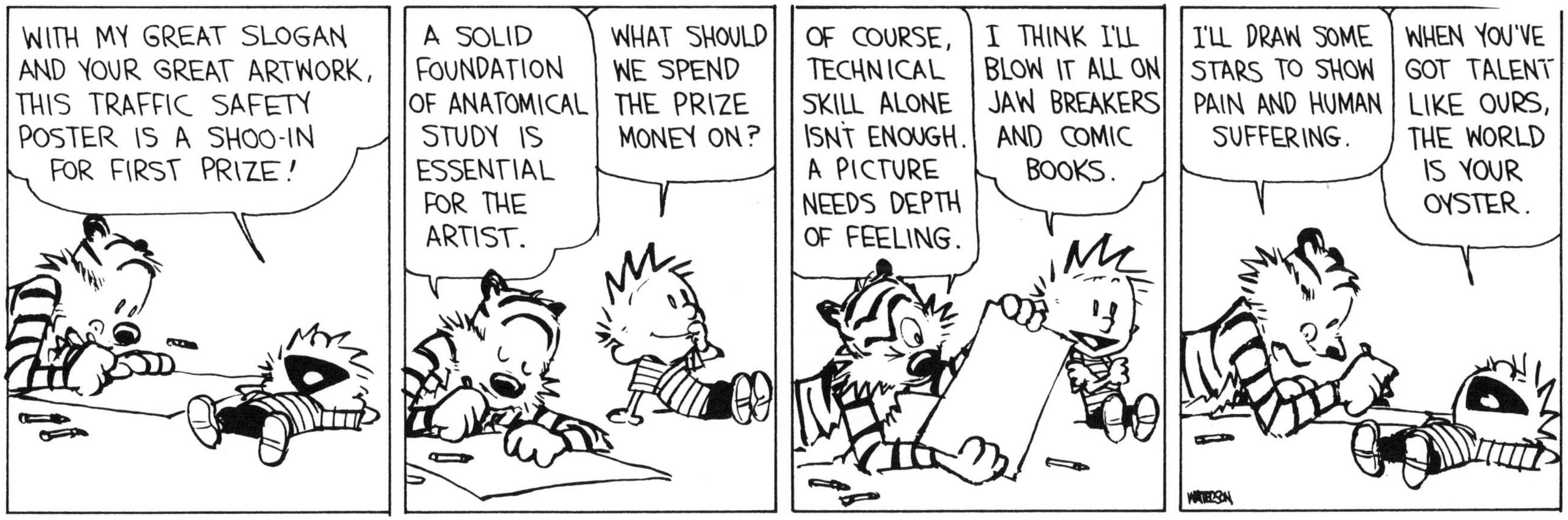
WITH MY GREAT SLOGAN AND YOUR GREAT ARTWORK, THIS TRAFFIC SAFETY POSTER IS A SHOO-IN FOR FIRST PRIZE!
A SOLID FOUNDATION OF ANATOMICAL STUDY IS ESSENTIAL FOR THE ARTIST.
WHAT SHOULD WE SPEND THE PRIZE MONEY ON?
OF COURSE, TECHNICAL SKILL ALONE ISN'T ENOUGH. A PICTURE NEEDS DEPTH OF FEELING.
I THINK I'LL BLOW IT ALL ON JAW BREAKERS AND COMIC BOOKS.
I'LL DRAW SOME STARS TO SHOW PAIN AND HUMAN SUFFERING.
WHEN YOU'VE GOT TALENT LIKE OURS, THE WORLD IS YOUR OYSTER.

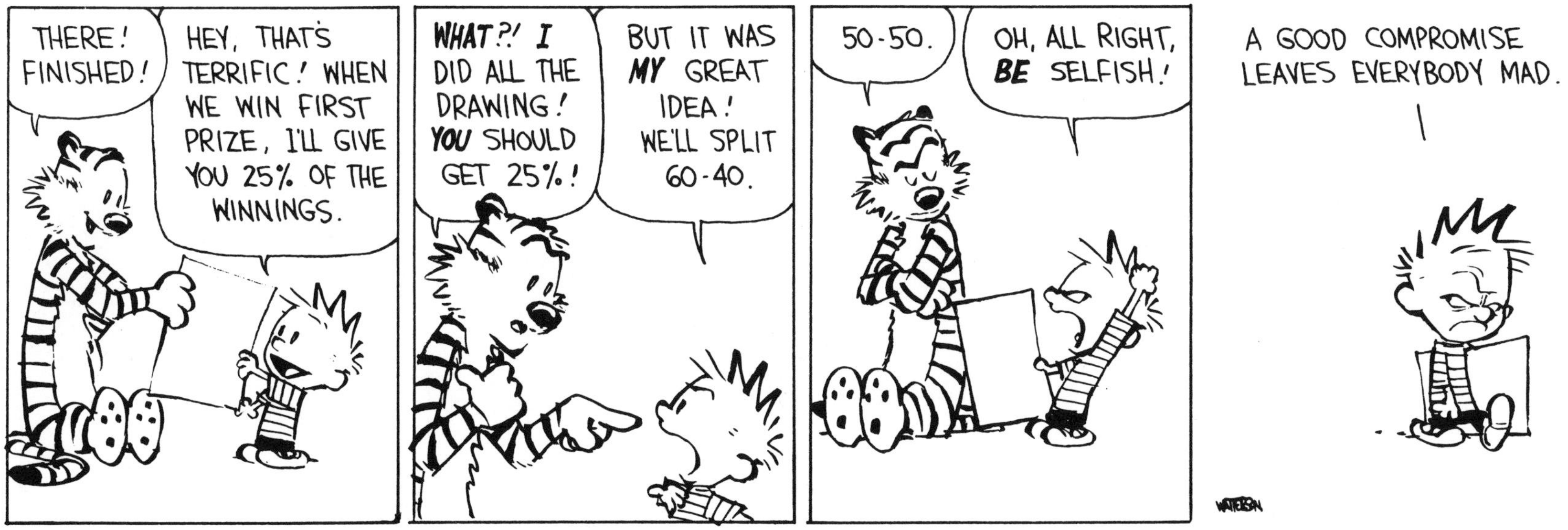
THERE! FINISHED!
HEY, THAT'S TERRIFIC! WHEN WE WIN FIRST PRIZE, I'LL GIVE YOU 25% OF THE WINNINGS.
WHAT?! I DID ALL THE DRAWING! YOU SHOULD GET 25%!
BUT IT WAS MY GREAT IDEA! WE'LL SPLIT 60-40.
50-50.
OH, ALL RIGHT, BE SELFISH!
A GOOD COMPROMISE LEAVES EVERYBODY MAD.

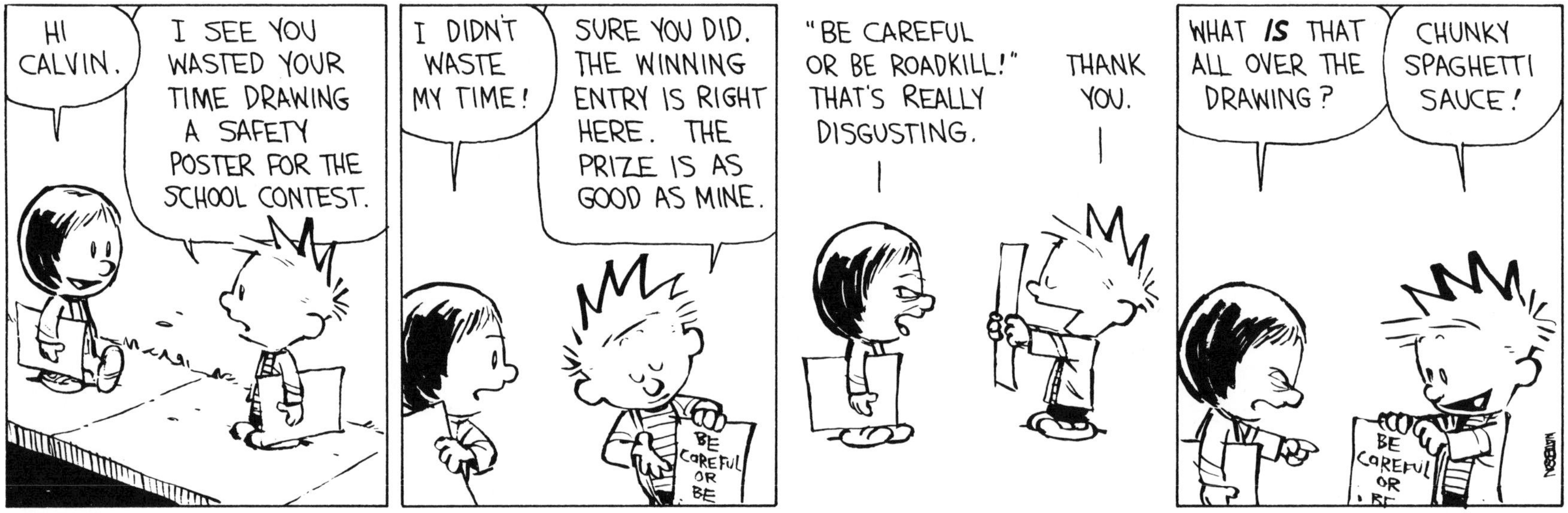
HI CALVIN.
I SEE YOU WASTED YOUR TIME DRAWING A SAFETY POSTER FOR THE SCHOOL CONTEST.
I DIDN'T WASTE MY TIME!
SURE YOU DID. THE WINNING ENTRY IS RIGHT HERE. THE PRIZE IS AS GOOD AS MINE.
BE CAREFUL OR BE
"BE CAREFUL OR BE ROADKILL!" THAT'S REALLY DISGUSTING.
THANK YOU.
WHAT IS THAT ALL OVER THE DRAWING?
CHUNKY SPAGHETTI SAUCE!
BE CAREFUL OR

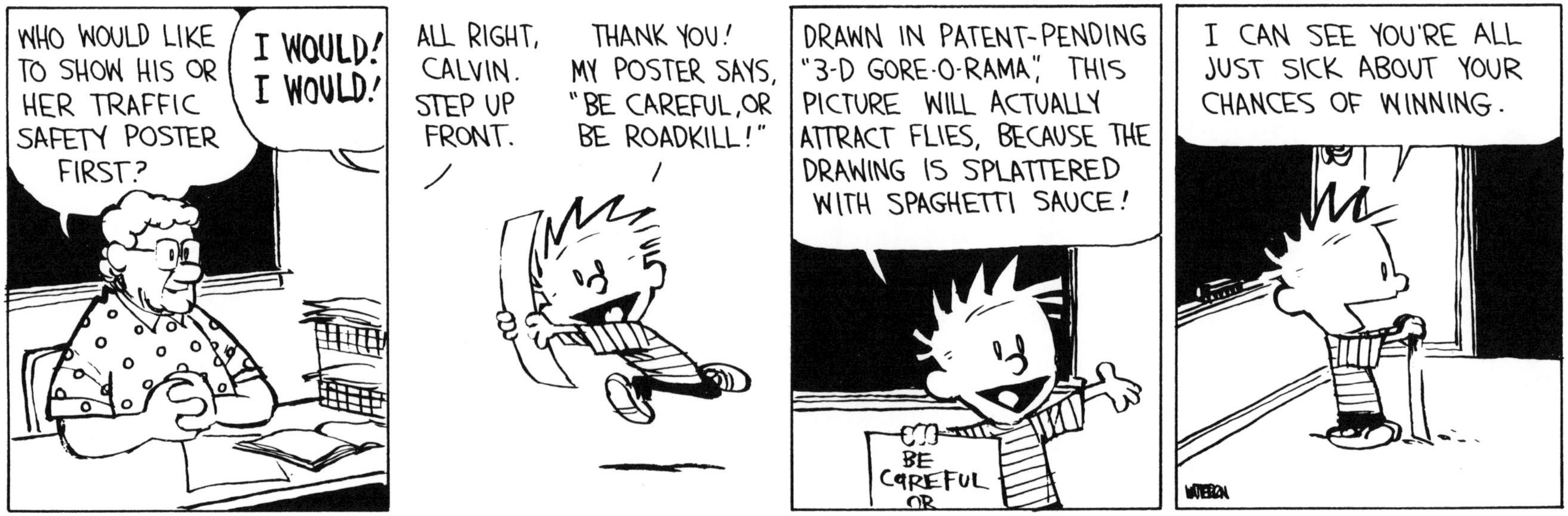
WHO WOULD LIKE TO SHOW HIS OR HER TRAFFIC SAFETY POSTER FIRST?
I WOULD! I WOULD!
ALL RIGHT, CALVIN. STEP UP FRONT.
THANK YOU! MY POSTER SAYS, "BE CAREFUL, OR BE ROADKILL!"
DRAWN IN PATENT-PENDING "3-D GORE-O-RAMA," THIS PICTURE WILL ACTUALLY ATTRACT FLIES, BECAUSE THE DRAWING IS SPLATTERED WITH SPAGHETTI SAUCE!
BE CAREFUL
I CAN SEE YOU'RE ALL JUST SICK ABOUT YOUR CHANCES OF WINNING.

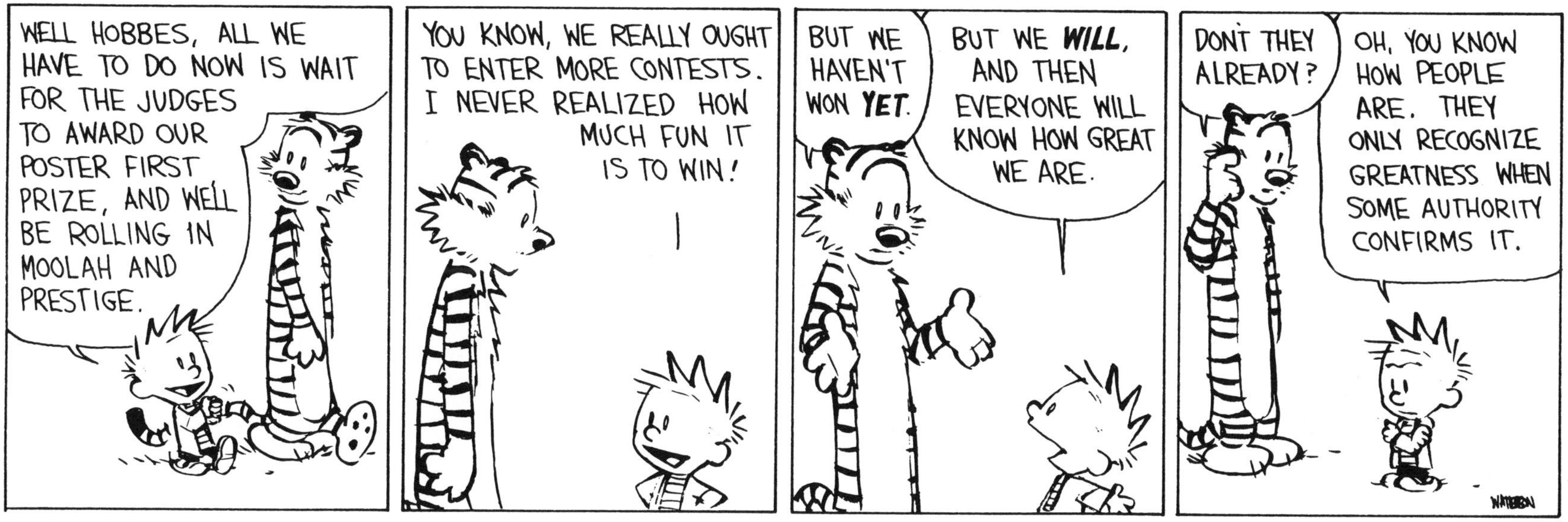
WELL HOBBES, ALL WE HAVE TO DO NOW IS WAIT FOR THE JUDGES TO AWARD OUR POSTER FIRST PRIZE, AND WE'LL BE ROLLING IN MOOLAH AND PRESTIGE.
YOU KNOW, WE REALLY OUGHT TO ENTER MORE CONTESTS. I NEVER REALIZED HOW MUCH FUN IT IS TO WIN!
BUT WE HAVEN'T WON YET.
BUT WE WILL, AND THEN EVERYONE WILL KNOW HOW GREAT WE ARE.
DON'T THEY ALREADY?
OH, YOU KNOW HOW PEOPLE ARE. THEY ONLY RECOGNIZE GREATNESS WHEN SOME AUTHORITY CONFIRMS IT.

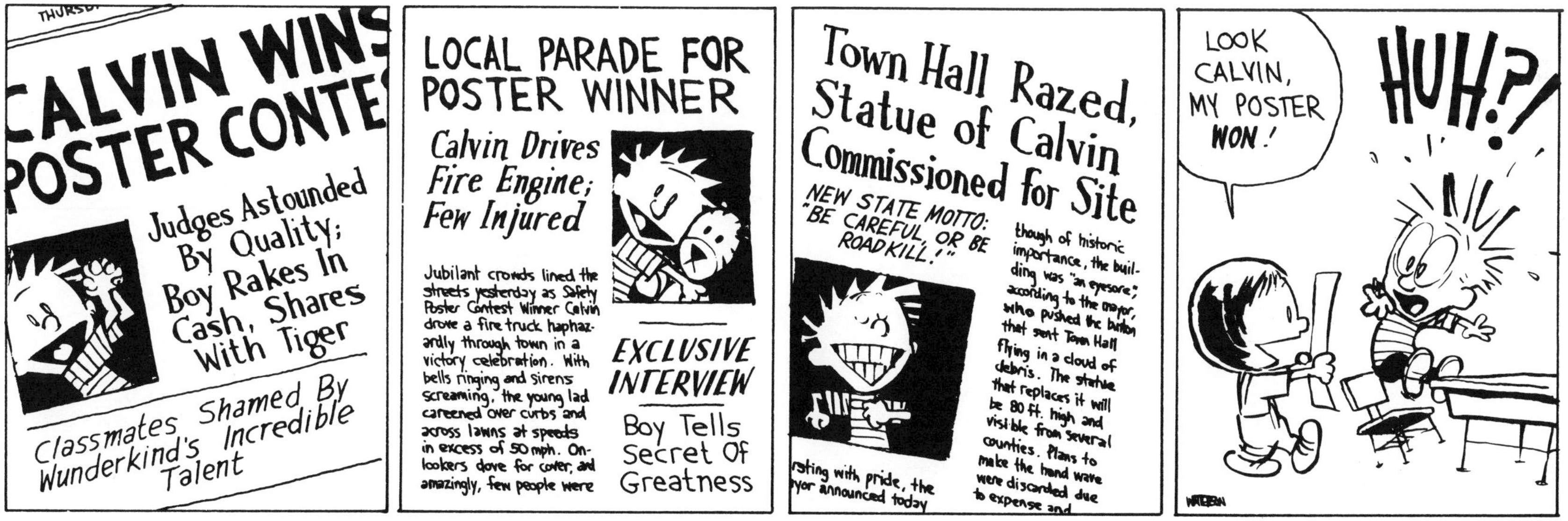
CALVIN WINS POSTER CONTE
Judges Astounded By Quality; Boy Rakes In Cash, Shares With Tiger
Classmates Shamed By Wunderkind's Incredible Talent
LOCAL PARADE FOR POSTER WINNER
Calvin Drives Fire Engine; Few Injured
Jubilant crowds lined the streets yesterday as Safety Poster Contest Winner Calvin drove a fire truck haphazardly through town in a victory celebration. With bells ringing and sirens screaming, the young lad careened over curbs and across lawns at speeds in excess of 50 mph. Onlookers dove for cover, and amazingly, few people were
EXCLUSIVE INTERVIEW
Boy Tells Secret Of Greatness
Town Hall Razed, Statue of Calvin Commissioned for Site
NEW STATE MOTTO: "BE CAREFUL, OR BE ROADKILL!"
rsting with pride, the yor announced today
though of historic importance, the building was "an eyesore," according to the mayor, who pushed the button that sent Town Hall flying in a cloud of debris. The statue that replaces it will be 80 ft. high and visible from several counties. Plans to make the hand wave were discarded due to expense and
LOOK CALVIN, MY POSTER WON!
HUH?!

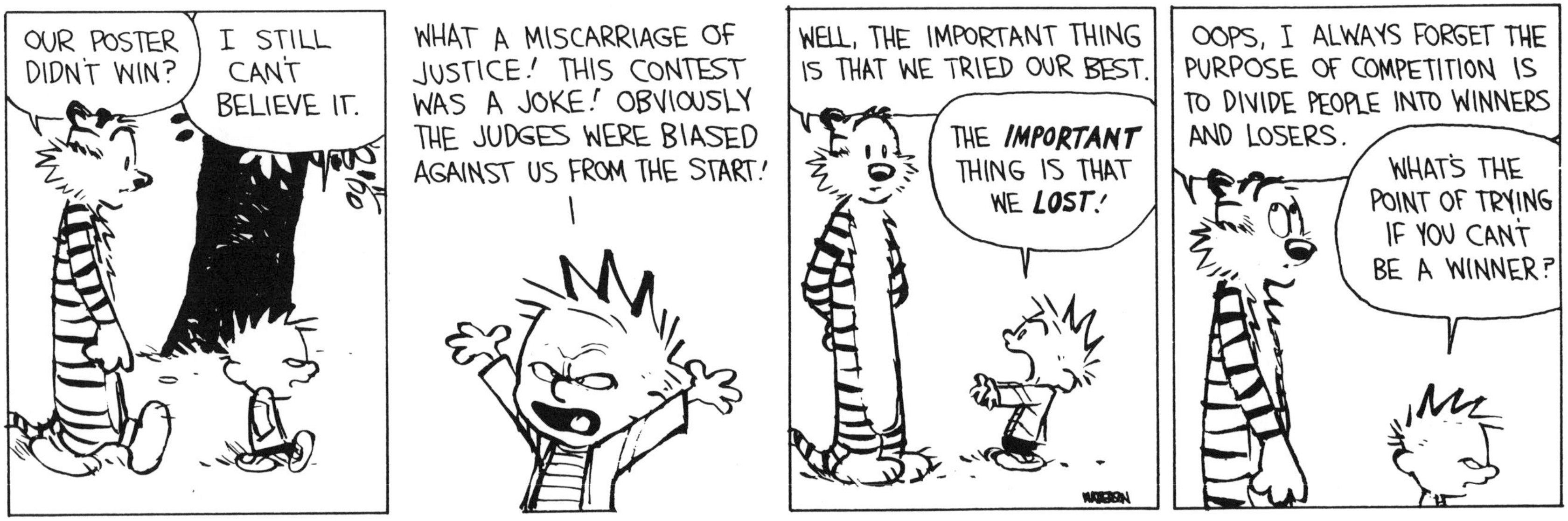
OUR POSTER DIDN'T WIN?
I STILL CAN'T BELIEVE IT.
WHAT A MISCARRIAGE OF JUSTICE! THIS CONTEST WAS A JOKE! OBVIOUSLY THE JUDGES WERE BIASED AGAINST US FROM THE START!
WELL, THE IMPORTANT THING IS THAT WE TRIED OUR BEST.
THE **IMPORTANT** THING IS THAT WE **LOST**!
OOPS, I ALWAYS FORGET THE PURPOSE OF COMPETITION IS TO DIVIDE PEOPLE INTO WINNERS AND LOSERS.
WHAT'S THE POINT OF TRYING IF YOU CAN'T BE A WINNER?

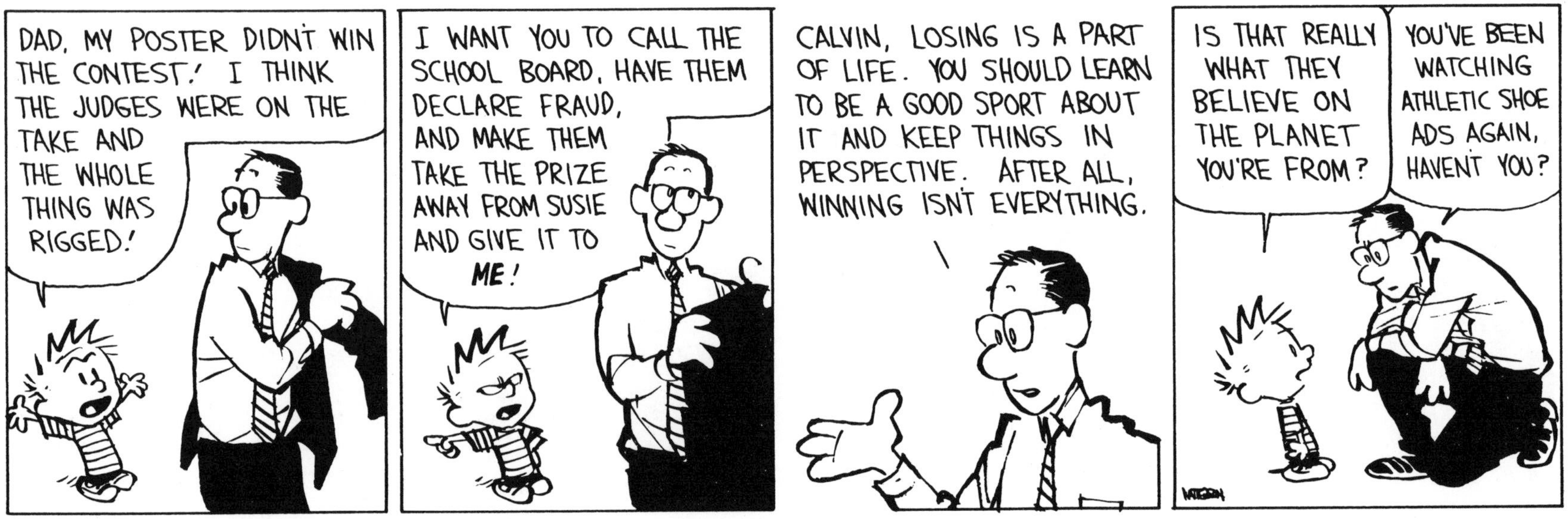
DAD, MY POSTER DIDN'T WIN THE CONTEST! I THINK THE JUDGES WERE ON THE TAKE AND THE WHOLE THING WAS RIGGED!
I WANT YOU TO CALL THE SCHOOL BOARD, HAVE THEM DECLARE FRAUD, AND MAKE THEM TAKE THE PRIZE AWAY FROM SUSIE AND GIVE IT TO **ME**!
CALVIN, LOSING IS A PART OF LIFE. YOU SHOULD LEARN TO BE A GOOD SPORT ABOUT IT AND KEEP THINGS IN PERSPECTIVE. AFTER ALL, WINNING ISN'T EVERYTHING.
IS THAT REALLY WHAT THEY BELIEVE ON THE PLANET YOU'RE FROM?
YOU'VE BEEN WATCHING ATHLETIC SHOE ADS AGAIN, HAVEN'T YOU?

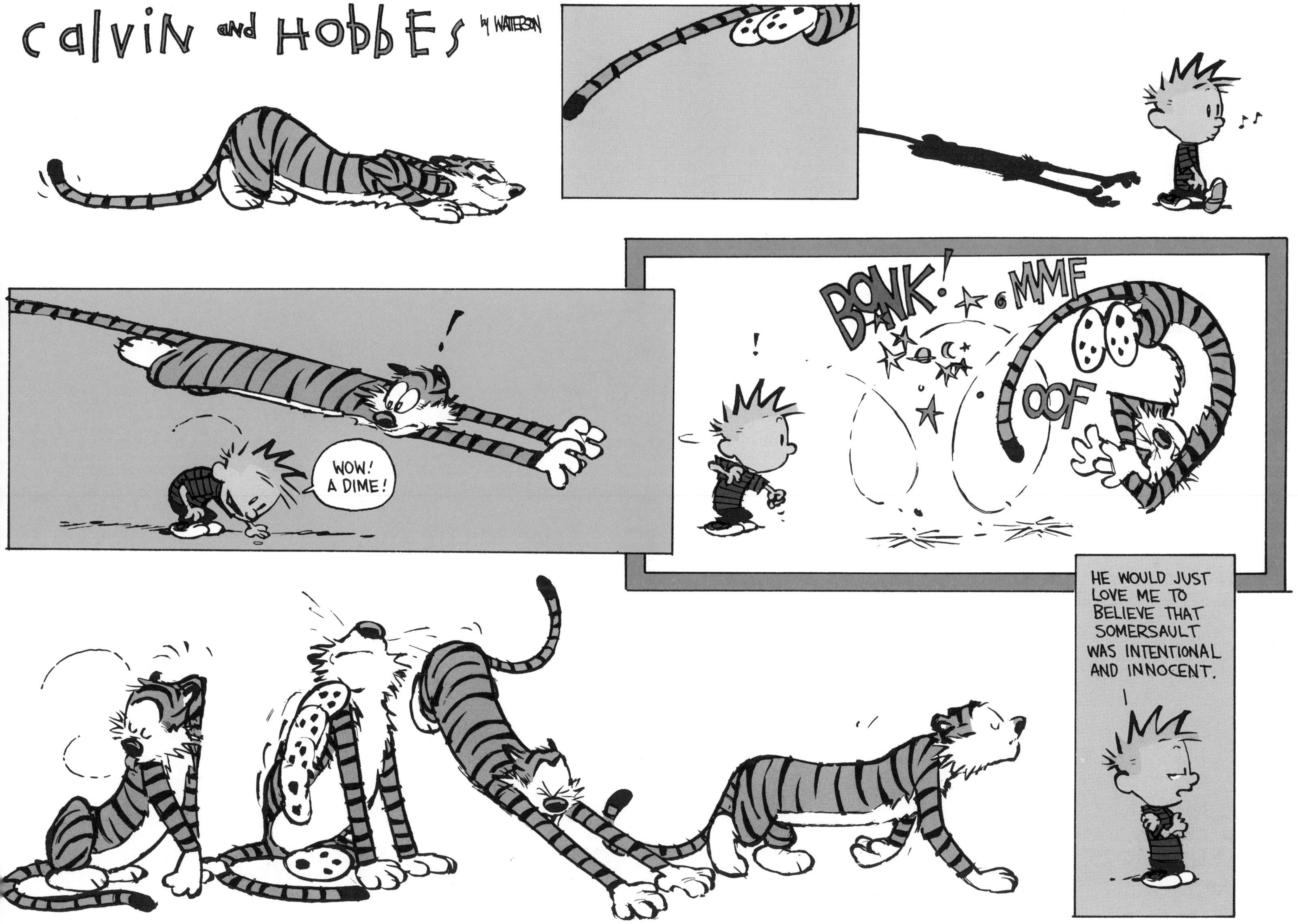
Calvin and HOBBES by WATTERSON
WOW! A DIME!
!
!
BONK!
MMF
OOF
HE WOULD JUST LOVE ME TO BELIEVE THAT SOMERSAULT WAS INTENTIONAL AND INNOCENT.

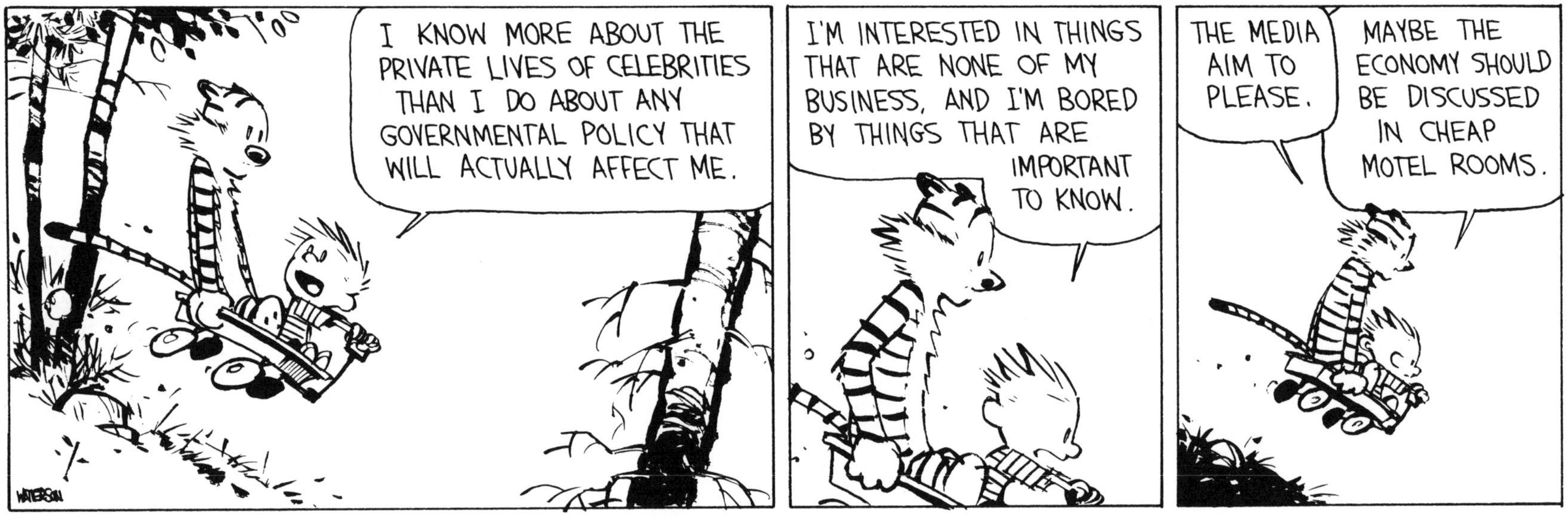
I KNOW MORE ABOUT THE PRIVATE LIVES OF CELEBRITIES THAN I DO ABOUT ANY GOVERNMENTAL POLICY THAT WILL ACTUALLY AFFECT ME.
I'M INTERESTED IN THINGS THAT ARE NONE OF MY BUSINESS, AND I'M BORED BY THINGS THAT ARE IMPORTANT TO KNOW.
THE MEDIA AIM TO PLEASE.
MAYBE THE ECONOMY SHOULD BE DISCUSSED IN CHEAP MOTEL ROOMS.

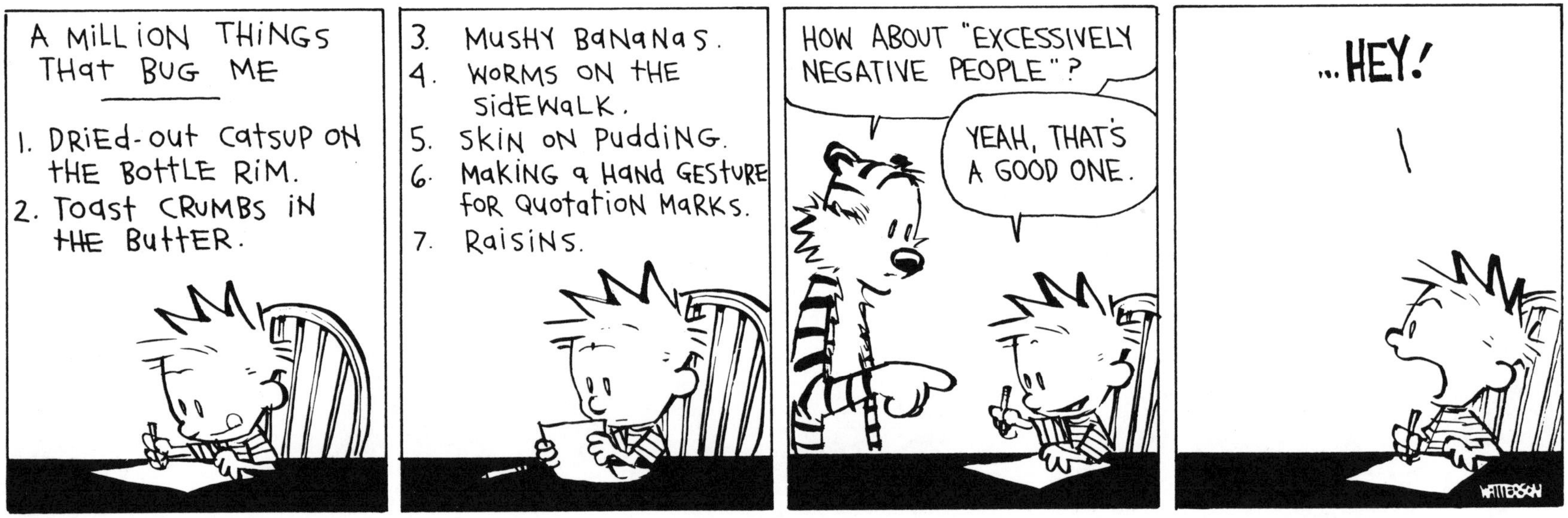
A MILLION THINGS THAT BUG ME
1. DRIED-OUT CATSUP ON THE BOTTLE RIM.
2. TOAST CRUMBS IN THE BUTTER.
3. MUSHY BANANAS.
4. WORMS ON THE SIDEWALK.
5. SKIN ON PUDDING.
6. MAKING A HAND GESTURE FOR QUOTATION MARKS.
7. RAISINS.
HOW ABOUT "EXCESSIVELY NEGATIVE PEOPLE"?
YEAH, THAT'S A GOOD ONE.
...HEY!

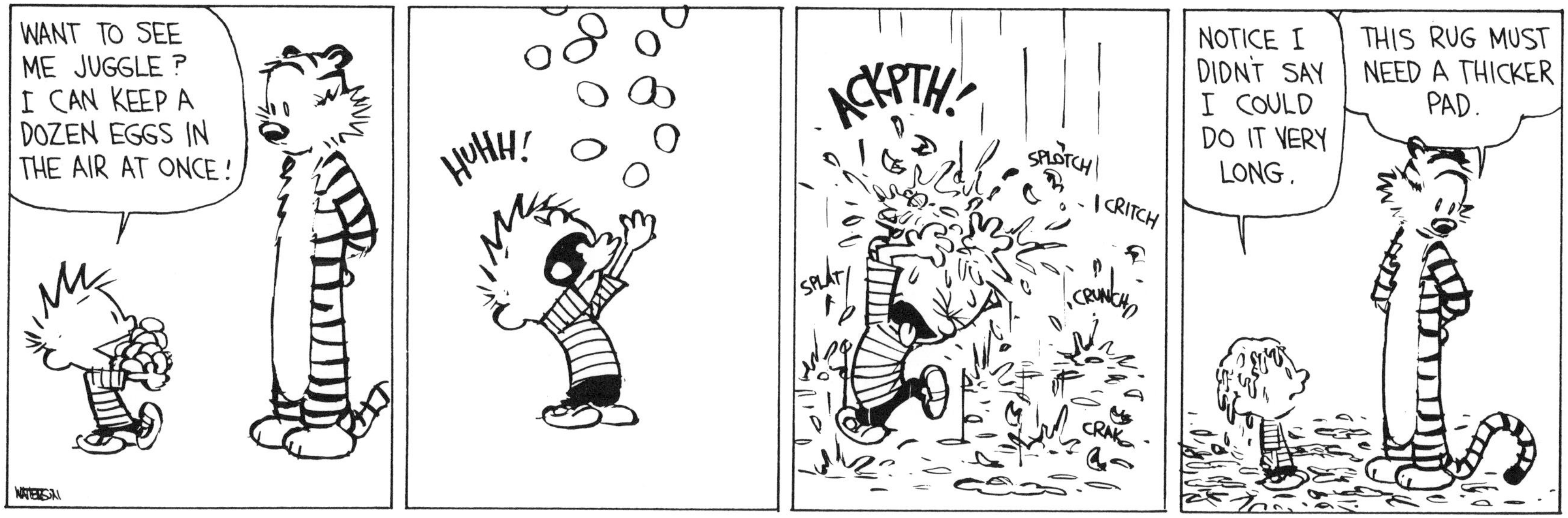
WANT TO SEE ME JUGGLE? I CAN KEEP A DOZEN EGGS IN THE AIR AT ONCE!
HUHH!
ACKPTH!
SPLOTCH
CRITCH
SPLAT
CRUNCH
CRAK
NOTICE I DIDN'T SAY I COULD DO IT VERY LONG.
THIS RUG MUST NEED A THICKER PAD.

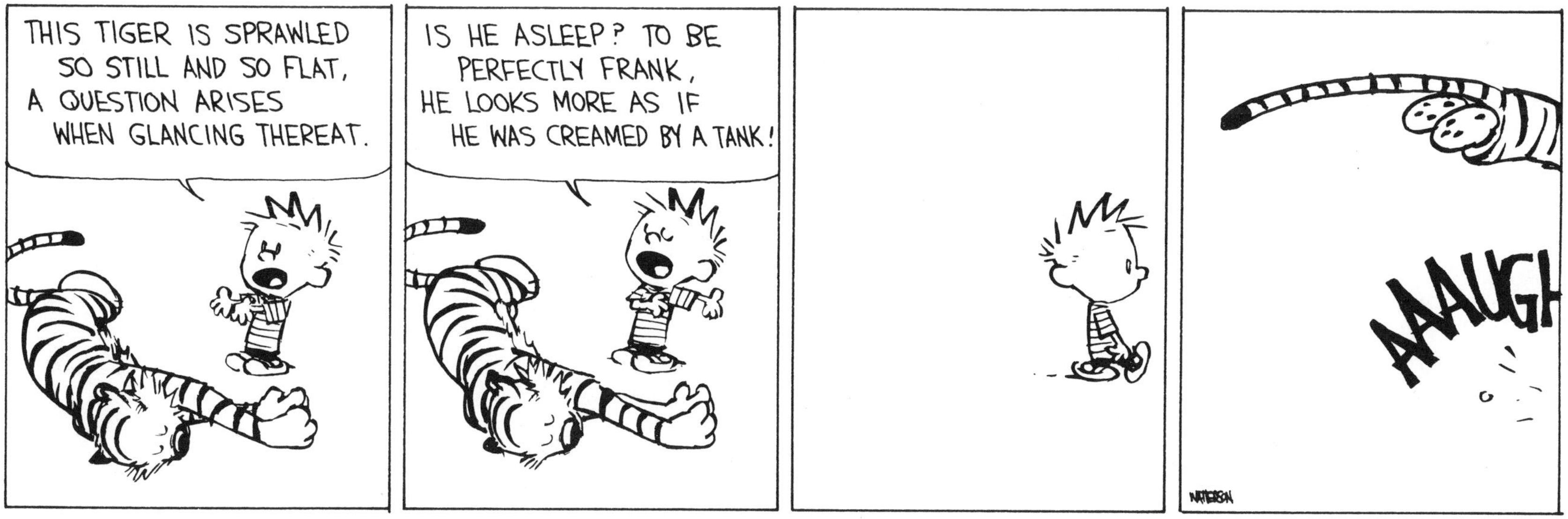
THIS TIGER IS SPRAWLED SO STILL AND SO FLAT, A QUESTION ARISES WHEN GLANCING THEREAT.
IS HE ASLEEP? TO BE PERFECTLY FRANK, HE LOOKS MORE AS IF HE WAS CREAMED BY A TANK!
AAAUGH

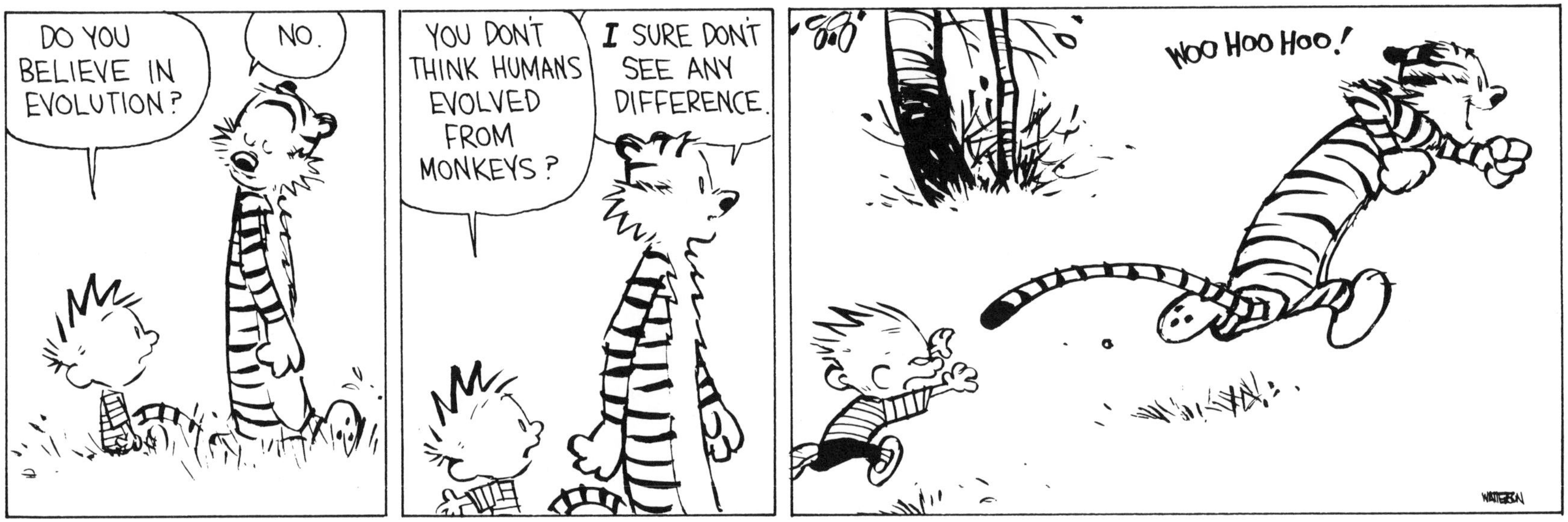
DO YOU BELIEVE IN EVOLUTION?
NO.
YOU DON'T THINK HUMANS EVOLVED FROM MONKEYS?
I SURE DON'T SEE ANY DIFFERENCE.
WOO HOO HOO!

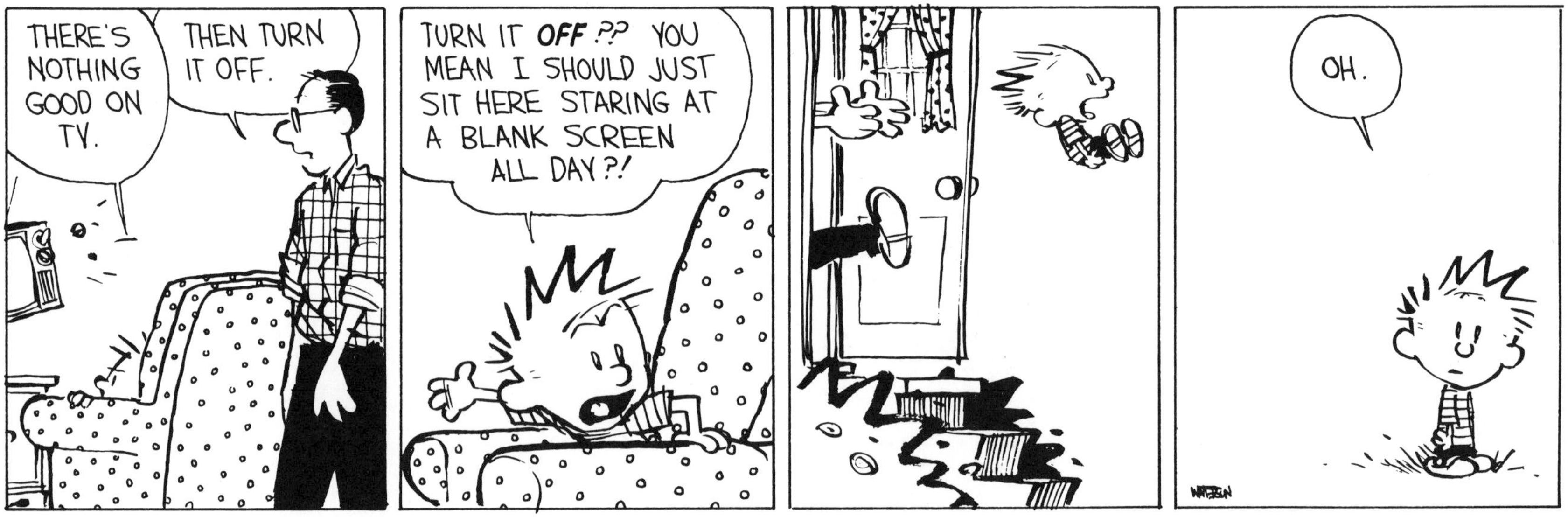
THERE'S NOTHING GOOD ON TV.
THEN TURN IT OFF.
TURN IT OFF?? YOU MEAN I SHOULD JUST SIT HERE STARING AT A BLANK SCREEN ALL DAY?!
OH.

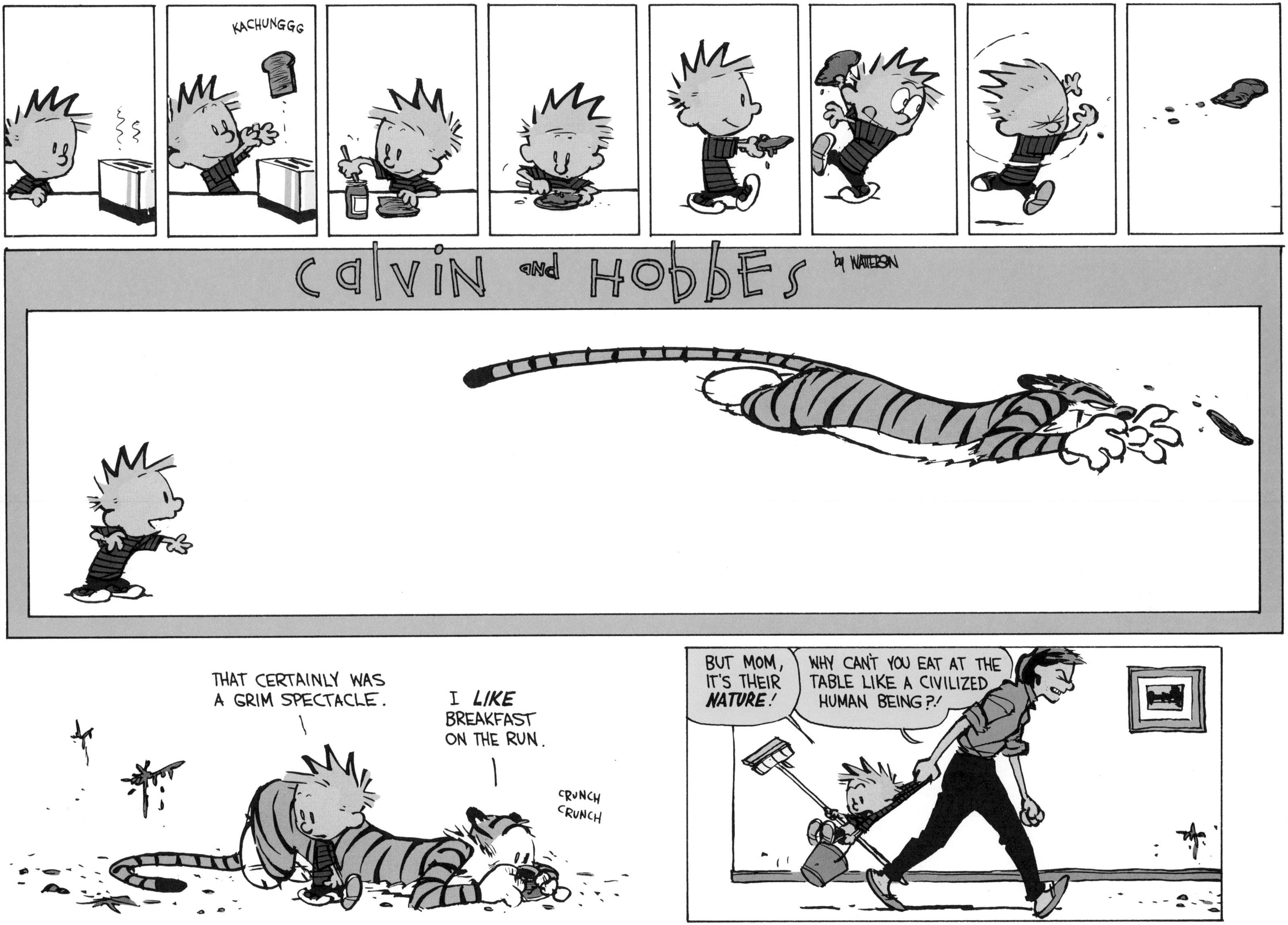
KACHUNGGG
Calvin and HOBBES
by WATTERSON
THAT CERTAINLY WAS A GRIM SPECTACLE.
I **LIKE** BREAKFAST ON THE RUN.
CRUNCH CRUNCH
WHY CAN'T YOU EAT AT THE TABLE LIKE A CIVILIZED HUMAN BEING?!
BUT MOM, IT'S THEIR ***NATURE***!

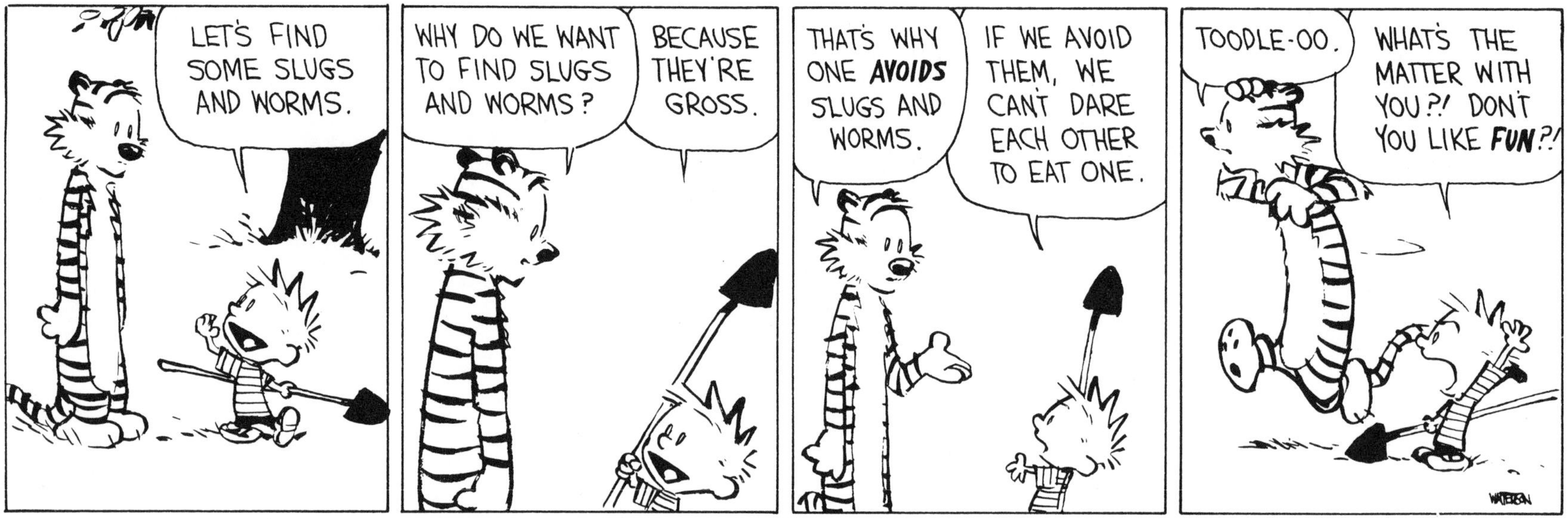
LET'S FIND SOME SLUGS AND WORMS.
WHY DO WE WANT TO FIND SLUGS AND WORMS?
BECAUSE THEY'RE GROSS.
THAT'S WHY ONE **AVOIDS** SLUGS AND WORMS.
IF WE AVOID THEM, WE CAN'T DARE EACH OTHER TO EAT ONE.
TOODLE-OO.
WHAT'S THE MATTER WITH YOU?! DON'T YOU LIKE **FUN**?!
WATTERSON

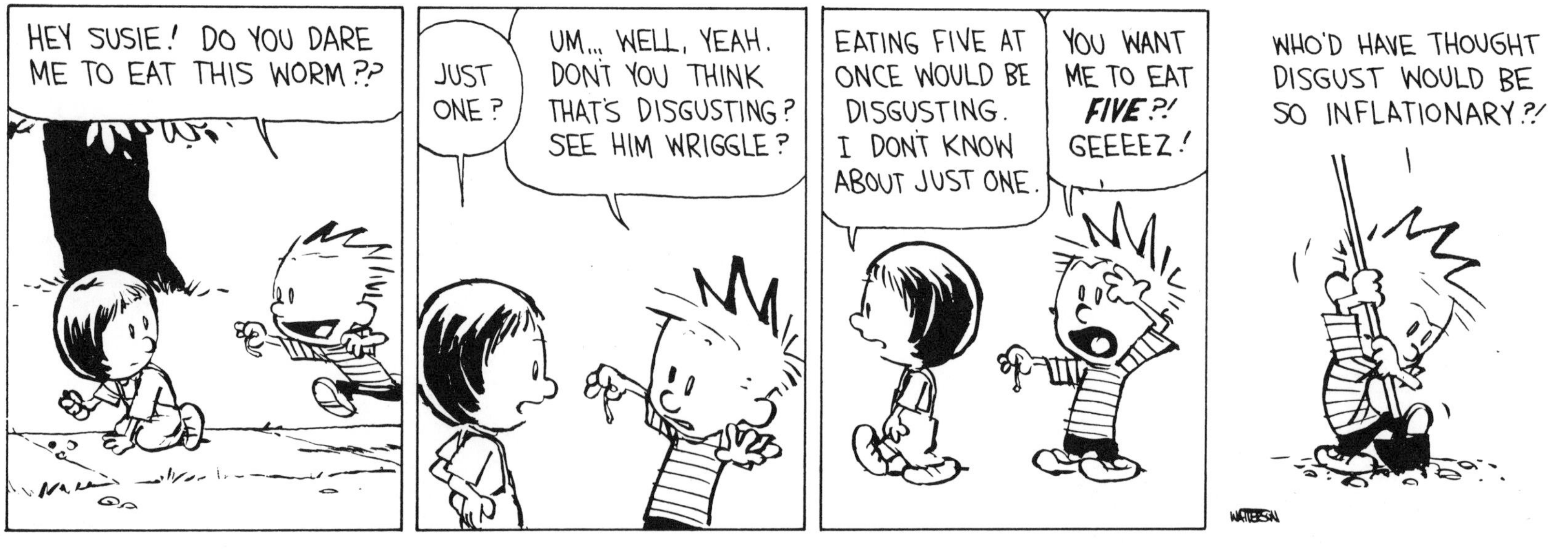
HEY SUSIE! DO YOU DARE ME TO EAT THIS WORM??
JUST ONE?
UM... WELL, YEAH. DON'T YOU THINK THAT'S DISGUSTING? SEE HIM WRIGGLE?
EATING FIVE AT ONCE WOULD BE DISGUSTING. I DON'T KNOW ABOUT JUST ONE.
YOU WANT ME TO EAT **FIVE**?! GEEEEZ!
WHO'D HAVE THOUGHT DISGUST WOULD BE SO INFLATIONARY?!
WATTERSON

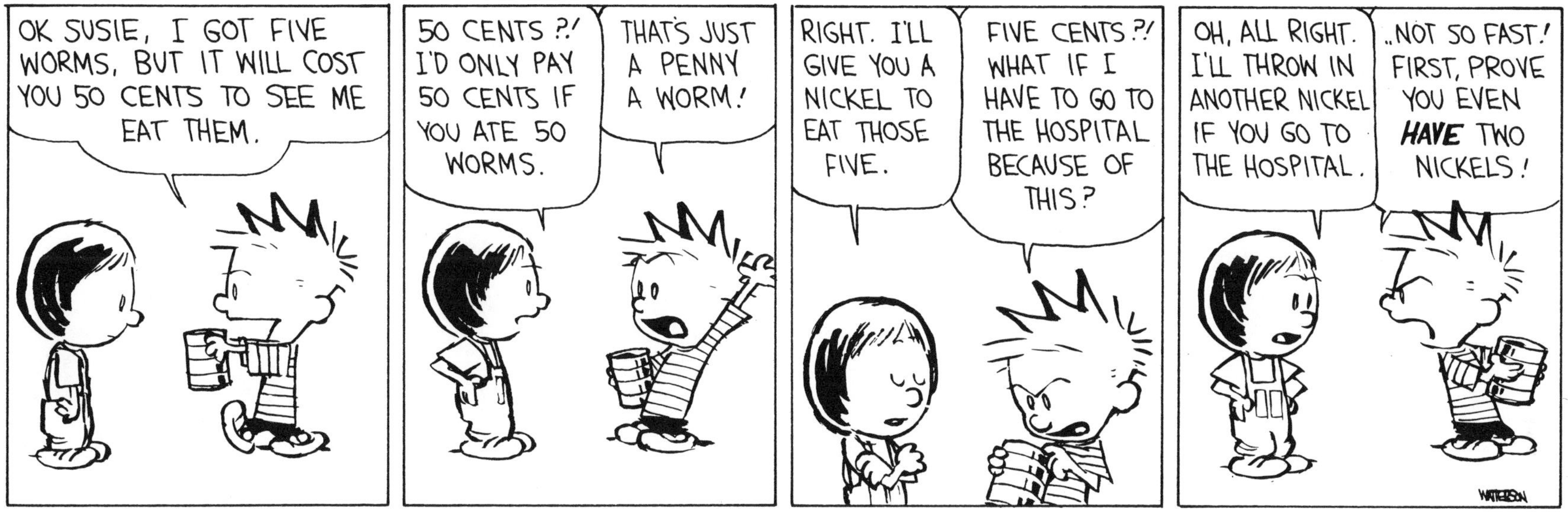
OK SUSIE, I GOT FIVE WORMS, BUT IT WILL COST YOU 50 CENTS TO SEE ME EAT THEM.
50 CENTS ?! I'D ONLY PAY 50 CENTS IF YOU ATE 50 WORMS.
THAT'S JUST A PENNY A WORM!
RIGHT. I'LL GIVE YOU A NICKEL TO EAT THOSE FIVE.
FIVE CENTS ?! WHAT IF I HAVE TO GO TO THE HOSPITAL BECAUSE OF THIS?
OH, ALL RIGHT. I'LL THROW IN ANOTHER NICKEL IF YOU GO TO THE HOSPITAL.
..NOT SO FAST! FIRST, PROVE YOU EVEN **HAVE** TWO NICKELS!
WATTERSON

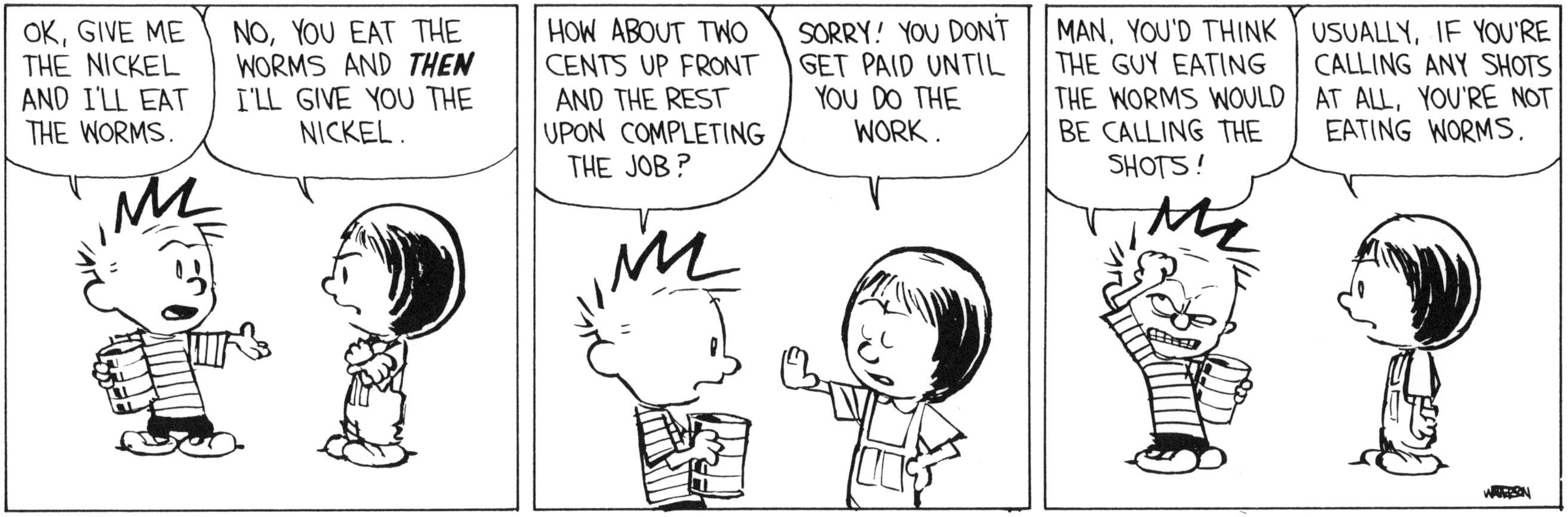
OK, GIVE ME THE NICKEL AND I'LL EAT THE WORMS.
NO, YOU EAT THE WORMS AND **THEN** I'LL GIVE YOU THE NICKEL.
HOW ABOUT TWO CENTS UP FRONT AND THE REST UPON COMPLETING THE JOB?
SORRY! YOU DON'T GET PAID UNTIL YOU DO THE WORK.
MAN, YOU'D THINK THE GUY EATING THE WORMS WOULD BE CALLING THE SHOTS!
USUALLY, IF YOU'RE CALLING ANY SHOTS AT ALL, YOU'RE NOT EATING WORMS.
WATTERSON

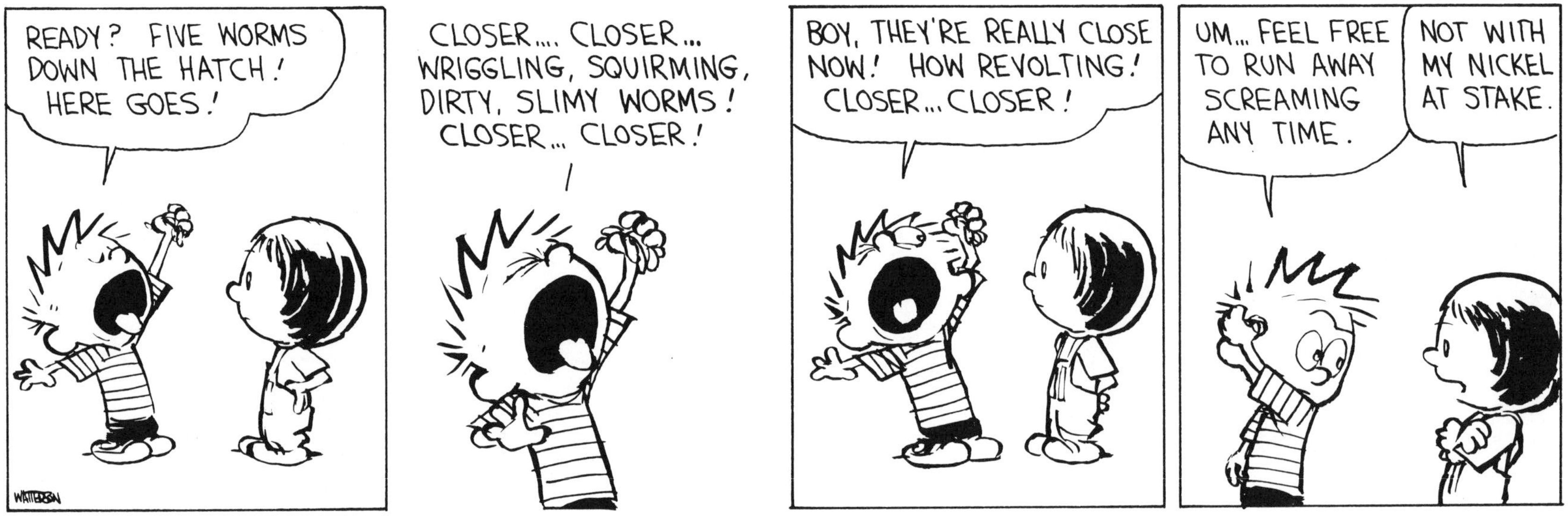
READY? FIVE WORMS DOWN THE HATCH! HERE GOES!
CLOSER.... CLOSER... ...WRIGGLING, SQUIRMING, DIRTY, SLIMY WORMS! CLOSER... CLOSER!
BOY, THEY'RE REALLY CLOSE NOW! HOW REVOLTING! CLOSER... CLOSER!
UM... FEEL FREE TO RUN AWAY SCREAMING ANY TIME.
NOT WITH MY NICKEL AT STAKE.

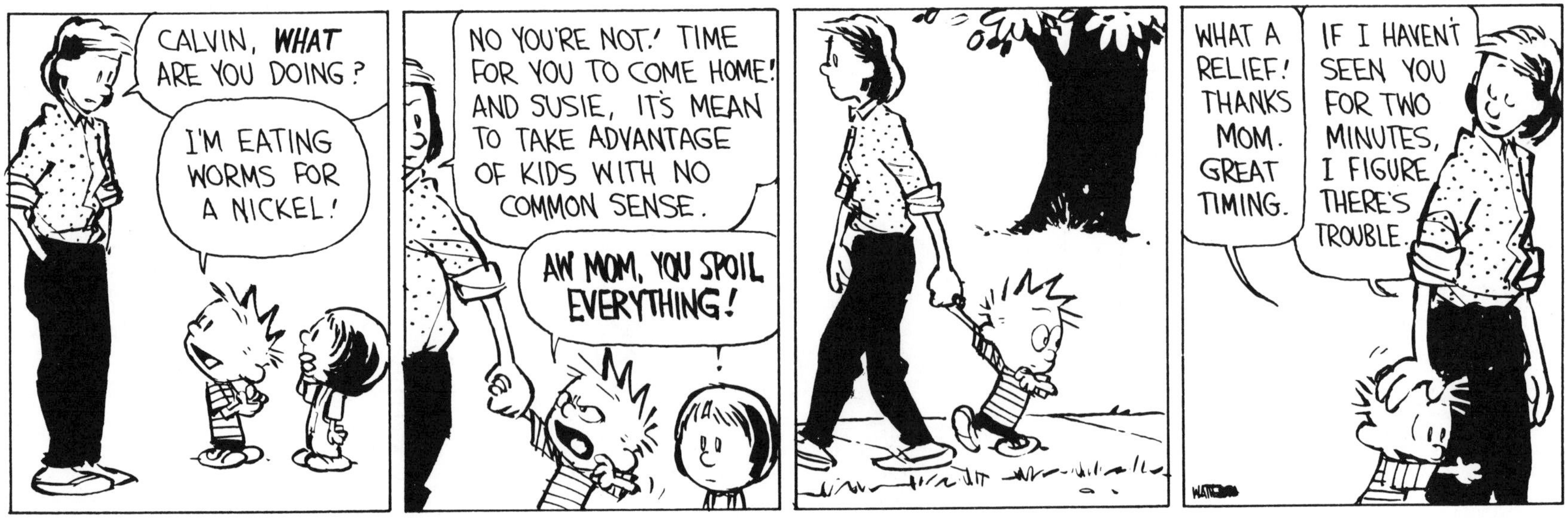
CALVIN, WHAT ARE YOU DOING?
I'M EATING WORMS FOR A NICKEL!
NO YOU'RE NOT! TIME FOR YOU TO COME HOME! AND SUSIE, IT'S MEAN TO TAKE ADVANTAGE OF KIDS WITH NO COMMON SENSE.
AW MOM, YOU SPOIL EVERYTHING!
WHAT A RELIEF! THANKS MOM. GREAT TIMING.
IF I HAVEN'T SEEN YOU FOR TWO MINUTES, I FIGURE THERE'S TROUBLE.

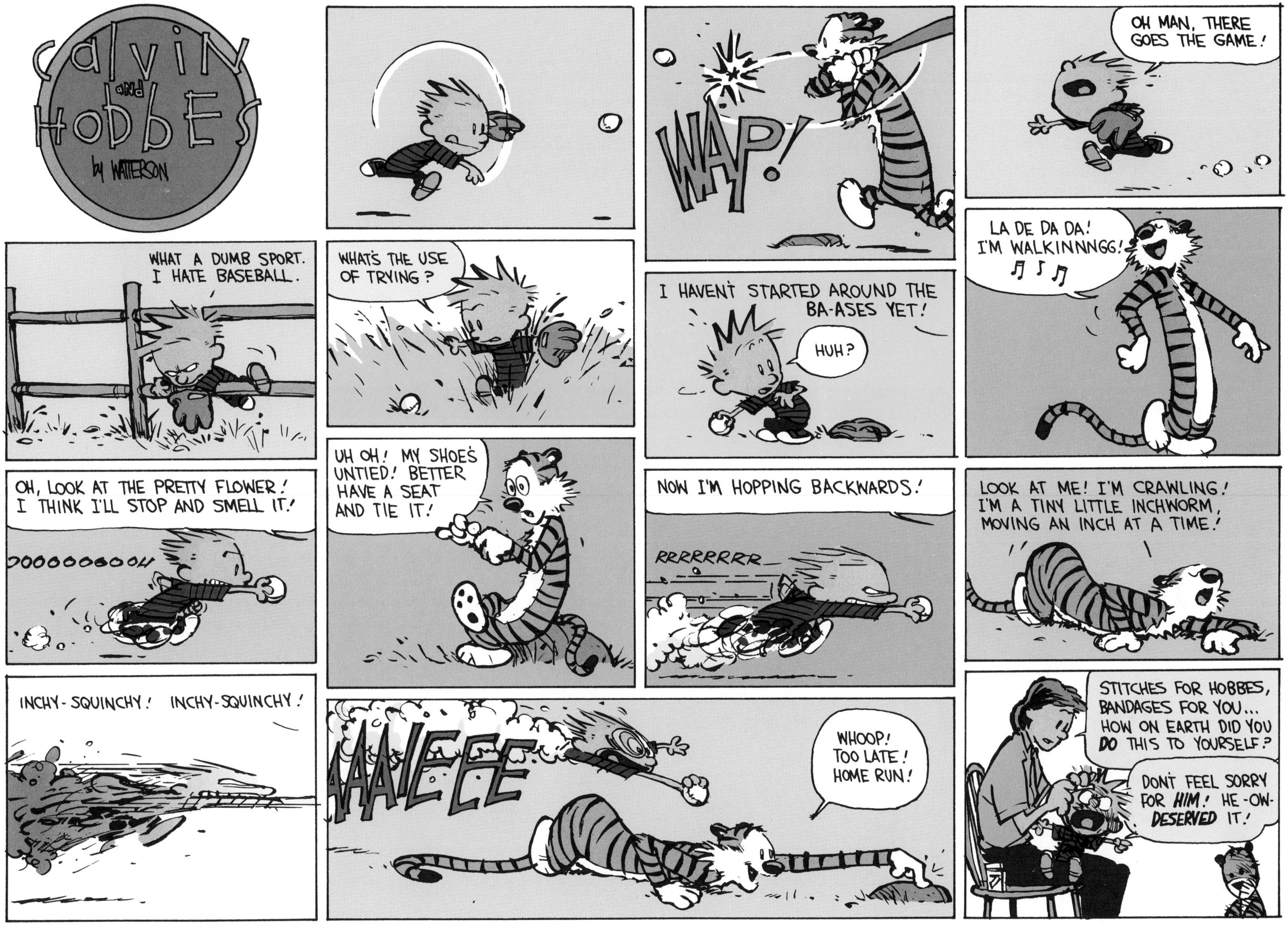
Calvin and Hobbes
by WATTERSON
WAP!
OH MAN, THERE GOES THE GAME!
WHAT A DUMB SPORT. I HATE BASEBALL.
WHAT'S THE USE OF TRYING?
I HAVEN'T STARTED AROUND THE BA-ASES YET!
HUH?
LA DE DA DA! I'M WALKINNNGG!
OH, LOOK AT THE PRETTY FLOWER! I THINK I'LL STOP AND SMELL IT!
OOOOOOOOOOH
UH OH! MY SHOE'S UNTIED! BETTER HAVE A SEAT AND TIE IT!
NOW I'M HOPPING BACKWARDS!
RRRRRRRR
LOOK AT ME! I'M CRAWLING! I'M A TINY LITTLE INCHWORM, MOVING AN INCH AT A TIME!
INCHY-SQUINCHY! INCHY-SQUINCHY!
AAAIEEE
WHOOP! TOO LATE! HOME RUN!
STITCHES FOR HOBBES, BANDAGES FOR YOU... HOW ON EARTH DID YOU DO THIS TO YOURSELF?
DON'T FEEL SORRY FOR HIM! HE-OW-DESERVED IT!

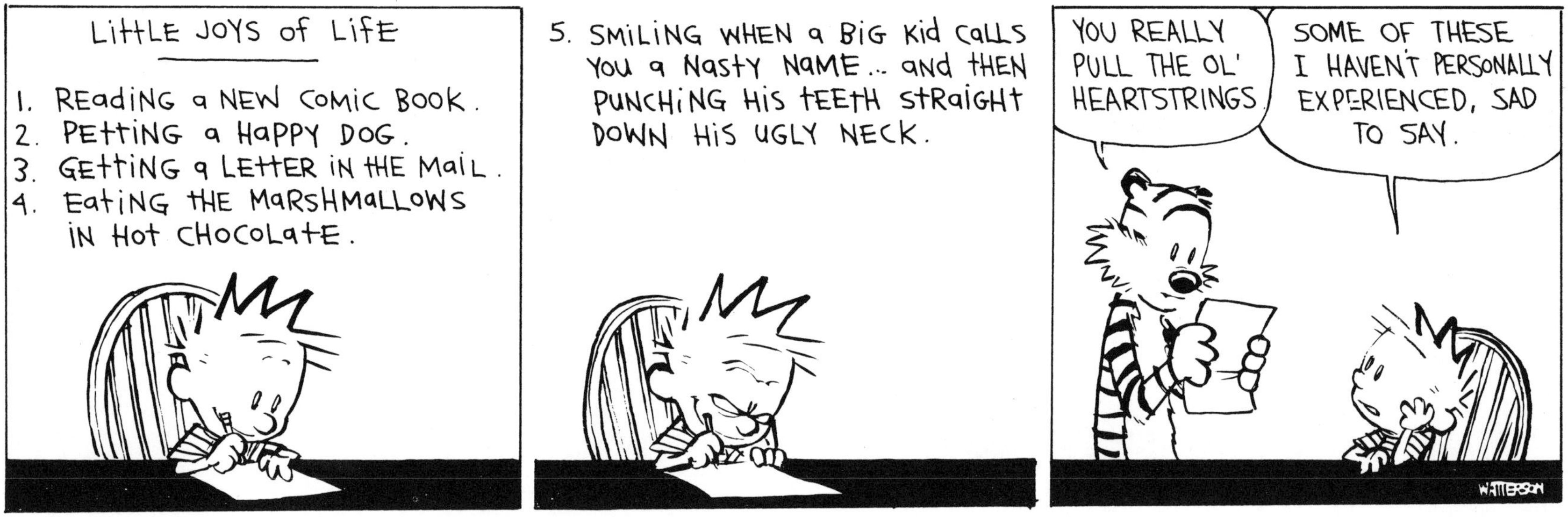
Little Joys of Life
1. Reading a New Comic Book.
2. Petting a Happy Dog.
3. Getting a Letter in the Mail.
4. Eating the Marshmallows in Hot Chocolate.
5. Smiling when a Big Kid calls you a Nasty Name... and then punching his teeth straight down his ugly neck.
YOU REALLY PULL THE OL' HEARTSTRINGS.
SOME OF THESE I HAVEN'T PERSONALLY EXPERIENCED, SAD TO SAY.
WATTERSON

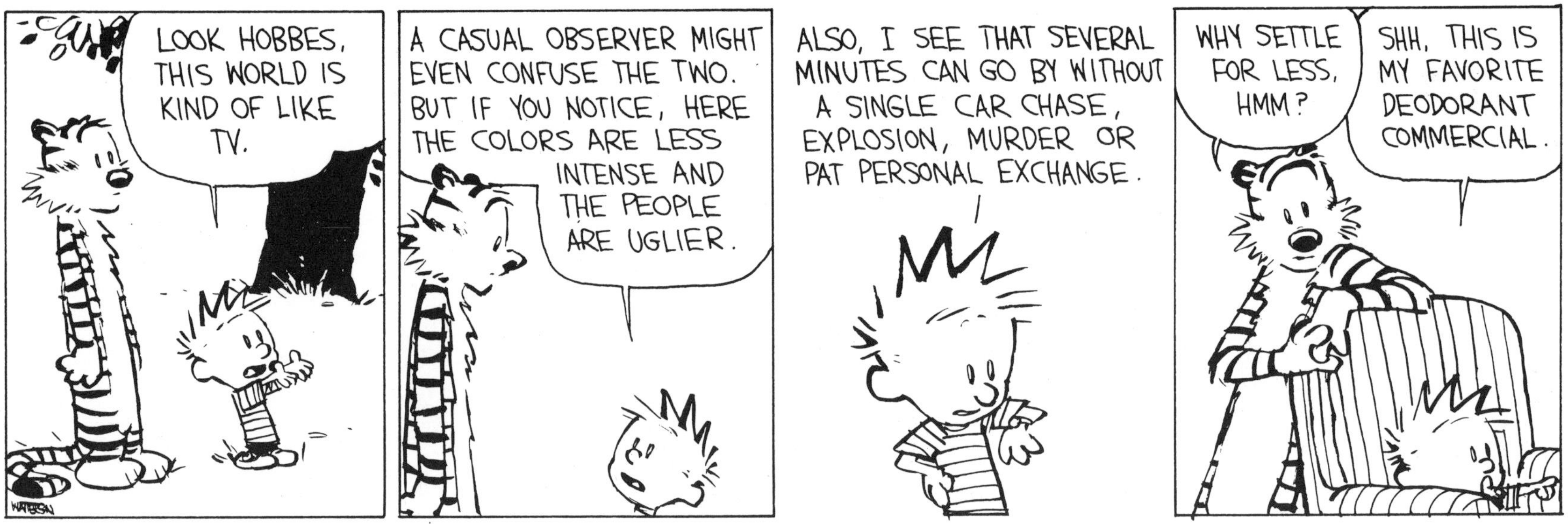
LOOK HOBBES, THIS WORLD IS KIND OF LIKE TV.
A CASUAL OBSERVER MIGHT EVEN CONFUSE THE TWO. BUT IF YOU NOTICE, HERE THE COLORS ARE LESS INTENSE AND THE PEOPLE ARE UGLIER.
ALSO, I SEE THAT SEVERAL MINUTES CAN GO BY WITHOUT A SINGLE CAR CHASE, EXPLOSION, MURDER OR PAT PERSONAL EXCHANGE.
WHY SETTLE FOR LESS, HMM?
SHH, THIS IS MY FAVORITE DEODORANT COMMERCIAL.
WATTERSON

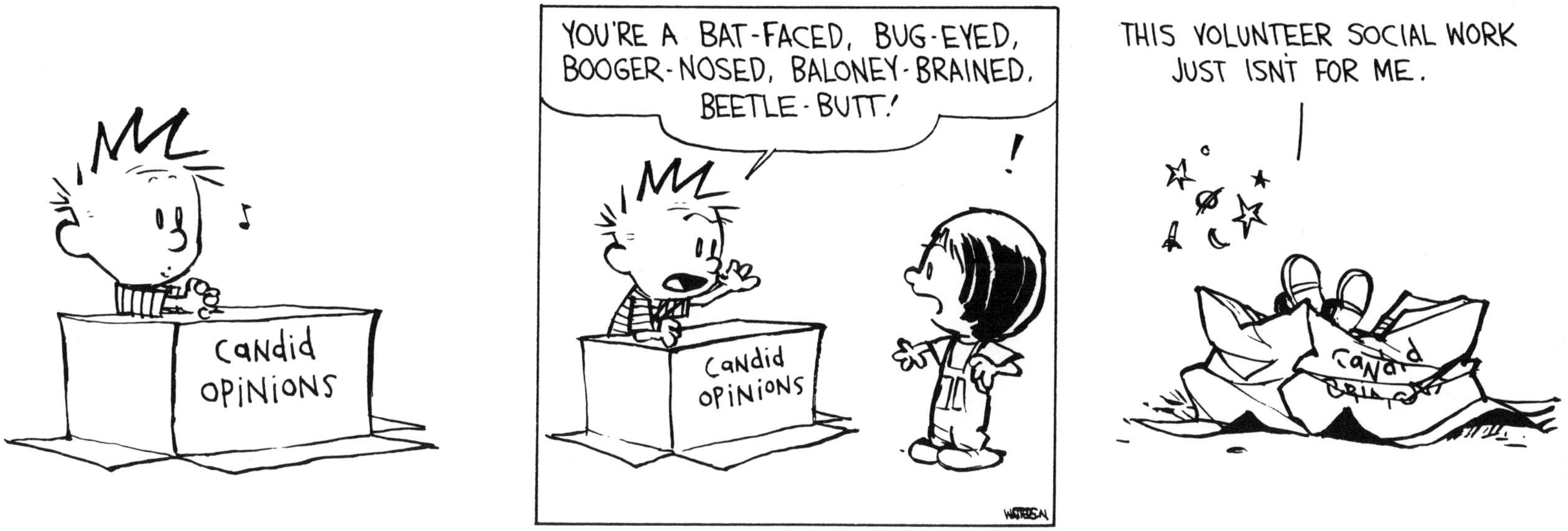
CANDID OPINIONS
YOU'RE A BAT-FACED, BUG-EYED, BOOGER-NOSED, BALONEY-BRAINED, BEETLE-BUTT!
!
THIS VOLUNTEER SOCIAL WORK JUST ISN'T FOR ME.

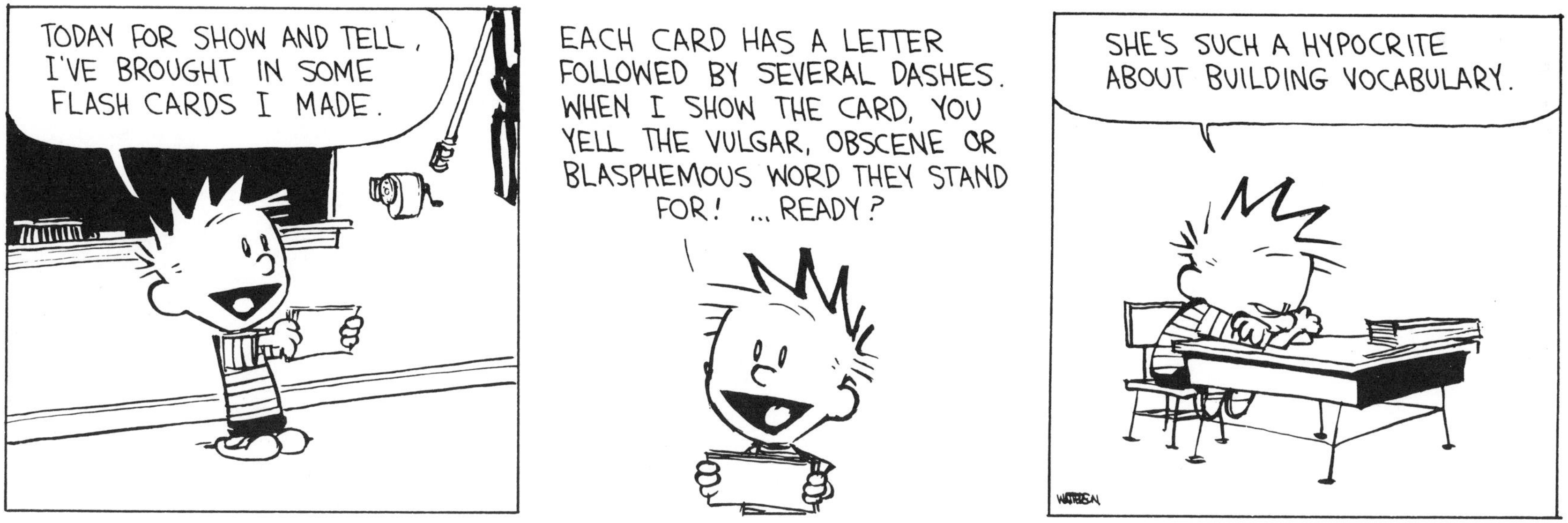
TODAY FOR SHOW AND TELL, I'VE BROUGHT IN SOME FLASH CARDS I MADE.
EACH CARD HAS A LETTER FOLLOWED BY SEVERAL DASHES. WHEN I SHOW THE CARD, YOU YELL THE VULGAR, OBSCENE OR BLASPHEMOUS WORD THEY STAND FOR! ...READY?
SHE'S SUCH A HYPOCRITE ABOUT BUILDING VOCABULARY.

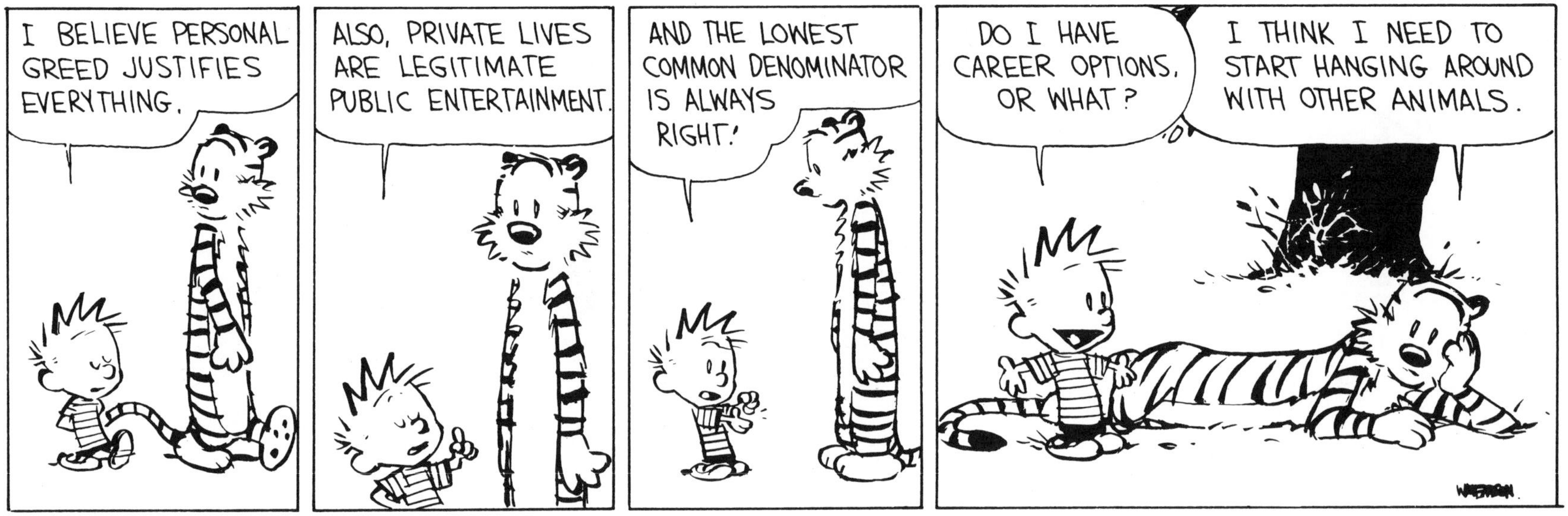
I BELIEVE PERSONAL GREED JUSTIFIES EVERYTHING.
ALSO, PRIVATE LIVES ARE LEGITIMATE PUBLIC ENTERTAINMENT.
AND THE LOWEST COMMON DENOMINATOR IS ALWAYS RIGHT!
DO I HAVE CAREER OPTIONS, OR WHAT?
I THINK I NEED TO START HANGING AROUND WITH OTHER ANIMALS.

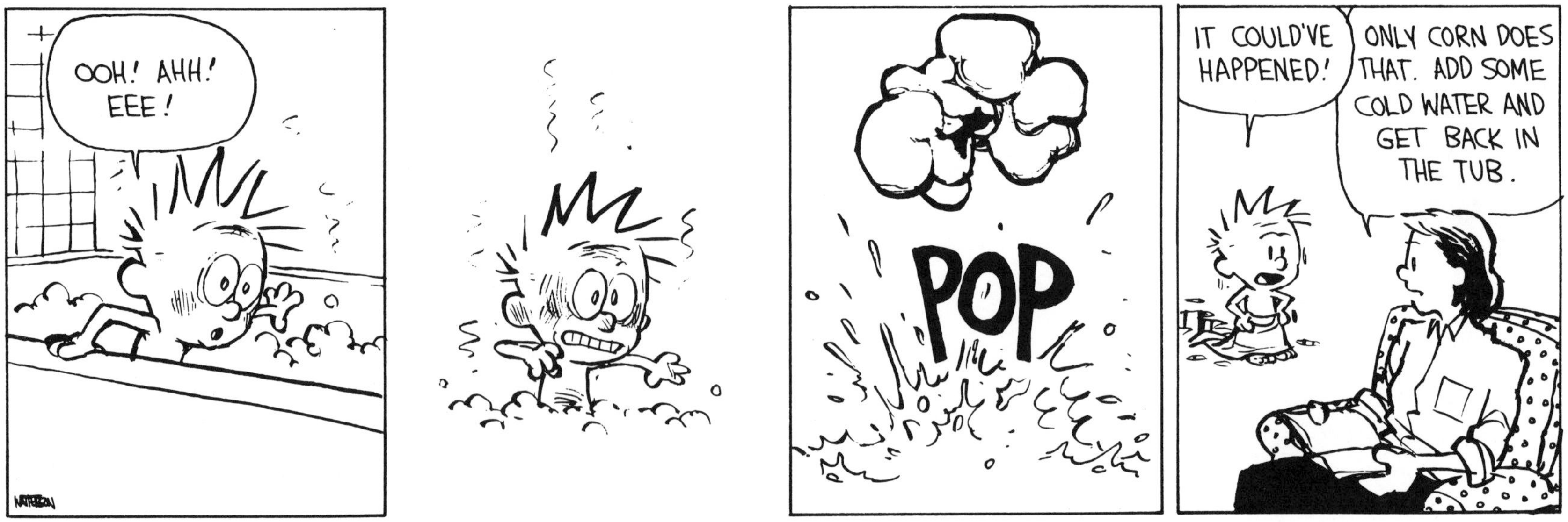
OOH! AHH! EEE!
POP
IT COULD'VE HAPPENED!
ONLY CORN DOES THAT. ADD SOME COLD WATER AND GET BACK IN THE TUB.

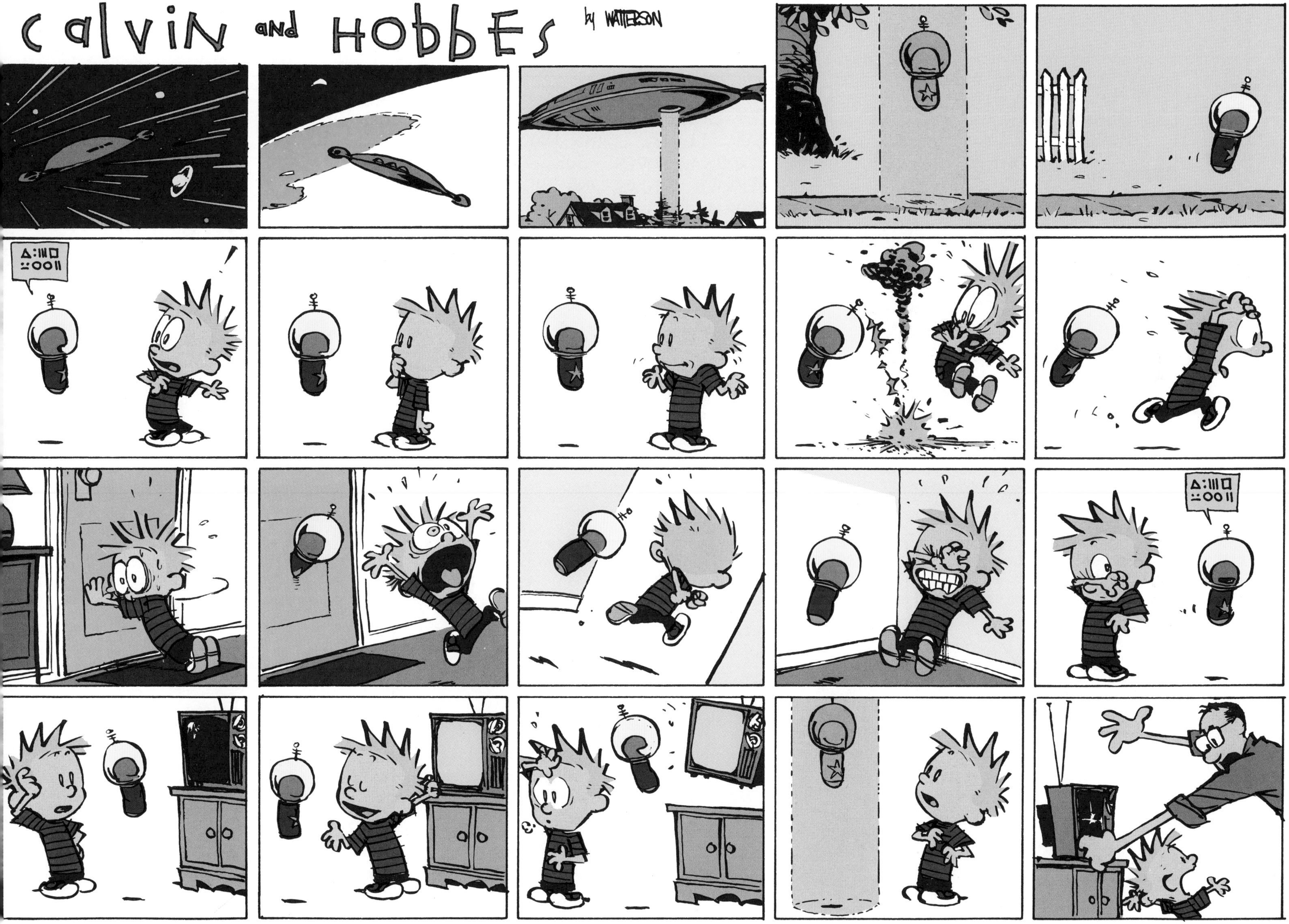
Calvin and Hobbes
by WATTERSON

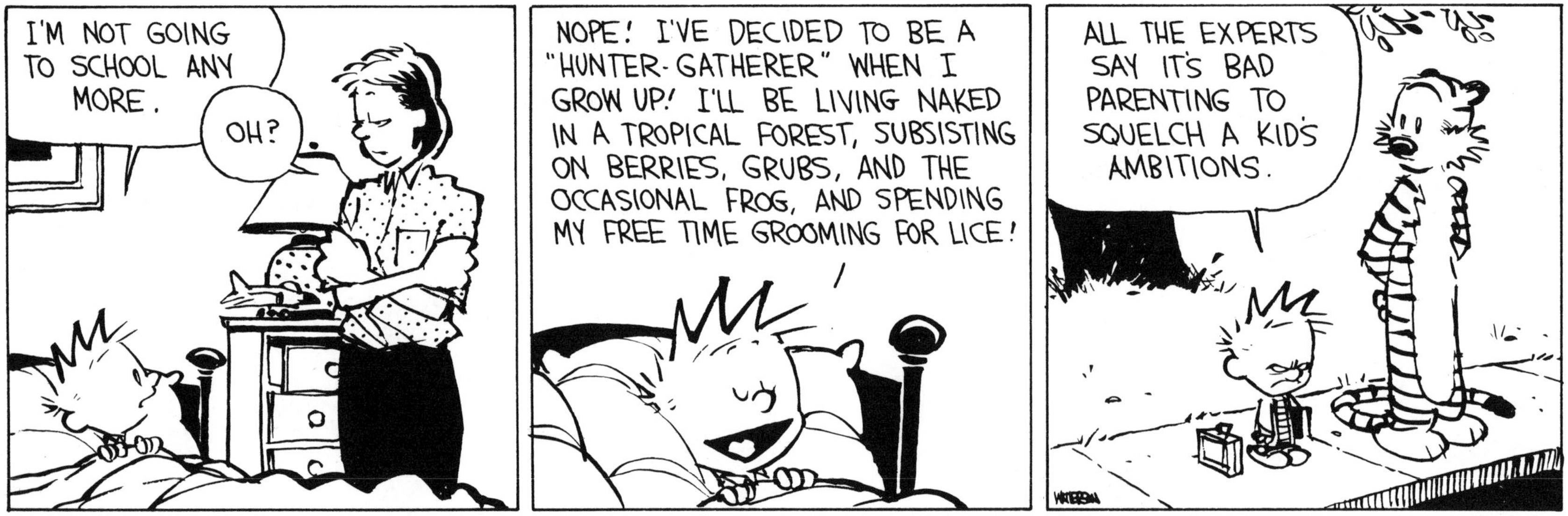
I'M NOT GOING TO SCHOOL ANY MORE.
OH?
NOPE! I'VE DECIDED TO BE A "HUNTER-GATHERER" WHEN I GROW UP! I'LL BE LIVING NAKED IN A TROPICAL FOREST, SUBSISTING ON BERRIES, GRUBS, AND THE OCCASIONAL FROG, AND SPENDING MY FREE TIME GROOMING FOR LICE!
ALL THE EXPERTS SAY IT'S BAD PARENTING TO SQUELCH A KID'S AMBITIONS.

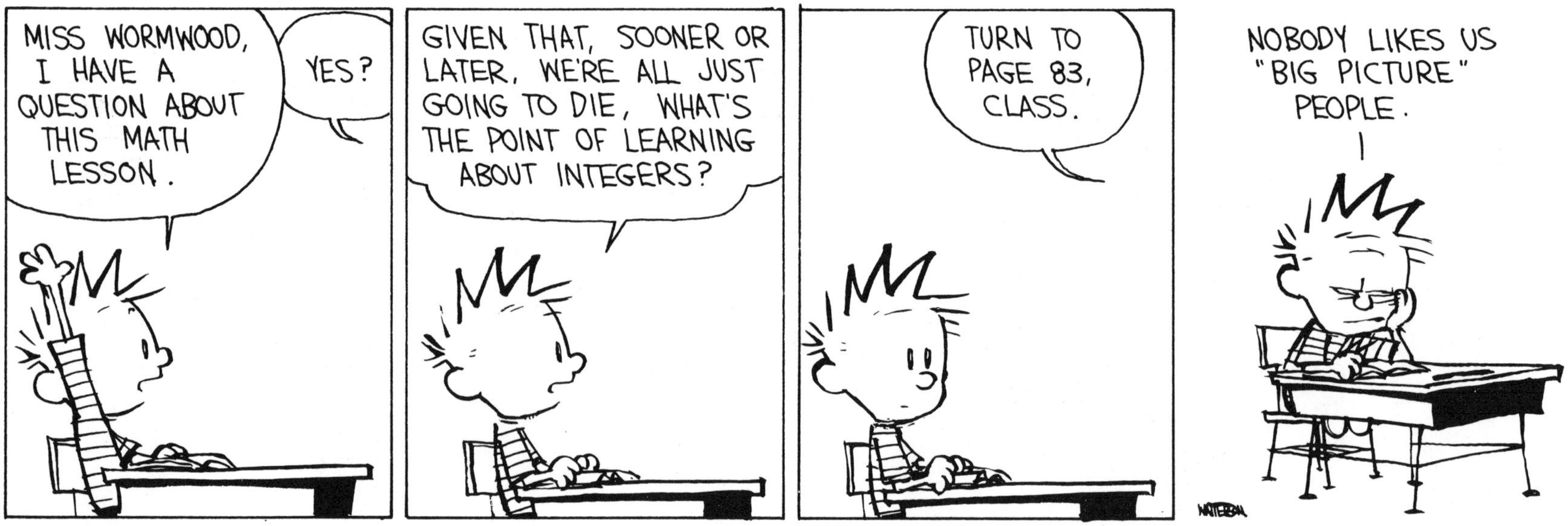
MISS WORMWOOD, I HAVE A QUESTION ABOUT THIS MATH LESSON.
YES?
GIVEN THAT, SOONER OR LATER, WE'RE ALL JUST GOING TO DIE, WHAT'S THE POINT OF LEARNING ABOUT INTEGERS?
TURN TO PAGE 83, CLASS.
NOBODY LIKES US "BIG PICTURE" PEOPLE.

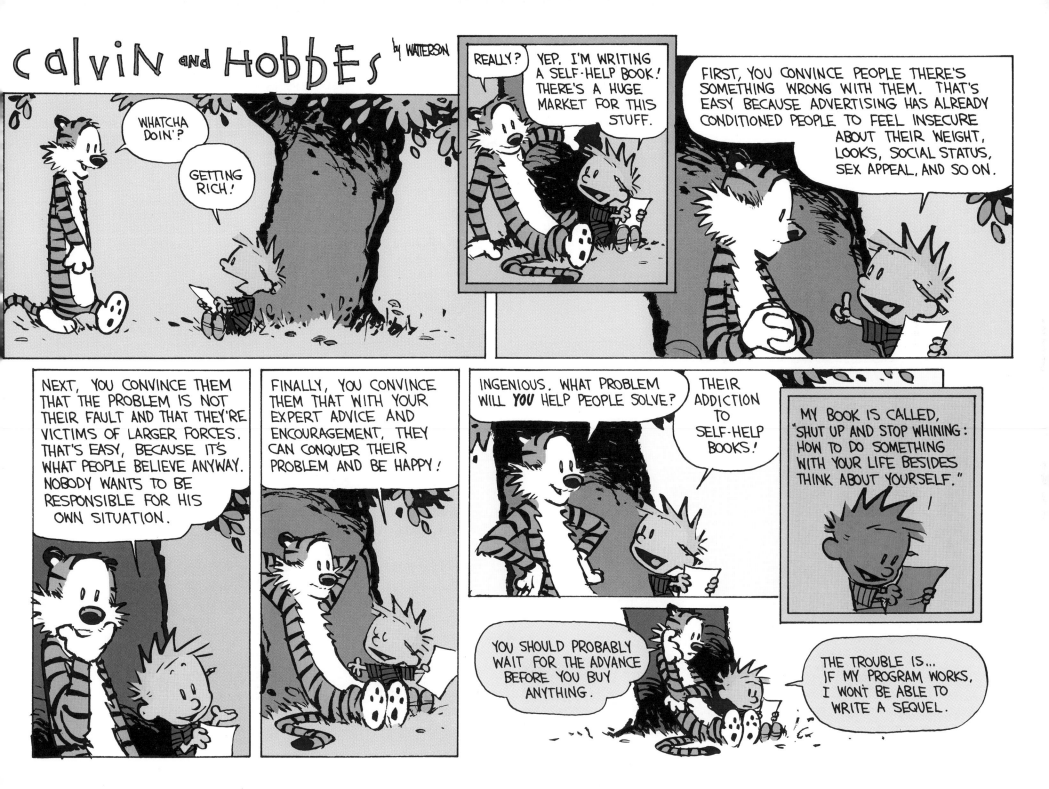

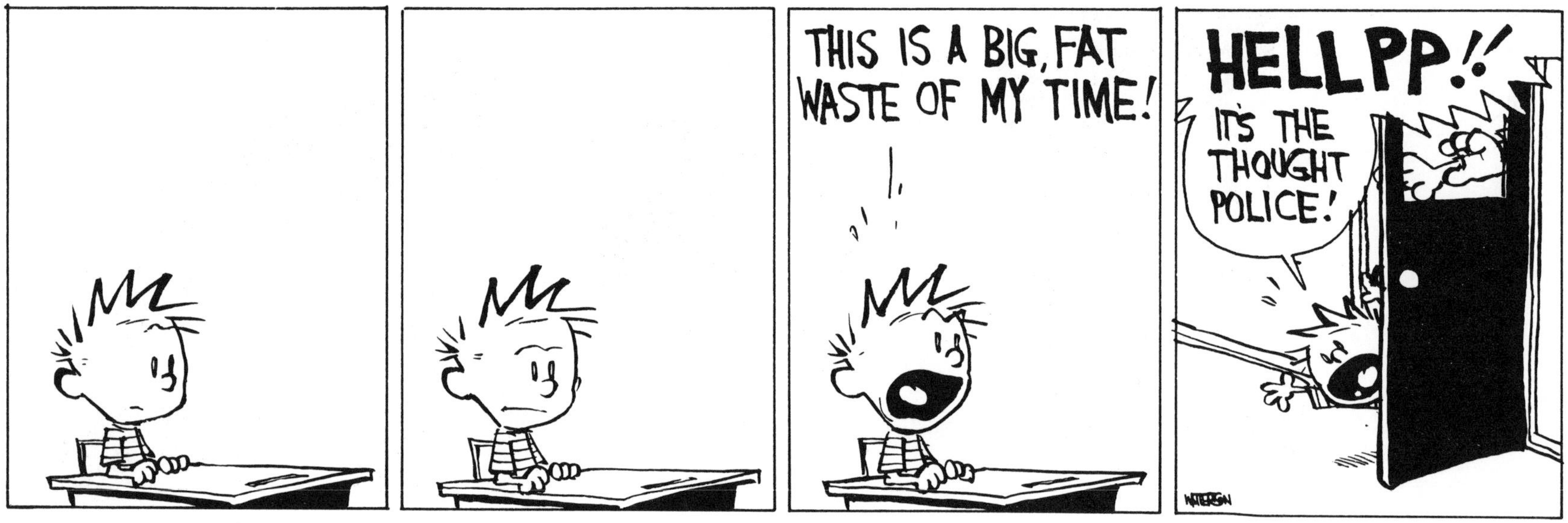
THIS IS A BIG, FAT WASTE OF MY TIME!
HELLPP!!
IT'S THE THOUGHT POLICE!
WATTERSON

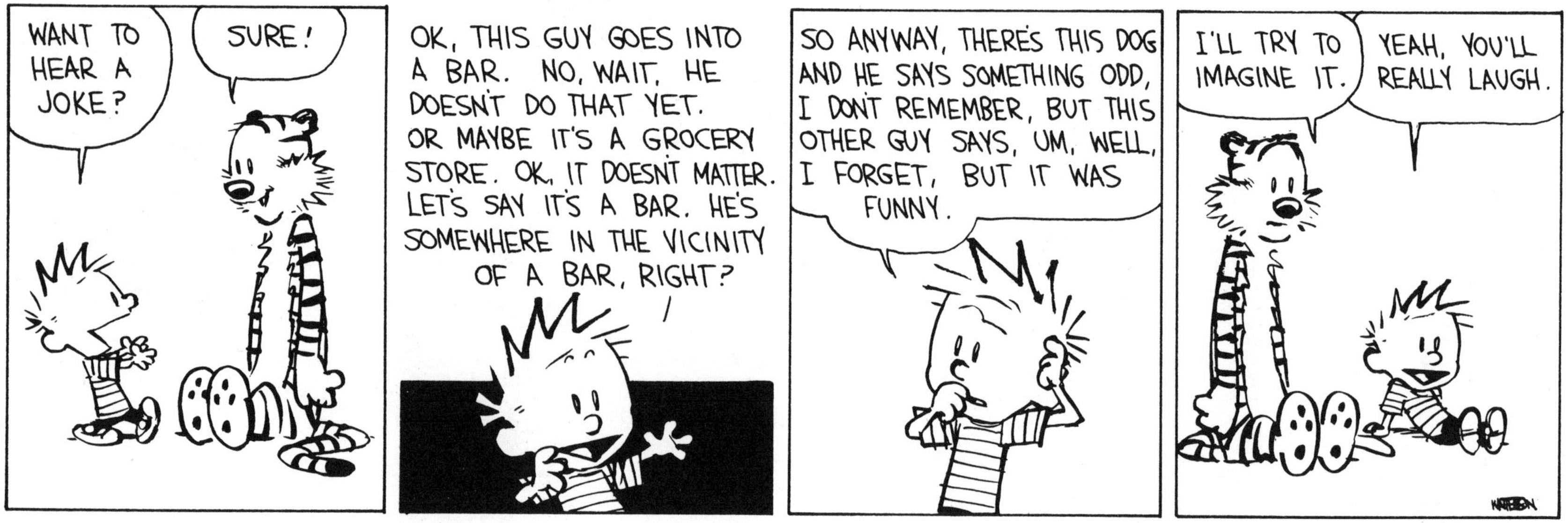
WANT TO HEAR A JOKE?
SURE!
OK, THIS GUY GOES INTO A BAR. NO, WAIT, HE DOESN'T DO THAT YET. OR MAYBE IT'S A GROCERY STORE. OK, IT DOESN'T MATTER. LET'S SAY IT'S A BAR. HE'S SOMEWHERE IN THE VICINITY OF A BAR, RIGHT?
SO ANYWAY, THERE'S THIS DOG AND HE SAYS SOMETHING ODD, I DON'T REMEMBER, BUT THIS OTHER GUY SAYS, UM, WELL, I FORGET, BUT IT WAS FUNNY.
I'LL TRY TO IMAGINE IT.
YEAH, YOU'LL REALLY LAUGH.
WATTERSON

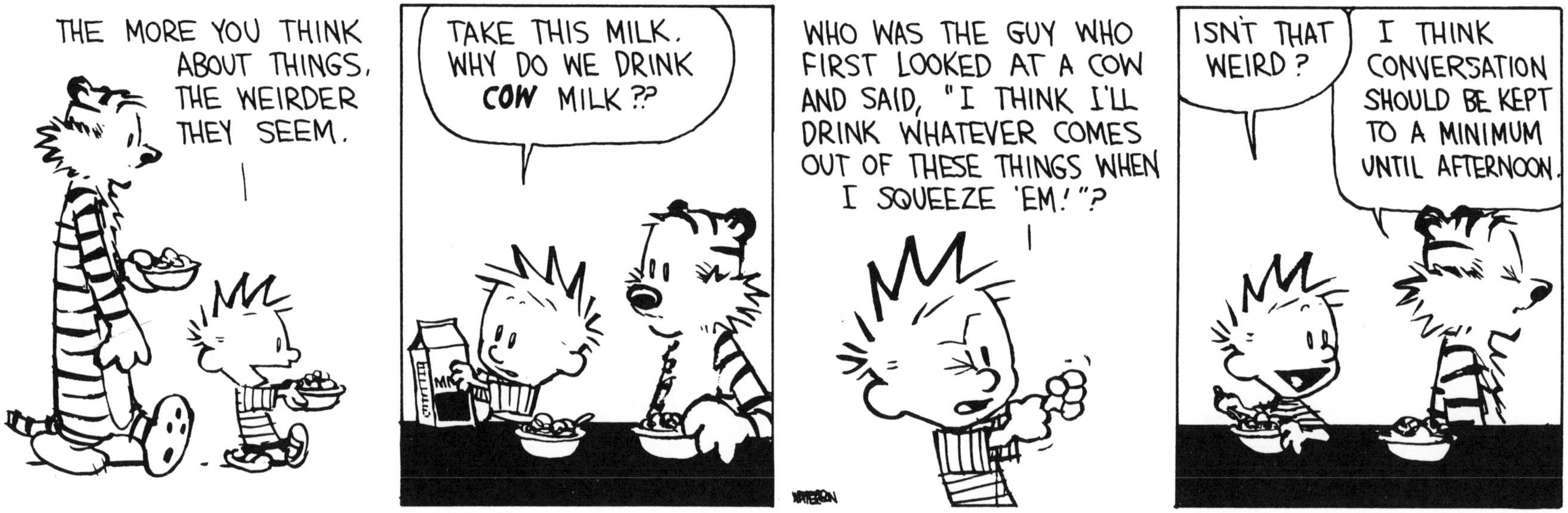
THE MORE YOU THINK ABOUT THINGS, THE WEIRDER THEY SEEM.
TAKE THIS MILK. WHY DO WE DRINK COW MILK ??
WHO WAS THE GUY WHO FIRST LOOKED AT A COW AND SAID, "I THINK I'LL DRINK WHATEVER COMES OUT OF THESE THINGS WHEN I SQUEEZE 'EM!"?
ISN'T THAT WEIRD?
I THINK CONVERSATION SHOULD BE KEPT TO A MINIMUM UNTIL AFTERNOON.

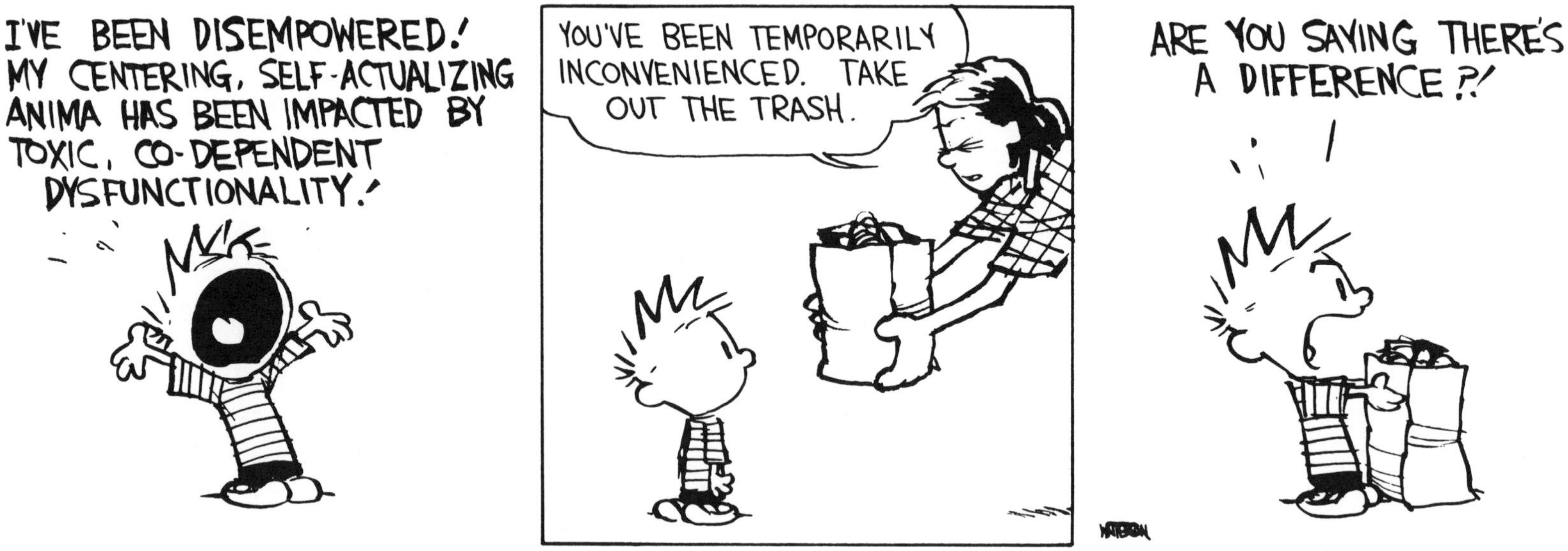
I'VE BEEN DISEMPOWERED! MY CENTERING, SELF-ACTUALIZING ANIMA HAS BEEN IMPACTED BY TOXIC, CO-DEPENDENT DYSFUNCTIONALITY!
YOU'VE BEEN TEMPORARILY INCONVENIENCED. TAKE OUT THE TRASH.
ARE YOU SAYING THERE'S A DIFFERENCE ?!

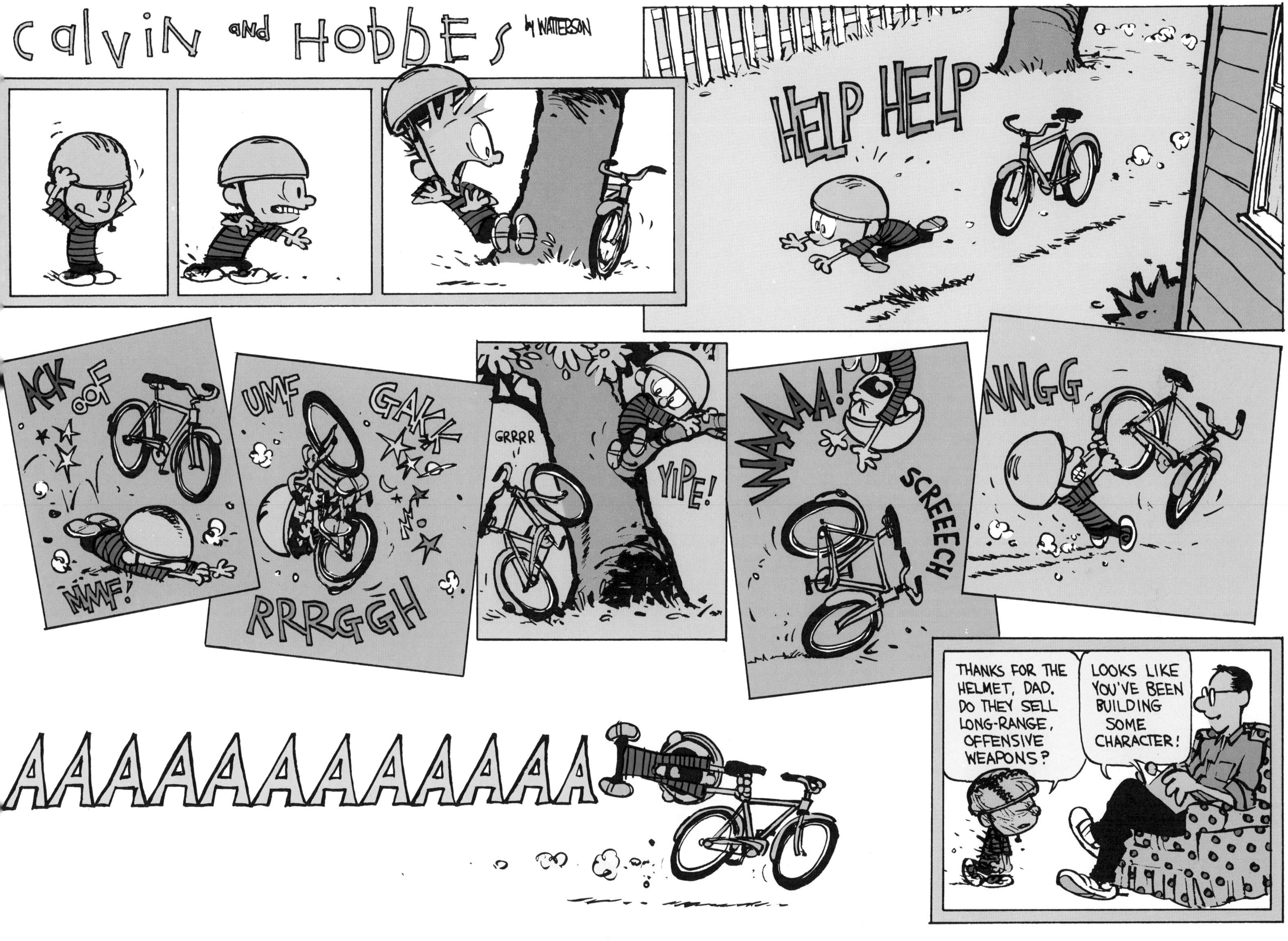
Calvin and HobbEs
by WATTERSON
HELP HELP
ACK
OOF
MMF!
UMF
GAKK
RRRGGH
GRRRR
YIPE!
WAAAA!
SCREEECH
NNGG
AAAAAAAAAAAA
THANKS FOR THE HELMET, DAD. DO THEY SELL LONG-RANGE, OFFENSIVE WEAPONS?
LOOKS LIKE YOU'VE BEEN BUILDING SOME CHARACTER!

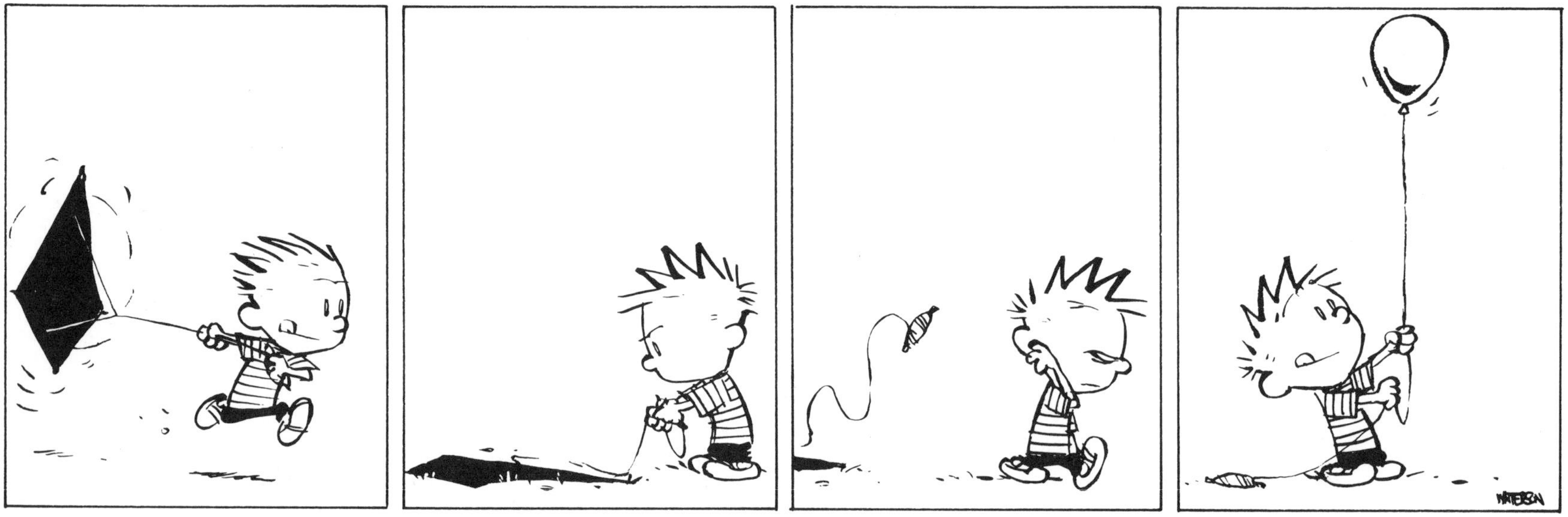

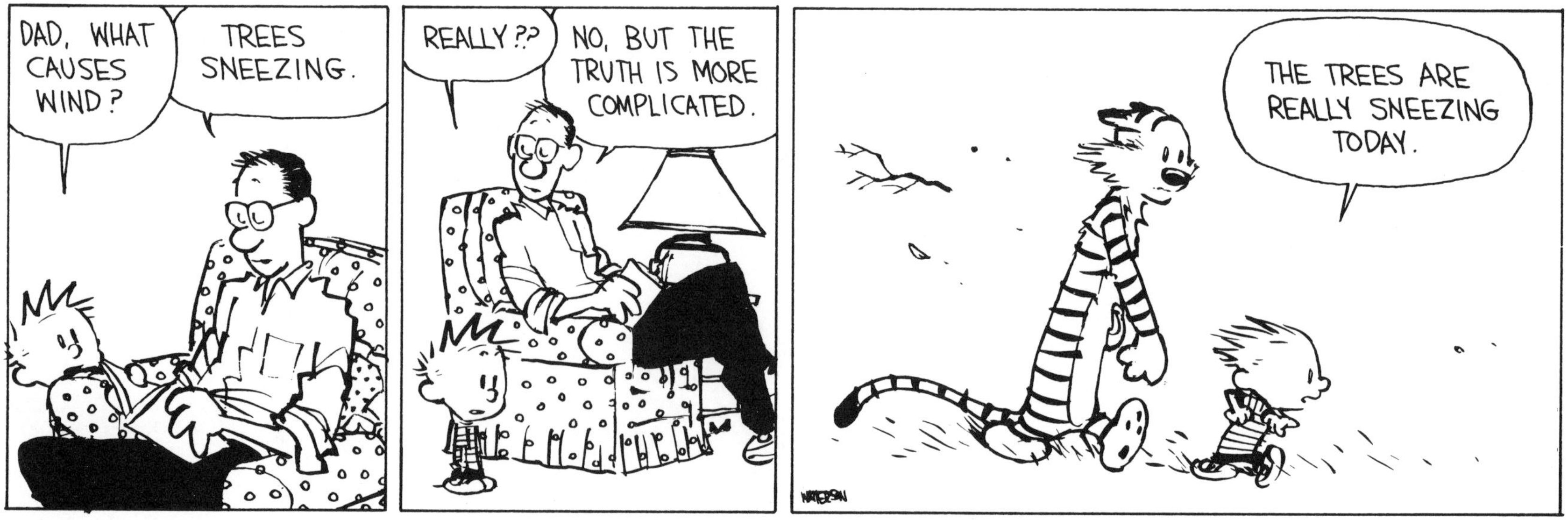
DAD, WHAT CAUSES WIND?
TREES SNEEZING.
REALLY??
NO, BUT THE TRUTH IS MORE COMPLICATED.
THE TREES ARE REALLY SNEEZING TODAY.

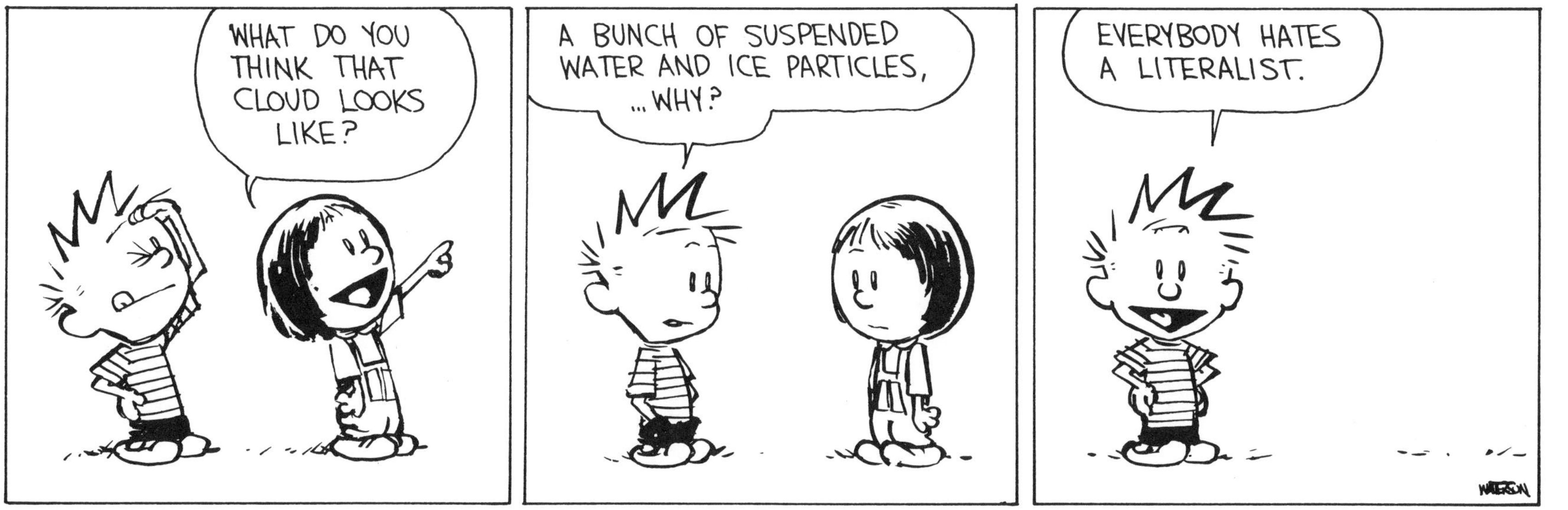
WHAT DO YOU THINK THAT CLOUD LOOKS LIKE?
A BUNCH OF SUSPENDED WATER AND ICE PARTICLES, ...WHY?
EVERYBODY HATES A LITERALIST.

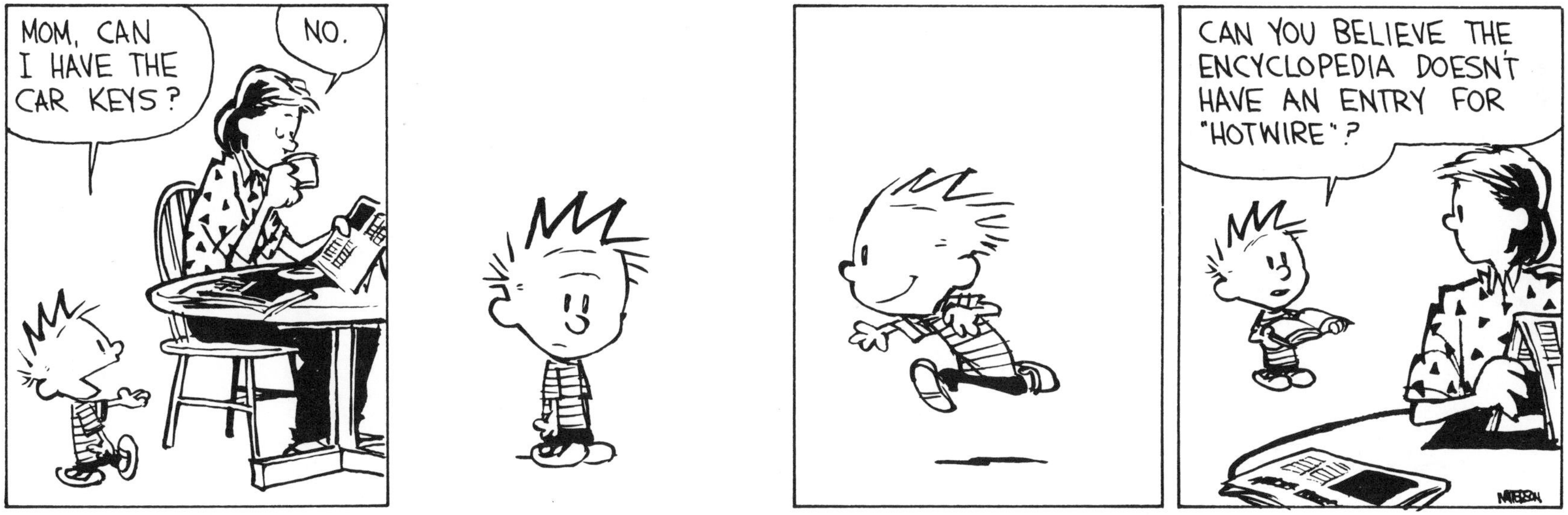
MOM, CAN I HAVE THE CAR KEYS?
NO.
CAN YOU BELIEVE THE ENCYCLOPEDIA DOESN'T HAVE AN ENTRY FOR "HOTWIRE"?

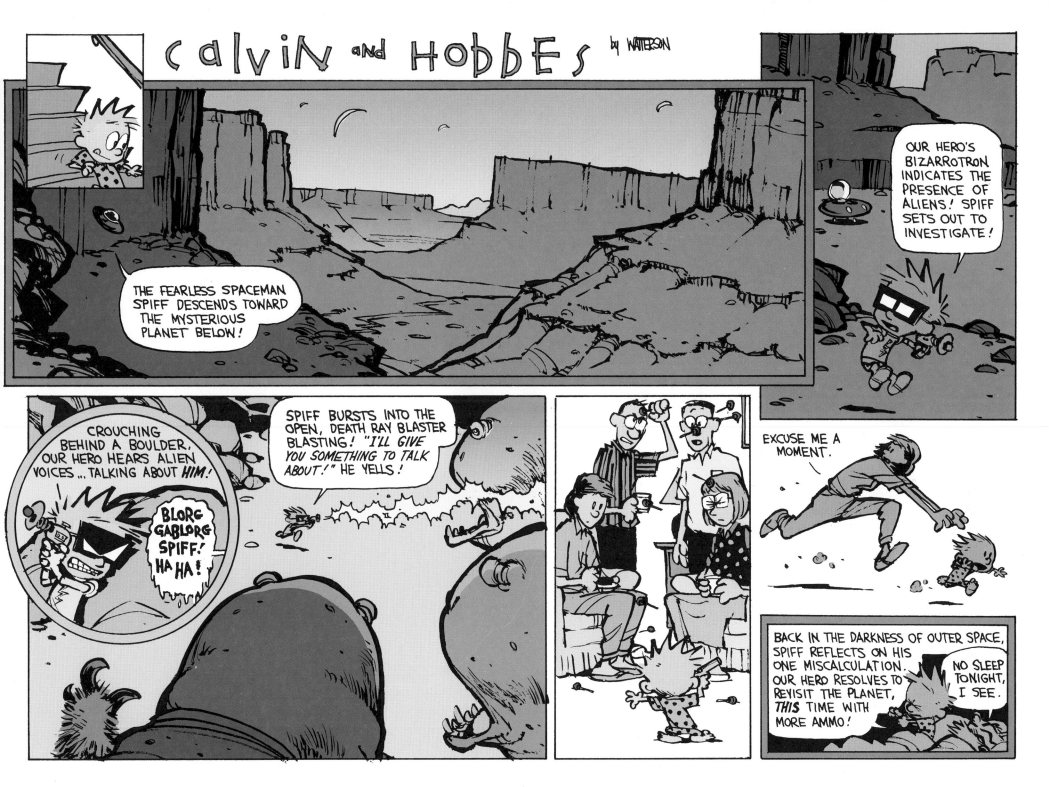

CALVIN AND HOBBES by WATTERSON

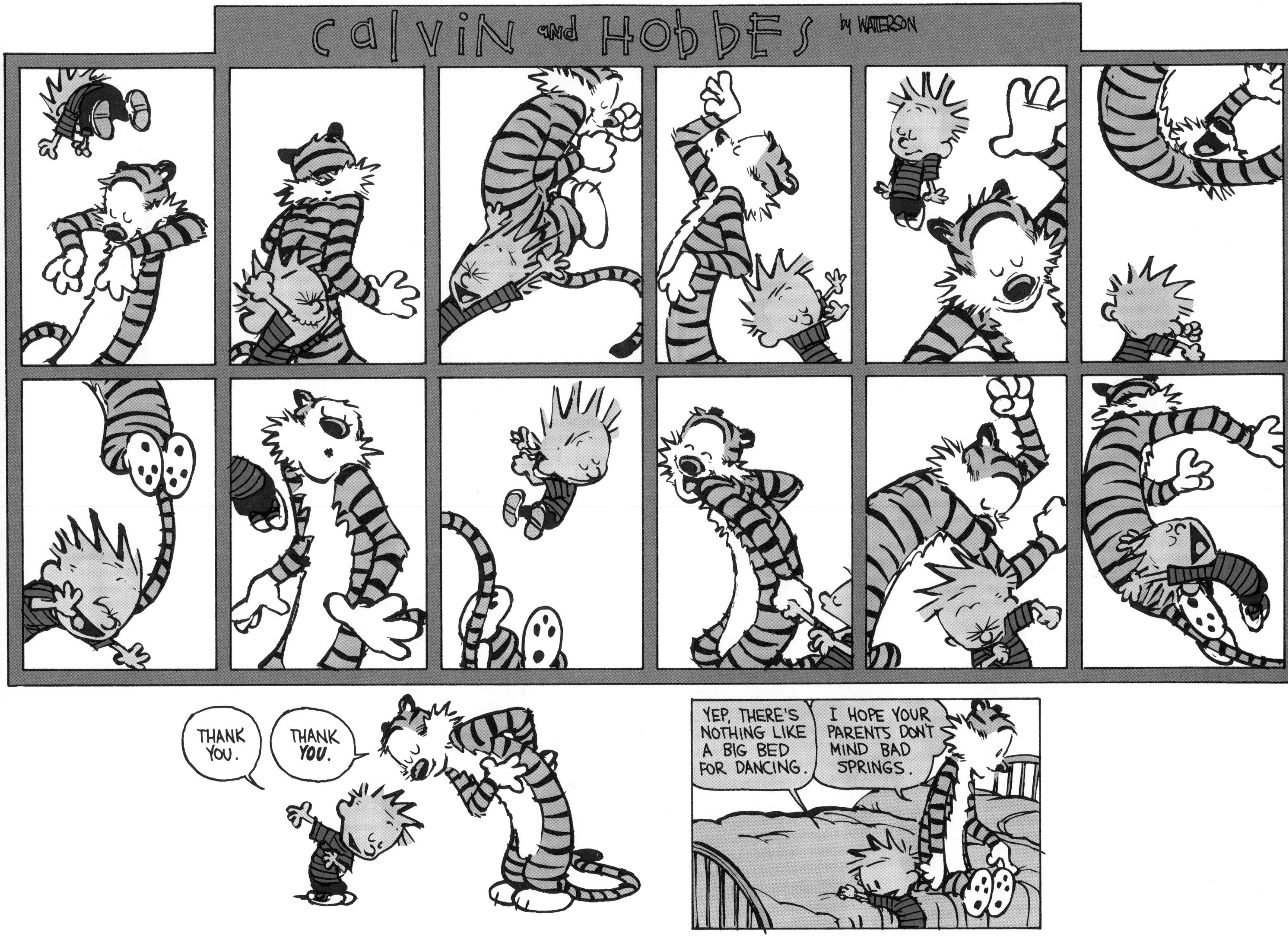

Calvin and HobbeS
by WATTERSON
THANK YOU.
THANK *YOU*.
YEP, THERE'S NOTHING LIKE A BIG BED FOR DANCING.
I HOPE YOUR PARENTS DON'T MIND BAD SPRINGS.

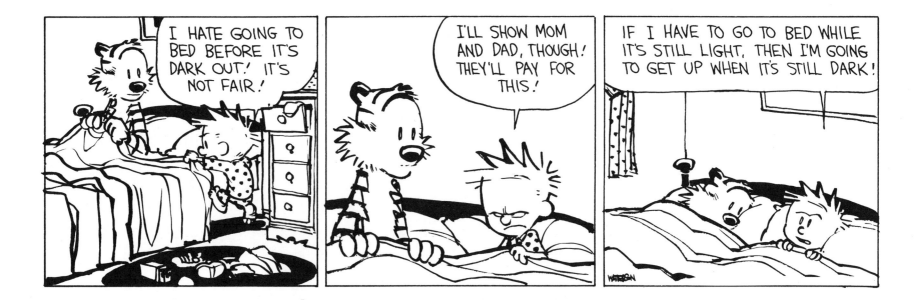

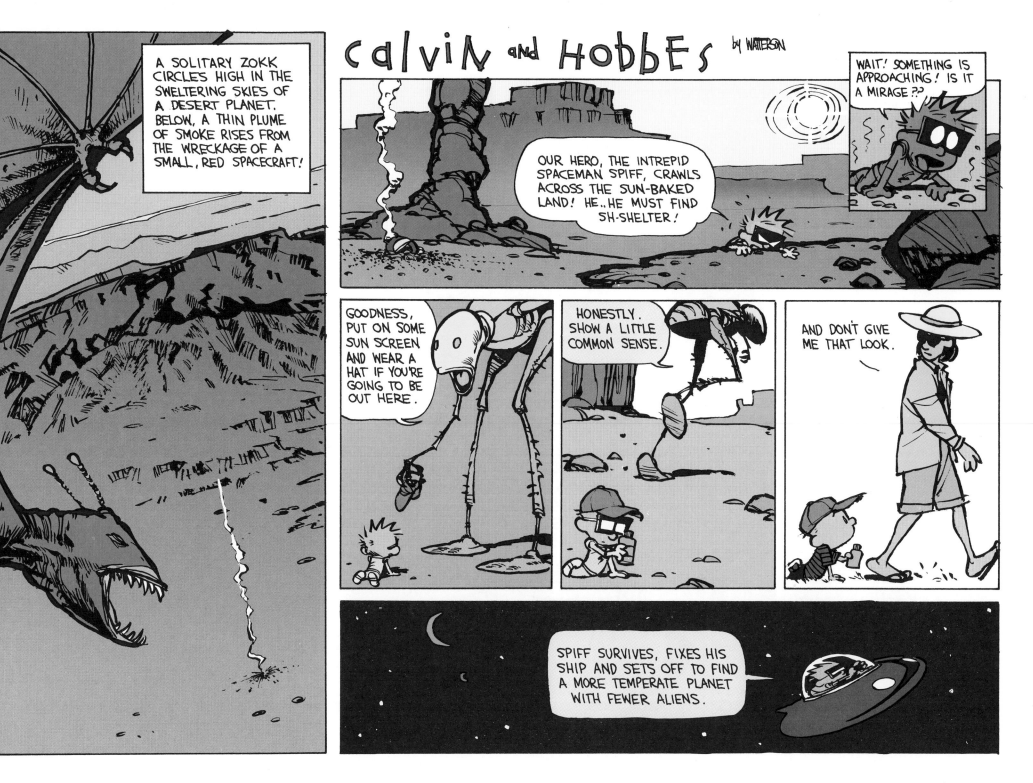

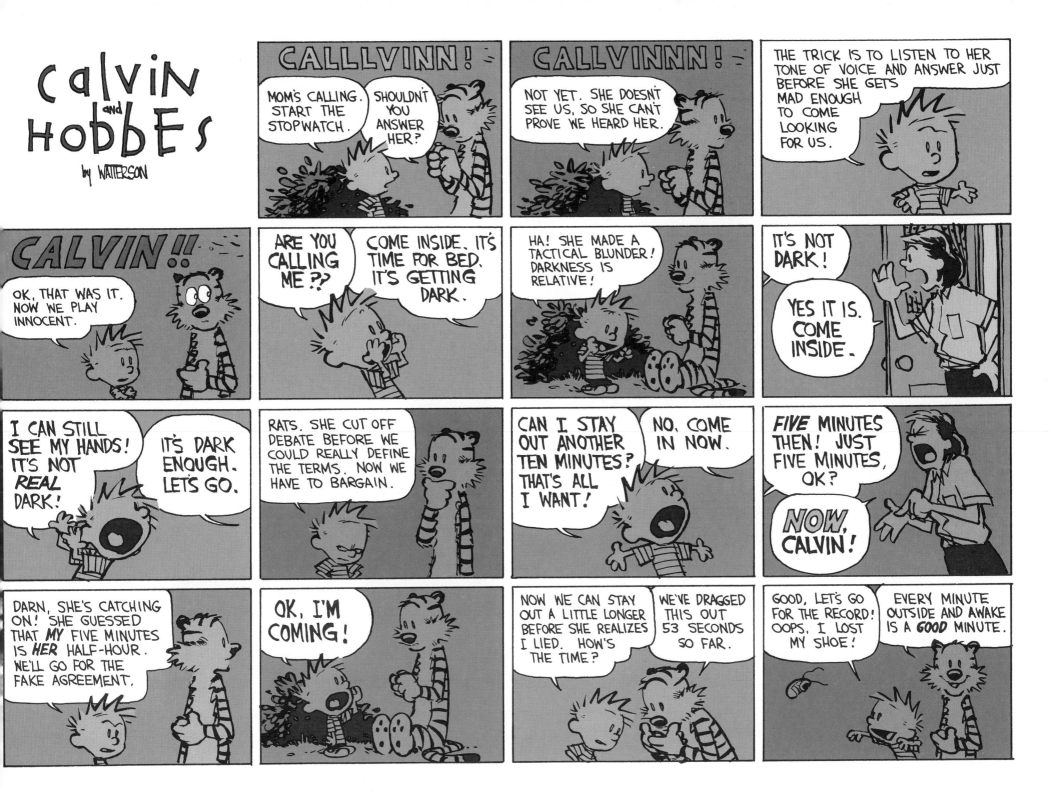

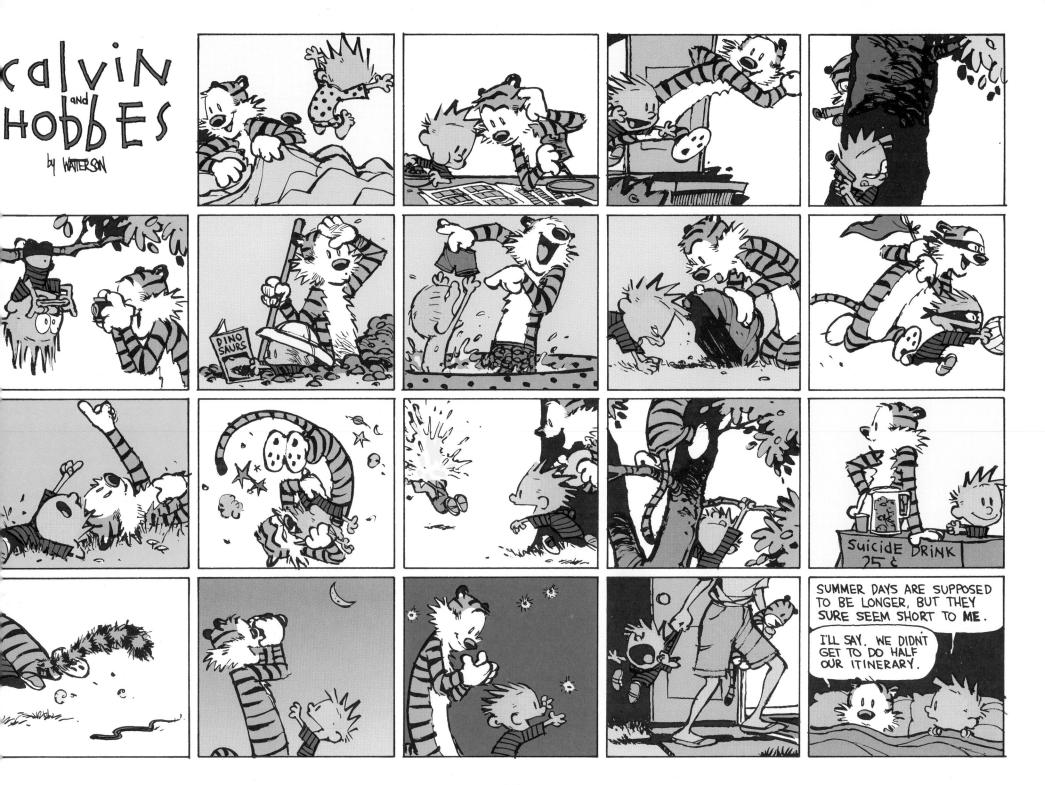